THE BLACK BOOK OF ENGLISH CANADA

THE BLACK BOOK OF ENGLISH CANADA

Normand Lester

Translated by Ray Conlogue

M&S

National Library of Canada Cataloguing in Publication

Lester, Normand
   The black book of English Canada / Normand Lester; Ray Conlogue,
translator.

Translation of: Le livre noir du Canada anglais.
Includes bibliographical references and index.
ISBN 0-7710-2259-X

1. Canada – English-French relations.   2. Canada – Race relations.
3. Canada – History.   I. Conlogue, Ray II. Title.

FC144.L4713 2002   971   C2002-902510-9
F1027.L55913 2002

We acknowledge the financial support of the Government of Canada
through the Book Publishing Industry Development Program for our
publishing activities. We further acknowledge the support of the
Canada Council for the Arts and the Ontario Arts council for our
publishing program.

The translation of this book was assisted by a grant from the Government
of Québec (SODEC).

Maple leaf illustration: Marie-Lynn Dionne
Designed by Blaine Herrmann
Typeset in Trump by M&S, Toronto
Printed and bound in Canada

This book is printed on acid-free paper that is 100% ancient forest friendly
(100% post-consumer recycled).

McClelland & Stewart Ltd.
The Canadian Publishers
481 University Avenue
Toronto, Ontario
M5G 2E9
www.mcclelland.com

1 2 3 4 5   06 05 04 03 02

"All history is contemporary."
　　　　　　– Benedetto Croce

"The past isn't dead, it isn't even past."
　　　　　　– William Faulkner

CONTENTS

INTRODUCTION

Normand Lester's *Black Book of English Canada* was a *cause célèbre* when it was published in Quebec in November 2001. Its attack on the history of anglophone misdeeds toward French Canada was considered so radical that its author, Radio-Canada reporter Normand Lester, was suspended from his duties. Accusations and lawyers' letters flew back and forth, and the media followed the story avidly.

What would make Lester feel so strongly as to write a book that would almost certainly place his career at risk?

The narrow explanation is that Lester, an investigative reporter with ten years' experience at Radio-Canada, had a difference of opinion with his employer. He had learned that the *Heritage Minutes*, patriotic capsules of Canadian history provided free by the Bronfman family foundation to television networks, including Radio-Canada, were actually aided by millions of dollars in hidden subsidies from the federal government. Informed that Radio-Canada would not broadcast his investigation of the matter, he went to the Montreal media with the story. He was duly suspended.

It was at this time that he began to research *The Black Book of English Canada*.

The CBC's ombudsman eventually vindicated him, declaring that it was highly improper for Radio-Canada and the CBC to conceal the federal funding behind the *Heritage Minutes*. The ombudsman asked that the series be discontinued.

If that were the whole story, Lester might have sought reinstatement. But by this time he had discovered much deeper reasons to write his book.

As he read into Canadian history, he came to feel that the *Heritage Minutes* were only a small part of a great and continuing injustice against French Canadians. Had they ever been fairly represented in Canadian history? he began to ask himself. Thinking themselves a people, they found themselves described as a linguistic minority. Thinking themselves equal partners in Confederation, they found themselves dismissed as a backward if colourful ethnic community.

English Canadians who feel Lester exaggerates should remember that our own historians have often expressed similar views. They too are troubled by pressure to create a "national unity" version of history which does violence to the facts. In a 1968 study called the *National History Project*, A. B. Hodgetts lamented that "the conflicts within our society have been swept under the classroom desk and greyed out in the textbooks. We have been unfavourably surprised by the number of teachers who believe that the answers to all our problems can be found in a Canadian history textbook that 'emphasizes our common achievements and eliminates controversy.'"

The problem has, if anything, grown worse since then. In his recent book *Misconceiving Canada*, political scientist Kenneth McRoberts argued that Pierre Trudeau's individual-based system of rights, including the Charter of Rights, was partially designed to obscure the fact that Canada was founded by two collectivities. Canadians are now encouraged to forget the undertakings that were made to the French as a group at the time of Confederation.

That is not to say that a new generation of historians working in English has not progressed beyond the partisan and Protestant tale recounted not so very long ago by historians like Donald Creighton. Younger anglophone historians have written an even-handed biography of Lionel Groulx, a book-length history of the Orange Order in Canada, and admirable texts on a dozen other sensitive issues.

But few Canadians read them. And few historians today attempt to write popular general histories.

Making matters worse has been the rise of separatism. It is worth remembering that in the past, when religion-based racism against the French was widespread and things were objectively much worse than today, few leaders in Quebec called for secession. The idea did not become widely popular until Quebec modernized during the Quiet Revolution of the 1960s. Self-confidence helped create the demand for political autonomy.

Some English Canadians, perhaps subconsciously, came to feel that if only French Canadians could be forced back into their insecure, pre–Quiet Revolution understanding of themselves, then separatism would go away. Books like *Oh Canada! Oh Quebec!* by Mordecai Richler and *Fighting for Canada* by Diane Francis try to put the French into a primitivist box by describing them in terms which recall the worst excesses of nineteenth-century assimilationists like D'Alton McCarthy.

These books are polemics. They purport to attack separatists, but in fact are attacking French Canadians generally. They give a relentlessly one-sided and negative picture of a people who make up one-quarter of Canada's population. And they are popular books, widely read and influential in English Canada.

More than that, however, they have an effect on French Canadians. As a minority, francophones are vulnerable (as every minority is) to the way in which they are represented by the majority. As Normand Lester has said to me, "The thing that made me the saddest was that French Quebeckers had started to believe this negative story about themselves."

The matter is serious. When a journalist like Diane Francis, represented in *Maclean's* magazine and the *National Post*, writes that "Quebec separatism . . . is a racially motivated conspiracy that has run roughshod over human rights . . . tampered with the armed forces of the nation. Stripped anglophones and allophones of their civil rights," then even French Canadians who know very well that none of this is true experience self-doubt. When celebrated novelist Mordecai Richler writes that Louis-Joseph Papineau's Patriote party plotted during the uprising of 1837 to slaughter all the Jews in Quebec, he is repeating a slur. But how can French readers – much less readers in Calgary or Vancouver – know that it is untrue? How many people remember that it was Papineau who won the vote for Quebec's Jews? It was, after all, a very long time ago.

The Black Book of English Canada is, then, a counter-polemic. It is Lester's attempt to restore the dignity and self-belief of his compatriots.

But it is one-sided. Lester does not deny the virtues or achievements of English Canada, but that is not the story he is telling. He wishes to set out what he calls the "dark story," the unpleasant history which every society softens, rationalizes and finally forgets with the passage of time.

Why should English Canadians read the *Black Book*? There are several reasons. The most agreeable is that they should read it for the same reason francophones read Richler's book: because of the crackle and sizzle of the arguments.

Lester's anger, like Richler's, can be seductive. Not for him the sobersided weighing of pro and con. Like a ferret he digs out the meatiest details to feed his indignation. Others may note that English Canadians lobbied for the execution of Louis Riel, but it is Normand Lester who slaps down on the table the Toronto newspaper which suggested he be hanged with a French flag. Look at that! he cries. And what about the twenty-pound weight the army attached to Riel's foot. Did they think God was going to levitate him out of jail?

The Black Book is also a rarity in that French Canadians do not often write polemics against English Canada. They are, however, often the target of such polemics, and the reader of *The Black Book* will soon gain a very good understanding of what that feels like.

There is a long history of anti-French writing in Canada. It begins with the first reports of British officials after the Conquest of 1760, and by the nineteenth century had settled into a literary sub-genre of lurid calumnies. The most celebrated was Maria Monk's false account of being kidnapped and raped by a cabal of Montreal Catholic priests, which became a North American best-seller in the late 1830s.

By the early twentieth century, when religious passions had moderated and the French had become a minority, the attacks softened into a charming but racist exoticism, best represented by William Henry Drummond's "Leetle Bateese" poems. These were still taught when I went to school in the 1960s.

By contrast, few anti-English polemics have appeared in French. In the decades after 1760, Quebec lost much of its educated leadership, and the population was in that state of shock which Alexis de Tocqueville described in 1831. Early historians such as François-Xavier Garneau were already on the defensive against Lord Durham's claim that French Canadians had no culture and ought to be assimilated. Later on, as French Canadians became a minority in a land they once had dominated, the astringent sense of reality possessed by minorities led them to understand that there was little point in troubling deaf heaven, or even deafer Winnipeg and Calgary, with their bootless cries.

In setting out to write a polemic against English Canada, Lester called upon a long tradition of aggrieved and vituperative writing. The word polemic comes from the Greek *polemos*, meaning war. It goes further than the customary refuting of an opponent's argument, seeking also to discredit him or her. It is a moral as well as an intellectual attack.

Whom is he attacking? All those who have advanced what he considers a dishonest picture of French Canadians. The book is largely a catalogue of such offences from 1750 through to the 1920s. But in its prologue he briefly reviews current diatribes against Quebec, especially those provoked by the rise of separatism in the 1990s. *The Black Book* is in some measure a response to them.

Does that mean that it is as unfair as the books by Richler, Francis, and others have been?

It is not, though it can certainly be annoying in its insistence that the British were hypocrites and their ideals of fair play a mockery. It rarely acknowledges that actions which offend us today were normal practice at the time, and the British far from the worst offenders. An extreme example is Lester's zeal in comparing Colonel Robert Monckton, who oversaw the expulsion of the Acadians in 1755, with the authors of twentieth-century genocides.

There is also, as one must expect in a polemic, a tendency to angelize where one's own side is concerned. In exculpating the nineteenth-century Quebec premier Honoré Mercier, who had been framed on a corruption charge by Quebec's English elite, he is forced to admit that one of Mercier's ministers was indeed guilty of the kickbacks in question. But he is not inclined to deal with the ingrained culture of corruption in Quebec political life.

There is, however, little outright distortion of historic fact. Lester is anxious to be credible, and he quotes extensively from sources in both English and French. Sometimes he is so generous with documentation as to undercut his own arguments. It can be reminiscent of the joke about the Québécois trying to impress a Frenchman by describing moose with huge antlers galloping through a forest where the trees grow chockablock. But, replies the Frenchman with nice logic, if the antlers are so wide, and the trees are that close together, how does the moose run? "Bien!" replies the injured Québécois. "Si tu ne veux pas comprendre!"

Lester's elaborate respect for the historical record is perhaps typical of an aggrieved minority. The majority, as Ernest Renan observed, does as much forgetting as remembering when it agrees upon a national identity. Certainly English Canadians are not inclined to remember anti-French racism or the unconstitutional laws which largely destroyed French minorities in Manitoba and Ontario. They are not even inclined, as sociologist John Conway pointed out in his book *Debts to Pay*, to feel badly about the stereotypes of French Canadians still common in our cultural life.

However, let us assume that most English Canadians really wish for a coherent nation where the two European founding peoples have a better understanding of each other. It is to our credit that we postulate in our laws the perfect equality of the French and English languages, knowing very well that we are a majority and they a minority, and that we shall always be obliged to restrain ourselves. We struggle to accept that, while immigrants in Toronto of course learn English, Quebec may very well have to force the ones in Montreal to learn French. We grapple desperately with Michael Ignatieff's suggestion that Canada can never be a "green baize pool table" where everybody has the same rights, but rather that it will be a lumpy place where the French, among others, have special rights.

How can Lester's book help us in this struggle?

Consider the two chapters he devotes to English Canada's dire treatment of the Japanese and the Jews. He is writing for French-speaking Québécois, of course, and he included these chapters as a kind of battle dressing for the wounds they have suffered. Do not listen to the English Canada that tells you that you are racist and inferior, he says to Quebeckers: the record shows that they were just as bad as we were, and arguably worse.

But for us these chapters can have an entirely different interest. They challenge our double consciousness concerning racism, where we store information in different places, and use it on different occasions.

Think of anti-Semitism. English Canada's own history of prejudice against Jews troubles many of us as we review the history of our families and communities. Quebec's anti-Semitism, however, leaps to the fore when we wish to attack a separatist leader, or to reinforce the ancient prejudice that the French cannot be trusted to govern themselves. The one is moral and personal; the other is an exercise in political expediency.

Normand Lester forces us to look at these two things together. He reveals the enormous popularity in English Canada of Quebec's most prominent pre-war anti-Semite, Adrien Arcand – a subject rarely treated in English, especially not in media commentaries which make use of Arcand to slander Quebec.

At the same time, Lester insists that Arcand was not that popular in Quebec. This you may take, as I do, with a grain of salt. It is enough if one comes away with the sense that anti-Semitism is a grim history in which we were as culpable as French Canadians, and one we ought in all conscience to stop using as a club against them.

Similarly with the capsule history of the Orange Order at the end of his chapter on Louis Riel. Lester exaggerates the influence of Orangemen in Canada today, and seems in fact not to know that they have become a relic of a vanished past. But just as he inflates their importance now, we tend to downplay their importance then. Lester is a useful corrective. He vividly recalls the Orange Order's racial and religious exclusivity, its influence on John A. Macdonald, and its stranglehold on nineteenth- and early-twentieth-century public opinion. In a brilliant rhetorical passage, he asks us to imagine the reaction of English Canada if Quebec had supported a racist secret society with thousands of members and links to an organization which kills schoolchildren in Ireland.

Normand Lester is very far from being the stereotypical *pure laine* Québécois. His father was a Romanian Jew who lived in

New York before moving to Quebec and who, recalls Lester, spoke English "with a Brooklyn accent" to the end of his life.

In spite of his mixed background, Lester identifies himself as a French Canadian. He is part of that large proportion of Québécois who are not ethnically French. These Algerians and Vietnamese and Haitians are rarely acknowledged in the English press because they are often separatist and demonstrate that Quebec nationalism is not ethnically exclusive. It is, as Lester emphasizes, a competing nationalism based on liberal principles similar to those of English Canada.

Like most minorities, the French in Canada are often bilingual. Lester reads and speaks English well, and relies on a high level of English literacy among his francophone readers. In the original *Livre noir du Canada anglais*, many long passages from the Montreal *Gazette*, the letters of John A. Macdonald, or the speeches of Mackenzie King are printed in English without translation.

At the same time, Lester does not live in English. This is an important distinction. It is possible to speak a language fluently without knowing the culture attached to it, as I learned one day when an impeccably bilingual Quebec friend asked me what on earth was meant by the expression "Huckleberry Finn."

In a similar vein, Lester sometimes misses nuances in English-language culture. He sees an Orange Lodge in Ontario named after the "famous thirteen" extremist members of parliament who tried to overrule the Quebec legislature in the 1880s, and wrongly imagines that people still know or care who they were. He sees an article in the English-language Montreal weekly *Hour* which compares Louis-Joseph Papineau with the Cambodian mass murderer Pol Pot, and fails to realize that the author's political views are of marginal significance.

But this, too, is instructive for English-speaking readers. If a man who understands English can miss these nuances, then what should one think of anglophone polemicists who neither speak nor read French?

I highly recommend reading Normand Lester. He is like a museum guide who is garrulous and grouchy, but he is at least inside the museum and not leading us down the garden path.

Ray Conlogue

PROLOGUE

"Canada loves you!" they cried out to the people of Quebec on the eve of the 1995 referendum. But English Canada's passion for us, as sudden as it was invasive, disappeared very quickly once the referendum was (from their point of view) won. In fact, with a narrow victory in hand, they unleashed a frenzy of verbal abuse against us such as we haven't seen in ages.

Not that Canada's anglophones have overwhelmed us with affection during our two long centuries of cohabitation. Domestic violence has been the norm.

So now they're at war with us again. We had the nerve to almost win a referendum on independence, and now we're to be punished. The Battle of the Plains of Abraham will be fought once more, and this time they hope to wash their hands of the Quebec problem once and for all: "In most epic battles – Waterloo, the Spanish Armada, Gettysburg – there is a clear winner and a loser. When Wolfe climbed the cliffs to the Plains of Abraham and beat Montcalm, the French thought it was a tie."[1]

A tie! Evidently, for them, we have not quite understood that we have been conquered, beaten, and humiliated. It gets their dander up! Shortly after the 1995 referendum Allan Fotheringham of *Maclean's* magazine bitterly noted that "we are back to the Plains of Abraham. A virtual tie is not going to do anyone any good."[2]

We are to understand, I suppose, that we have been indulged long enough. That's what Pierre Trudeau believed. And now Canada has generally decided that Quebec's place is on its belly. That, having being conquered, we exist thanks to its forebearance.

It seems the English-speaking public will approve just about any measure which deals slightingly with Quebec. Just as it approved the War Measures Act in 1970. No punch is illegal in this boxing match. Whether they call it Plan A, B, or C, it is always about the flag, and no quarter will be given. Anglo pundits and their docile French-speaking auxiliaries are on the warpath, launching campaign after campaign to put down French Quebec with avid pleasure.

Just like the good old days! Reading the newspaper is like a cold shower that sprays us with bad faith and manipulated facts. The opinion makers of English Canada have assigned themselves the mission of needling English-Canadian public opinion into a sectarian frenzy, making use of age-old anti-Quebec and anti-French-Canadian prejudices.

There is nothing new about this. Since the very beginning the English-Canadian press has prided itself on persecuting minorities, and there's no sign of enlightenment.

Consider this: In January 1997 in Toronto, Conrad Black launched a diatribe against the French Language Charter (Charte de la langue française), which he indirectly compared to the Nazism Canada struggled against during the Second World War. The newspaper he will found, the *National Post*, will become English Canada's main forum for race-based anti-Quebec obsession. Conrad Black's wife, Barbara Amiel, underlines the point in *Maclean's*:

> If the members of the PQ want to be indignant when I describe
> their party as neofascist, let them. Any party which supports a law

condemning a citizen to pay a $7,000 fine for putting out a sign inscribed "Today's special/Specialité du jour" carries within itself a dirty totalitarian tendency. Of course this law was approved by the Liberals of Quebec and illustrates another fact, which is that francophone culture itself is not as intrinsically democratic as cultures based on British traditions. If the separatists one day obtain their State, it will be a disagreeable, bureaucratic, statist and intolerant place.[3]

It's characteristic of racist discourse to demonize the group it attacks while attributing all virtue to itself. It claims to represent universal rights while the group it targets is untrustworthy. This in turn means that any complaint from that group can be dismissed out of hand, since it is by definition undemocratic and without merit.[4]

The similarities between pre–Civil War America and Canada today are more than coincidental, and cause for concern. . . . The "self-image" of the Québécois is "communitarian" and emphasizes *la survivance* of francophone society as an "organic and coherent" community. That is exactly ethnic nationalism. When anglophone critics branded as ethnocentric Quebec's language laws, Quebec's minister of culture replied unabashedly: "All nations are founded on the principle of ethnocentricity." In contrast, English Canadians subscribe to values of "egalitarian individualism" that emphasize "civil liberties and the classical liberal individualism of Anglo-Saxon cultures."[5]

For Bill Johnson, the Péquistes and the Liberals are Tweedledum and Tweedledee: if Quebec's francophones affirm a group identity, that in itself is subversion.

The two principal political parties [of Quebec] and the majority of the articulate French media wish to overturn the Constitution, ignore the decisions of the courts, debase the rights of Crees,

Inuit, Mohawks and the Canadian citizens of Quebec. It's a recipe for chaos, economic ruin, violent inter-citizen conflict, the partition of Quebec, and even civil war.[6]

And of course *Cité libre*, the venerable review founded by Pierre Elliott Trudeau, joined the anti-Quebec campaign:

> In Quebec, the nationalist upwelling has given birth to the most powerful secession movement in the western hemisphere, at the same time preventing Quebec's most talented people from helping it to progress economically, intellectually, scientifically, or technologically, or to help it evolve a lifestyle distinct from American-style consumerism. The Québécois possesses immense riches but, generation after generation, has not been able fully to exploit these gifts due to the retrograde aspect of his collective cultural personality. They can nonetheless transcend this nationalist passion as well as the minority complex which feeds it.[7]

DIANE FRANCIS: THE SEASON OF SCORN

Diane Francis, the editor in chief of the *Financial Post*, the most influential business newspaper in English Canada (now part of the *National Post*), stands alone in her particular vindictiveness. For her, the Québécois are contemptible creatures: "They whine and moan and damage our economy. They plot and scheme and dream about creating an ethnocentric, francophone state. They revise history. They fabricate claims about recent injustices. They irritate English Canadians to help their case. They are, in a word, despicable."[8]

It would seem we Québécois are a mass of ignoramuses and imbeciles who let ourselves be manipulated by a few hundred separatists, whose elimination alone would return peace and harmony to Canada. Like Conrad Black, Diane Francis advocates the partition of Quebec and the use of violence to block its independence: "grassroots fires in favor of partition and human rights have been lit all across the province. Anglos are standing their ground at long last. . . . Mohawks revealed for the first time last month that they will take up arms if Quebec tries to leave Canada. That means violence is certain."[9]

As she explains in her book, the sovereignist movement in Quebec is a racist and criminal conspiracy which violates human rights:

> Quebec separatism is not a legitimate struggle for self-determination. It is a racially motivated conspiracy that has run roughshod over human rights, fair play, the Quebec economy, and democracy. The separatists should be treated like the ruthless elite that they are.
>
> Because of superior intellect and single-mindedness, the separatists have controlled Quebec's French language media and the country's political agenda, and by so doing have been allowed to run virtually rampant, by successive Quebec-born prime ministers, for more than three decades. . . .
>
> English Canadians still remain in the dark and do not fully understand the extent of separatist wrongdoing. The separatists have cheated. Lied. Hidden facts. Revised history. Disenfranchised thousands of voters. Fraudulently spoiled ballots, then covered up their crimes. They have tampered with the armed forces of the nation. Stripped anglophones and allophones of their civil rights for more than three decades. Purposely driven anglophones out of Quebec. Passed laws that legalized employment discrimination and educational discrimination.[10]

Did she mention educational discrimination? This oppressed English minority, numbering less than a million, has three universities. Yet it received 23.6 per cent of Quebec's and 36.7 per cent of Ottawa's post-secondary educational subsidy while making up 8.8 per cent of the province's population. Michel Moisan, a researcher at the Université de Montréal, points to this extraordinarily generous financing as a factor in anglicization. It partly explains why 60 per cent of allophones and 21 per cent of franco-phones pursue higher education in English, while only 1.3 per cent of anglophones study in French institutions.[11]

Even today, 40 per cent of Quebec's anglophones are unilingual. In a province which is 82-per-cent French-speaking they go from cradle to grave without taking the trouble to learn the language. Could such a thing happen in New Brunswick? Ontario? Quebec alone is still evolving within a colonial situation.

Ray Conlogue, one of the few Anglo-Canadian journalists to present a fair picture of Quebec society – he has been accused of being a victim of Stockholm Syndrome, where the hostage is converted to his captors' point of view – finds that English Quebeckers are a minority divorced from the social reality in which it lives:

> It's a minority with a schizophrenic outlook. It won't face facts.
> It's a local minority making up part of a national majority. Living
> in Quebec, these people do not watch popular television, read
> French-language newspapers, and find little but popular American
> culture in the *Gazette*. They have little contact with the franco-
> phone culture around them. To resist assimilation they need only
> grab the TV zapper. English is, after all, the only language in the
> world which has succeeded in monopolizing an entire continent.
> Francophones ask these anglophones to look on Quebec as their
> country. But they can't. The young are a little better, but still
> affected by their parents' presumption of superior status. It's sad.[12]

So it's all the more to the credit of the hundred-or-so young Anglo-Quebeckers in a group called Forum Québec that they had the courage to confront the hostile frenzy of English Canada and lodge a complaint against Diane Francis with the Ontario Press Council on May 21, 1996:

> the anglophone pressure group affirmed that Ms. Francis's editori-
> als were bristling "with gross mistakes, false representation, and

gratuitous claims." Forum Québec reviewed Ms. Francis's articles over a period of a year. Its spokesman, Daniel-Robert Gooch [director of a Montreal public-relations firm] particularly reproached Ms. Francis for having compared the Quebec referendum with tactics used by Hitler and Mussolini to seize power in the 1930s.

Among numerous factual errors in the *Financial Post*, Forum Québec cites a text of November 23, 1995, in which Diane Francis declared that there had been a "dramatic" drop in Quebec's credit rating in New York. Moody's had actually set Quebec's rating twenty days earlier, and no other agency had modified it since. Francis had deliberately misled readers. "As a newspaper of reference for Canadians and foreign business circles, the *Post* ought to be certain its information is fair and correct," wrote Gooch in his letter. "Provoking anti-Quebec feelings is unproductive."[13]

As Francis's newspaper is not a member of the Press Council, the complaint went nowhere. Ray Conlogue accuses the English-Canadian financial press of an "insane hostility" where Quebec is concerned. He describes the "Rest of Canada's" coverage of Quebec as follows:

> They exploit Quebec coverage to play to popular prejudice. Mordecai Richler's *Saturday Night* commentaries are not intended to clarify matters, but to sharpen prejudices. Since the referendum, attitudes have hardened everywhere in Canada, including my own newspaper. There is more space for Anglo-Quebec complaints about their presumed persecution. Anglo-Canadians increasingly feel it is their right to interfere in the life of Quebec. It is troubling.[14]

LUCIEN BOUCHARD, ENGLISH CANADA'S PUBLIC ENEMY NUMBER ONE

According to Diane Francis, Lucien Bouchard was the devil incarnate while premier of Quebec. "Bouchard must go. The man is a menace, a demagogue and, possibly, a criminal."[15] There was general concern about his sanity across the country. The *Vancouver Sun* one day captioned his photo as follows: "Is this man insane?" Vivian Rakoff, a Toronto psychiatrist, drew a devastating psychological portrait of the premier, whom he had not met. Very likely he simply read the stories invented by Diane Francis and William Johnson.

But the English-language press was apparently untroubled by this ignoble operation, and happy to exploit it: "It doesn't matter if Bouchard's unflattering portrait is unscientific and biased by its author's federalist loyalties. If it walks like a duck and quacks like a duck, then it's a duck. This isn't news. It's reality."[16]

Dr. Rakoff goes further than "analyzing" Lucien Bouchard. He psychoanalyzes Quebec as a whole, maintaining that the PQ's political platform and its modern and pluralist idea of Quebec are little more than sovereignist trickery. In his own mind Rakoff knows exactly what Quebec wants: "Quebec really wants a nineteenth-century ethnic state, but the leaders and intellectuals try to square the circle by packaging it into a late-twentieth-century notion of a pluralist society. . . ."[17]

For his part, Lawrence Martin, author of *The Antagonist*, a biography of Bouchard relying heavily on Rakoff's profile, gets right to the point in the *Globe and Mail*: "Lucien, Lucifer of our land."[18]

English Canada welcomes these outrages with pleasure. On phone-in radio shows, callers applaud and reinforce the most excessive statements of the media junta. Jean Paré, editor in chief of *L'Actualité* at the time, notes the harm done by media demagogues: "To many Canadians, Quebec is an ethnocentric backwater filled with racists who snack on anglophones gathered up the night before by the Gestapo of Bill 101. . . . This ambient hostility is much more than the usual prejudice one associates with ignorance. . . . the worst of it is the character-assassinating accusation of racism. One feels dirtied by it."[19]

The object is to link the Québécois, sovereignists especially, with fascism by whatever means, and always to sully Quebec's movement of national affirmation. Mordecai Richler, William Johnson, Diane Francis, and – with rare exceptions – the editorialists and columnists of the *Globe and Mail*, *National Post*, Montreal *Gazette*, *Ottawa Citizen*, and *Maclean's* magazine, repeat these comments without reflection. It's possible, in fact, to indict the entirety of the Anglo-Canadian media:

> It has become acceptable in this country to denigrate French Canadians by taxing them with a profound (and perhaps genetic?) xenophobia, mulishness, and racism. It's being done with a threadbare intellectual mediocrity that wouldn't be worth wasting time over, except that it's become a model of how to instill contempt for francophones. Cultivating hatred toward Quebec's sovereignty becomes the willy-nilly slandering of an entire population.
>
> Is it a coincidence that the majority of these analyses originate in Conrad Black's publications? His pages shelter nearly every habitué of the genre, from Diane Francis to Mordecai Richler.
>
> Those who René Lévesque called Canada's "Rhodesians" are on the way to inventing a subtle, insinuating racism. Sheltering behind the rubric of multiculturalism is the old nostalgia for the days when Anglo-Saxons ran the show. The very idea that Quebec might be an exception to North American cultural hegemony infuriates them.[20]

Even Jean-Paul Marchand, a Franco-Ontarian unfriendly to the Bloc Québécois's policy on official languages, writes: "A surprising number of English-Canadian journalists feel obliged to belittle Quebec, using language of a ferocity which evokes violence. Why should it surprise us to find most English Canadians harbouring a bleak idea of Quebec, given that they're not too fond of the French fact in Canada to begin with?"[21]

LIES ARE NEVER IN SHORT SUPPLY

Mordecai Richler once told readers of the *Atlantic Monthly* that young Parti Québécois members chanted "'Tomorrow belongs to us,' the chilling Hitler Youth song from *Cabaret*,"[22] on the evening of the party's 1976 victory. *La Presse* columnist Pierre Foglia recently recalled this astonishing propaganda. Could there be anything more defamatory?

Imagine, claiming that the "Nazis" of the Parti Québécois borrow their ditties from the Hitler Youth! Of course the song in question is part of a musical theatre show called *Cabaret* and has nothing to do with Hitler Youth. And in any event it was not the song used by the PQ in the 1976 election campaign. That was Quebec composer Stéphane Venne's "À partir d'aujourdh'ui, demain nous appartient" (Starting today, tomorrow belongs to us). This jingle, which the Mouvement Desjardins financial group had once considered using in an ad campaign, caught on in PQ rallies everywhere.

But the trifling fact that his allegation was false did not dissuade Richler from dragging Quebec into the mud once again:

> That didn't stop Mordecai from repeating the story to the CBC.
> So it cropped up finally in the American journal *Commentary*,
> where two McGill professors, Ruth Wisse and Irwin Cotler,
> recalled in an article on Quebec anti-Semitism that it was the
> "Nazi Party song from *Cabaret* that had unfortunately been
> adopted as a French Canadian nationalist anthem."[23]

Composer Stéphane Venne sent his musical score together with the song from *Cabaret* to warn Wisse and Cotler that they had inadvertently been caught up in a defamatory fabulation which had harmed him.[24] Did they apologize? Did they sent a correction to *Commentary*? No. They informed Venne that they would stand by their conclusions.

Irwin Cotler is the federal Liberal member for Mont-Royal, a former director of the Human Rights program at McGill University's Faculty of Law, a professor at Harvard and Yale, and doctor honoris causa of five universities. Wisse is a Harvard professor and has written or edited five books. Who would doubt the intellectual honesty of such people?

According to Richler, one of the goals of the Rebellion of 1837–38 was to impound the goods of all the Jews of Upper and Lower Canada and "strangle" them.[25] This accusation sullied both a progressive political movement and its leader, Louis-Joseph Papineau. This "strangler" of Jews had in fact persuaded Quebec's Legislative Assembly to give civic and political rights to Quebec's Jewish community in 1832. It was the first such legislation in the British Empire, and the English government referred to it when it finally enfranchised England's Jews in 1859.

So where is Richler's source for this dreadful accusation? Nowhere. He cites no document. Nothing.

The myth does have a historical source, though. Researcher Gary Caldwell mentions a British informer named Joseph Bourdon, who infiltrated a secret society called the Frères chasseurs on behalf of Montreal's police chief around the time of the 1837 Rebellion. In a deposition Bourdon said he had his information from a certain Glackmeyer, who had claimed on another occasion that the majority of British soldiers in Quebec had also sworn loyalty to the Frères chasseurs: a patent absurdity.

What we're talking about is hearsay reported by a paid police informer. And the information in question was heard two weeks earlier from a non-French-Canadian who was working with an organizer of the Patriote Rebellion. Glackmeyer had a history of exaggerated declarations unsupported by witnesses or documents. So the imputation to the Patriotes of a plan to exterminate Jews comes from the hearsay of an informer not in direct contact with French-Canadian Patriote leaders rather than a written document concerning the movement or its leaders.[26]

But never mind: Richler's tittle-tattle spread like crabgrass. It inspired M. J. Milloy, a columnist in one of Montreal's cultural weeklies, to compare Papineau to Cambodia's Pol Pot, whose genocidal regime left two million dead:

> Most importantly, the Patriotes were hardly liberty-seeking rev-
> olutionaries, despite the final cries of the condemned on the
> gallows. Patriote leader Joseph Papineau saw the decolonization
> of Quebec as the most necessary means of returning Quebec to
> its preconquest, feudal, agricultural roots, cleansed of the
> influence of English merchants, ruled by the common law and
> the Catholic clergy.
>   In that sense, Papineau is less Che Guevara – a quote from the
> icon of rebellious undergrads ends the flick – and more Pol Pot,
> the nationalist Khmer Rouge leader who, as justification for the
> killing fields, set the clocks to a "year zero" to purge Cambodia
> of foreign influences and return to the mythical glory of the
> Angkor empire.[27]

ONE MUDSLINGING METHOD, AMONG OTHERS

Of all the unfair procedures used by English-Canadian journalists, there is one so ubiquitous that you might imagine it as a separate course in journalism school. Let's call it Quebec Mudslinging 101. To use this time-tested method, the journalist starts by finding an ethnic Montrealer, somebody humble like a taxi driver or shop-keeper. Somebody who only speaks English. Then he encourages this person to make sweeping accusations against French Quebec: racism, exclusivity, whatever.

The next ingredient is to remind the reader about Bill 101, and to make sure of getting a quote from an Alliance Quebec or Equality Party spokesperson.

Finally, the article is given excellent play in the newspaper, ideally with a photograph of the unfortunate cabby. He should look as foreign and un-Quebecish as possible.

Needless to say, it would never occur to the article's intended readers that any Quebec journalist could spend an afternoon in an ethnic or native neighbourhood of Toronto, Winnipeg, or Vancouver and come back with equally lurid, and probably better-founded, tales of racism and harassment. Self-awareness is not English Canada's strong suit.

BEATING UP QUEBEC:
THE KEY TO ELECTORAL SUCCESS

The anti-Quebec fever inevitably spread from journalists and thinkers to politicians. Speaking in Nova Scotia, the Liberal MP for Simcoe North explained that "the separatists want to prevent Quebeckers from travelling outside Quebec." Anna Terrana, Liberal MP for Vancouver East, detailed the similarities she saw between Lucien Bouchard and Adolf Hitler in the *Globe and Mail*, lingering on a supposedly shared thirst for power:

> There's a parallel between what happened in Europe and what's happening here. [The Nazis] first founded a party, then infiltrated the unions and institutions before finding a charismatic leader.
>
> What's happening today [in Quebec] corresponds to what happened in Germany before the war. Now we're moving toward ethnic cleansing. . . . Hitler was crazy; I don't think Bouchard is.[28]

And why should Ms. Terrana regret such remarks? You don't get expelled from the Liberal caucus for a peccadillo like uttering racist remarks about the premier of Quebec. Jean Chrétien did not ask Anna Terrana to recant, and certainly not to apologize. He *did* ask her not to do it again. As Bloc MP Jean-Paul Marchand said: "Imagine the outburst in English Canada if a Quebec member said that kind of thing about Ralph Klein or Mike Harris."[29]

Journalist Barbara Yaffe, who interviewed Terrana, found her remarks "not wholly unreasonable." And it's true that the comparison had been made before, notably by people "as reputable" as Professor Robert Lecker of McGill University, who had already written:

> in its quest for sovereignty the Parti Québécois is endorsing a
> view of linguistic and ethnic dominance that is responsible for
> the ongoing violation of democratic principles and human rights.
> Tensions are rising every day as the separatists get more and more
> confrontational in their demands. If Quebec secedes illegally by
> making a unilateral declaration of independence – the likely sce-
> nario – there will be a revolution and large parts of Canada will
> be ungovernable.[30]

At the end of 1996 federal Liberal Doug Young, then minister of national defence, took umbrage with Bloc deputy Osvaldo Núñez, who comes from Chile. He accused him of being an immigrant who came to Canada intending to destroy it, and declared Núñez ought to return home if he couldn't stop behaving that way. Here's a federal MP having a racist rant about an immigrant, and not a peep out of the Anglo media. No theatrical indignation! Not the tiniest disavowal! Perhaps out in the corridor they were cheering Mr. Young for slapping down this troublesome newcomer. After all, every Anglo-Canadian pundit had cried from the rooftops that sep-aratists didn't like immigrants. Hadn't anybody told this Chilean not to confuse everybody by getting himself elected a PQ deputy?

On August 28, 1997, Gerry Weiner, once a Conservative min-ister of immigration, has a press scrum in Ottawa. The order of the day is to accuse Quebec's government of a racist preference for French-speaking immigrants:

> This country had a non-discriminatory immigration policy. It's
> clear that Quebec is building an ethnocentric French-speaking
> enclave by a careful method of selecting immigrants. . . . The
> federal government is sitting by, silently, watching the separatists
> ram their agenda down the throats of Canadians by imposing
> racist and discriminatory immigration policies.[31]

It's worth remembering, as political theorist Maryse Potvin reminds us, that Quebec's immigration policy is "the fruit of policies set in place by the Quebec Liberal Party, which Gerry Weiner certainly did not denounce when he was federal immigration minister. And they haven't changed since."[32] But why bother with logic when the real job is dirtying Quebec's reputation?

THE LEVINE AFFAIR

The "national unity" psychosis went critical in spring of 1998, with the David Levine affair. Nourished for years by Anglo pundits and opinion makers, hostility to Quebec by now is part and parcel of most Anglo-Canadians' cultural baggage.

When David Levine, former PQ candidate and one-time Quebec delegate to New York, was named director of Ottawa's new hospital, there was a regular revolt among the region's English-speaking people. They were duly egged on by the local media.

> This hiring [of Levine] paves the way for Ernst Zündel [a notorious Holocaust-denier] to head up the Human Rights Commission. . . . Ottawa's anglophones are in the front line of the battle for the country's survival: up till now, a solitary struggle. Betrayed by wet-hen Liberal politicos who lace up their jogging shoes and take off when a separatist appears, these citizens are no longer able to struggle alone. What they're not used to, and, I suppose, can't stand, is to see themselves so stupidly provoked by the system.[33]

In English Canada, having been a separatist and having been a Nazi are just about the same thing. Péquiste equals Nazi. Never mind that Levine was no longer politically active, he is permanently marked by having once belonged to the Parti Québécois. "Not knowing he is one isn't the same thing as knowing he isn't one . . . If you ran for the nazis in 1979, never repudiated them, and won't say if you're one now, you are one, right?"[34] Ontario premier

Mike Harris joined the chorus: "Surely, there is an administrative capability within Ontario or at least within Canada, or even a non-Canadian, who believes in Canada and keeping Canada together."[35] Any foreigner would be a better hospital administrator than a Quebec sovereignist!

The hospital board fought back courageously against the racism in the media and the streets. David Levine remained in place.

> In the "Levine Affair," racism even became a principle of political action and mobilization in a part of the population, soon to be taken up by certain politicians. Now, there's three real dangers when universal ideals are cheapened by racialist sloganeering. First, it trivializes racism in the popular mind; second, it leads to a fixation on supposedly "irreducible" identities; and finally, there's its use as a "political weapon."[36]

English Canada's view of the country's history has been falsified by Panglossian historians. Today, Canadians manifest a serene sense of moral superiority with regard to Québécois and Americans alike. They have become a self-important clutch of Pharisees. Consider how even noted historian Jack Granatstein, in collaboration with Robert Bothwell[37], can write in good faith that Canada is a healthier place than a United States marked by racism, assassination, and warfare. . . .

> In the past, numerous Canadian historians have too frequently presented our history in a self-righteous and selective way. These historians have written about the positive aspects of our past and have ignored the negative. . . .
> A possible rationale for such an approach to Canadian history was national unity. In a bi-national, multi-cultural society, emphasis was placed on the positive aspects of our history in the belief that this was necessary to achieve a national unity. Unfortunately, the consequence of such historical selectivity has

been the development of Canadian historical myths. For example, not only have we been taught that Canada was free of racial bigotry, but also that Canada always treated aboriginal people fairly and with justice. We cannot, however, understand the Canadian contemporary situation if these historical myths are not analyzed or our past examined for historical truths.[38]

The *Heritage Minutes*, broadcast for the last ten years on television and in movie houses, are the popular version of this Ottawa-sponsored project of historical denial. Using dummy foundations, Heritage Minister Sheila Copps has paid out $7.2 million for a historical whitewashing meant to make the country feel better about itself.

This book is my reply to the *Heritage Minutes*, a journalist's investigation of the dark and bloody side of Canada's history, and a refusal to put up with this organized lying by omission.

In recent years Quebec has been the victim of a campaign led by prominent English Canadians which can only be described as contemptible. We are accused of racism, of irredeemable bigotry. We have to sit still while ignoramuses tell us that these defects are rooted in our culture, and then spread the same lie abroad. These self-appointed prefects really must forget a good deal of their own history in order to wag a finger at us.

Let's be clear: since 1760, anybody in this country who wasn't white, Anglo-Saxon, and Protestant was the target of shunning, racism, and human-rights violations. Our high-spirited attackers suffer historical amnesia. You'll read in these pages whatever History has truly retained of our predecessors and their society.

1

PAYBACK TIME

Though they've long coveted the women of France, together with its cuisine, geography, and climate, the English have always rather considered the French as enemies. Favourite enemies, in fact! The Conquest of New France was a mere episode in a millenarian rivalry going back to William the Conqueror. He subdued England's barons, imposing a Franco-Norman military caste and, it really must be said, civilization upon the raffish Anglo-Saxon countryfolk.

During the Hundred Years War (1337–1453), the English tried to return the favour by laying hands on the French throne and establishing a continental zone of influence. Only when half of France belonged to them did the Franks, rallying behind the Virgin of Orleans, hustle them back to their foggy island.

This deep-rooted dislike took on a lubricious dimension with Henry VIII. He broke with Roman Catholicism. Now France's Catholicism became an additional reason for antagonism.

Colonial conflicts in the seventeenth and eighteenth centuries, French support for U.S. independence, the French Revolution, and the Napoleonic epic kept the quarrel hale and hearty. Confrontations in Africa early in the twentieth century abraded both countries' nerve endings to the point they were amazed to find themselves allies in the First World War.

By the time the Seven Years War (1756–63) arrived, France and England had already been disputing the North American continent for a century and a half. Seventy thousand Canadiens and their native allies, together with a few thousand soldiers and French administrators, controlled the continent with the exception of a slender coastal strip where nearly two million English colonists were squeezed together. Understandably, the British longed to clear out this handful of heavily outnumbered "French papists" who nonetheless blocked their way and raided them incessantly. Also understandable is the pent-up frustration they unleashed on the French once they succeeded. The Acadians were the first to feel it.

ATTEMPTED GENOCIDE AGAINST THE ACADIANS

Longfellow's poem *Evangeline* is the enduring chronicle of the Acadian drama. Let's go back to the town of Grand-Pré on September 5, 1755. The men are jammed into the little village church. Lieutenant colonel John Winslow reads the edict of deportation:

> Gentlemen I have received from His Excellency Governor
> Lawrence the King's commission which I have in my hand and
> whose orders you are conveyed together to manifest to you His
> Majesty's final resolution to the French inhabitants of this His
> province of Nova Scotia. . . . Your lands and tenements, cattle of
> all kinds, and livestock of all sorts, are forfeited to the Crown . . .
> and you, yourselves are to be removed from this, His Province. I
> am, through His Majesty's goodness, directed to allow you liberty
> to carry off your money and household goods. . . . You are now
> the King's prisoners.[1]

The scene repeated itself through Acadia. The price they were to pay had been minutely arrived at a year earlier by Nova Scotia's governor, the war criminal Charles Lawrence. His "final solution" to the Acadian question was thought through with the perfidious spirit we have so often attributed to Albion.

> The only way to prevent them fleeing with their livestock is to conceal our plans, and to ensure that all the men, young and old, above all heads of families, fall into our power.
>
> You will then detain them until the transport ships are ready to embark them. No fear of the women and children fleeing with the animals once the men are in hand. Even so, prudence suggests our detachments keep a watch on the villages and roads, as well as seizing boats, canoes, small craft, and any other vessels which come to hand.
>
> Foodstuffs and livestock are confiscated to the profit of the Crown, in view of the rebellion, and must be applied toward the expense of deporting them. No person is to be permitted to acquire them under any pretext, and any such purchase is legally nullified since the French are stripped of title to all property and shall be permitted to take nothing with them apart from furniture and money presently in their possession.[2]

Lawrence is lying when he uses the word rebellion. It is true, however, that the Acadians had refused to renew their pledge of allegiance to England, and they had indeed been British subjects since their land was ceded to England in the Treaty of Utrecht (1713). At that time Queen Anne had proclaimed the safety of their property titles, and London had asked them to remain where they were.

> It is our wish and pleasure that all who hold land under our government in Newfoundland and Acadia, who have become our subjects through the last treaty of peace, and who have wished to remain under our authority, have the right to possess and enjoy

the said lands and leases without hindrance, as fully and freely as our other subjects do.[3]

In 1730 the Acadians swore to remain strictly neutral in French–English conflicts and they did so right through the war of 1744–48. But they were an encumbrance! A French Catholic majority in an Anglo Protestant colony! "London fretted about Nova Scotia, a British colony which, to all intents and purposes, was still French territory. Only one thing to do: inundate it with English colonists and 'Britannify' it."[4]

A policy we'll also see applied in the St. Lawrence Valley after the Conquest. But the immediate problem was the feeble interest of English colonists in the equally feeble soil of Nova Scotia. Lawrence therefore decided to eliminate the French. In 1754 France and England were enjoying a rare moment of peaceful cohabitation before the eruption of the Seven Years War (1756). Lawrence chose this moment to suggest the simple theft of Acadian lands. "They possess the prettiest and largest lands in the province, leaving us quite simply no place to put our colonists. . . . I cannot help thinking it would be best . . . to drive them out."[5]

Once he had the green light, Lawrence secretly prepared his plans for ethnic cleansing. On July 28, 1755, he had his council ratify the expulsion of the Acadians, French-speaking British subjects who by unhappy chance owned the prettiest land in Nova Scotia: "After ripe deliberation it was unanimously agreed that preventing the French inhabitants from returning and molesting those who might settle on their lands was best achieved by dispersing them in several colonies on this Continent, and to immediately engage a number of vessels for their transport."[6]

Colonel Robert Monckton put Lawrence's ethnic cleansing into effect. In June 1755, ignoring treaties signed with France, he seized the forts of Beauséjour and Gaspereau. In the adjacent areas he began the destruction of French Acadia. On August 8, 1755, Lawrence sent him new orders to hasten the final solution of the Acadian question:

you may have difficulty seizing the inhabitants, and should therefore destroy all villages on the north and northwest coasts of the
isthmus near Fort Beauséjour. Those who flee to the forest should
be starved. Be diligent, however, in sparing animals and unharvested
fields, so that your men may return in safety. Above all, do what
you can to prevent French and Savages from destroying animals.[7]

Like Nazi officers, Monckton enacted his orders without pangs
of conscience and with not a little pride in a job well done. Many
tiny villages were scattered through the sector for which he was
responsible. The men, perhaps naively, sought shelter in the
nearby forests in the belief the soldiers would never take out their
frustration on the women and children. They were wrong. In a
typical case, at Boishébert, on the Petcoudiac River, a British
detachment seized twenty-three women and children and burned
every building they could find, about 200 in all, together with a
quantity of wheat and flax. Lawrence's indifference to the fate of
these people is clear enough in this directive to Monckton: "I
would have you not wait for the wives and children coming in, but
ship off the men without them."[8]

On August 9, 1755, not a single person appears at the gathering
place designated by Monckton for the population of the
Beaubassin region. The Acadian countryfolk defy the British. So
he decides on a trick, summoning them the next day to a meeting
which, he assures them, "will concern the governor at Halifax's
measures for the safeguarding of their lands." All who appeared
the next day were imprisoned at his orders and forcibly placed on
the deportation ships.[9]

In Nazi fashion, the British took reprisals against the parents of
those who had rebelliously hidden in the woods, the better to
force them out. "If within two days the absent ones are not delivered up, military execution would be immediately visited upon
the next of kin."[10]

In the course of undertaking this "ethnic cleansing," Monckton deported more than 2,100 Acadians from Beaubassin, Beauséjour, and the Chignecto isthmus. He confiscated their lands and goods, burned the dwellings, barns, and outbuildings, and seized the livestock.

Monckton's odious actions constituted, under the circumstances, a clear crime of genocide as defined by the United Nations. This stipulates that genocide occurs where there is "assassination, extermination, enslaving, deportation and other inhuman acts committed against a civilian population, before or during a war; or persecution for political, racial or religious reasons."

Monckton's efficiency earned him the post of lieutenant-governor of Nova Scotia after it was vacated by Lawrence, in December 1755. This made him the head of the chain of command which captured and deported a further 3,000 Acadians from the Île Saint-Jean [Prince Edward Island] in 1758.[11]

Spelled "Moncton," the New Brunswick city and its francoph one university constitute an eternal memorial to the glory of this odious man. There's even a street named for him in Quebec City. On September 24, 1999, Richard Gervais asked Quebec mayor Jean-Paul l'Allier to put an end to this absurd situation:

> An avenue of Quebec carries the name of Moncton, that is to say Monckton, colonel of the British colonial army. Since the city disgraces itself in offering him this unearned honour, I hereby demand that Moncton Avenue become the "Avenue of the Acadians." Running from the Chemin Sainte-Foy to the Plains of Abraham, this road carries the name of a principal executor of the Acadian genocide perpetrated in the mid-eighteenth century.
>
> Colonel Monckton organized and directed the first deportations, notably of the 6,500 inhabitants of Grand-Pré, Annapolis, Beauséjour, and Piziquid, who were locked into rotting hulks

bound for unfriendly American colonies. He condemned them to
misery, diaspora, and death. This same Colonel Monckton, in
December of the same year – now graced with the title of governor of Nova Scotia after Lawrence – once again pursued the "final
solution" to the "Acadian problem." And this at a time when no
state of war existed.

Three-quarters of the Acadian population would vanish during
the seven years of deportation, leaving in 1762 only 2,500 of the
15,000 who had lived there in 1755. Between 5,000 and 6,000,
about a third of the population, will meet their deaths. Colonel
Robert Monckton directed half these deportations, not to
mention the accompanying exactions, terror, house burnings and
barn burnings, seizure of land, goods, cattle, and grain.

It is ignominious that Quebec preserves the name of the
author of this ethnic cleansing in its toponymy. The hateful
homonym "Moncton" dishonours us and harms Quebec's
friendship with the people of Acadia. Worse, it shocks historic
memory to see this name adjacent to the Plains of Abraham,
knowing as we do that 150 exiled Acadians stood with Quebec's
defenders in 1759, and that opposing them was the selfsame
Monckton, second in command to the siege general, James
Wolfe. It's only fair that Moncton's avenue become the Avenue
of the Acadians.[12]

François Baby of the Université Laval wrote in *Le Devoir*:

As a soldier in Acadia and Quebec, Monckton's actions were of
great and unacceptable cruelty, quite equivalent to crimes of
genocide and war, to crimes against peace and humanity, in the
sense we understand those terms today.

Canada is one of the rare countries to join with the former
Soviet Union in arrogantly and permanently afflicting those
whom it defeated with symbols of humiliation. Whether through
cynicism or shamelessness, it reminds them of their conquest and

glorifies their conquerors. Towns are named Moncton or Colborne, streets become Wolfe, Amherst, Murray, Fraser, Moncton, and so on.

Would Paris name a street after Adolf Hitler, or so honour the commander of the Reich tank division, which carried out the massacre at Oradour-sur-Glane in June 1944? Do we see French towns called Rommel or Goering?[13]

Is it appropriate to accuse Lawrence and his subaltern Monckton of crimes which didn't exist at the time? François Baby insists that "even in distant times, military tribunals routinely punished those who committed acts nowadays described as crimes of war, genocide, and inhumanity."[14] He cites the jurist Mario Bettati, who says such acts of infamy were first defined "in customary fashion, arising from the laws of war, and were ratified by ancient military jurisprudence."[15]

Isn't it a national shame to see the roads and institutions of Quebec commemorating our enemies and their hangmen? What people on earth, apart from us, would tolerate it? It's a question of self-respect! Hereabouts, what is demeaning is thought to be normal. How do Acadians deal with the fact their university is named after the persecutor of their ancestors?

Monckton is, of course, a hero in English Canada. The *Dictionary of Canadian Biography*, François Baby tells us, speaks of the criminal Monckton's "humane perspective"[16] and his lack of enthusiasm for the orders he must carry out. Just obeying orders, sir! . . . It's a familiar melody, isn't it?

So the English thought they'd finished with the bad, bad French . . . not reckoning with a certain tenacity on the part of the Acadians. For they would return to New Brunswick. But they'd never get back the fine lands which had been stripped from them, nor to this day have they been compensated for their enormous losses. A lot of effort, however, has since been expended on assimilating them rather than having to deport them again.

THE CONQUEST

After the final destruction of French Acadia, the British turned
their attention to the St. Lawrence Valley and the Great Lakes;
that is to say, New France.

General James Wolfe, hero of the Plains of Abraham, began the
year 1758 by pillaging the Gaspé Peninsula in preparation for the
attack on Quebec the next year. With 12,000 soldiers he moved
up the river in June 1759, sowing terror in leisurely fashion, until
he arrived at the Île d'Orléans, where he evicted the farmers and
established his headquarters. This is from the proclamation he
issued that summer in the parish of St.-Laurent:

> The King my master, justly angered by France, resolves to punish
> her pride and revenge her abuses against England's colonies. . . .
>
> Therefore it pleases him to send me into this country at the
> head of a redoubtable army. Labourers, settlers, and countryfolk,
> women, children, and sacred ministers are in no way the object of
> the King of Great Britain's resentment. . . . Such inhabitants may
> remain with their families in their homes. I promise to protect
> them and assure them that they may continue to enjoy their
> property and follow their religion without molestation; in a word,
> to enjoy in the midst of war the sweet diversions of peace.[17]

Some, to their later woe, took Wolfe at his word. Three men
were scalped and a house into which women and children fled was
set ablaze – they were burned alive. The entire length of the South
Shore was similarly sacked.

War criminal Robert Monckton, fresh from the ruins of Acadia,
prepared himself as Wolfe's second in command to ravage the
Quebec that still glorifies his memory.

> On August 6, Wolfe ordered Monckton to devastate the country-
> side on the South Shore. First Monckton torched the houses,

barns, and outbuildings, together with the crops, in the region from Beaumont to the Chaudière River.

Then he ordered Major George Scott, an officer, to destroy the South Shore. Though the seige had ended five days earlier, Scott's soldiers burnt 998 houses, barns, and buildings from Kamouraska to Cap-Saint-Ignace between September 9 and 17. He was considered a specialist in this art, and his diligence brought him rapid promotion to lieutenant colonel. . . .

The true motivations behind the barbarity of Monckton and the British are crystal clear. They took the mass of civilians hostage by leaving them nothing but "famine and devastation."[18]

A soldier's journal highlights the satisfaction felt by the perpetrators of this misery: "Having mastery of that country through the siege, we burned and destroyed fourteen hundred fine farms. We sent out troops continuously to devastate the country up and down the river, and did such a superb job they'll need a half-century to set things right again."[19]

This was total war against the French population on Wolfe's part, indistinguishable from Lawrence's methods against the Acadians. Nor did Wolfe delude himself about this, as a letter to Amherst shows:

> If . . . we find that Quebec is not likely to fall into our hands (persevering however to the last moment), I propose to set the Town on fire with Shells, to destroy the Harvest, Houses, & Cattle both above and below, to send off as many Canadians as possible to Europe, & to leave famine and desolation behind me; belle resolution, & tres chretienne! but we must teach these Scoundrels to make war in a more gentlemanlike manner.[20]

Historians such as Laurier Lapierre[21] have claimed this war was between France and Great Britain, and had nothing to do with the Canadiens. France's eviction from North America meant nothing to them, says Lapierre, tears in his eyes, during Jacques Godbout's film *Le Sort de l'Amérique* (The Fate of America). False, false, false! How can anyone not see that this war touched every civilian, and that every civilian knew that England considered them the enemy? The French-speaking population fought alongside the regular French army. What village in the St. Lawrence Valley didn't send a militia to stiffen the French lines? Even the military commander, Governor Vaudreuil, was born in Quebec.[22] These people were defending a way of life, a religion, and a country against the hereditary English enemy. And why was a volunteer regiment of Acadians battling the English on the Plains of Abraham if the subject didn't concern them? Count on Lapierre and the priceless René Daniel Dubois (another star of Godbout's painfully extended "Heritage Minute") to tell us that the Conquest was nothing but an administrative changeover after a scrappy election campaign. Saying that the Canadiens weren't defending their national existence isn't far from intellectual dishonesty.

In the articles of the capitulation of Montreal, the Canadiens are treated as a group separate from the French. In particular, they are given the right to remain on their land, unlike the Acadians, who still suffer the malice of the English. The deportation order is still in force.

Seeking to minimize the Conquest's impact on Quebec society is part of a large-scale political rewriting of history, financed through the various propaganda arms of the federal government, together with the trusts and foundations that enjoy its emoluments.

Meanwhile, back to the story. Wolfe continued the siege of Quebec into September, setting the night of the thirteenth for his attack. By the time the sun rose on this dark day, his soldiers were on the Plains of Abraham, and by 9 a.m. were locked in battle. An hour later the army of French and Canadiens was in flight. New France was lost and Quebec had capitulated. Lévis's expedition against the English on those same plains the following year would make no difference because Britain had been quicker than France in sending new supplies to Quebec . . . Britannia ruled the waves! The defenceless country and its exhausted people are haunted by famine. Vaudreuil surrenders. On September 8, 1760, he signs the capitulation of New France in front of Wolfe's successor, Amherst.

AMHERST AND THE ATTEMPTED GENOCIDE OF FRANCE'S NATIVE ALLIES

The new military administration governs by decree. Its commander is General Jeffrey Amherst, commander of all His Majesty's troops in North America.

Shortly after Montreal's surrender, Sir William Johnson, the famous Indian affairs commissioner, who was married to a Mohawk, suggests that Amherst would do well to continue France's commercial arrangements with the natives. But Amherst loathes the natives. Instead, he makes them pay for the necessities (gunpowder, to begin with) that they had received for free from the French: "Lord Jeffrey Amherst, the British commander-in-chief for America, believed . . . that the best way to control Indians was through a system of strict regulations and punishment when necessary, not 'bribery,' as he called the granting of provisions."[23] He also cut the supply of powder and upped the price of goods, which immediately sent the tribes of the old French Alliance to the edge of famine. They had grown dependent on this merchandise, having forgotten the art of hunting and the striking of arrowheads.

Nor did Amherst stop there. His contempt for the natives was such that he summarily turned over Seneca lands to his officers, a decision which London was later obliged to overturn. But not before Amherst's disdain had provoked a terrible uprising which would last until 1764. It was led by the high chief Pontiac, long a French ally, and his Ottawa warriors. Pontiac's Conspiracy[24] gambled on recurring hostility between France and England, given that they were still technically at war. And France still had useful military resources in Louisiana and in the Illinois country, where the outlying fort of Chartres was located.

But in the end, only 300 French Canadians, commanded by Zachary Chicot, supported Pontiac. They were the last Canadiens to take up arms against the English during the Seven Years War, allying themselves with the ten insurgent tribes of the American Midwest. Amherst's biographer, J. C. Long, said the general was aroused "to a frenzy, a frenzy almost hysterical in its impotence" by Pontiac's attacks on the forts of Detroit and Presqu'Isle: "it would be happy for the provinces there was not an Indian settlement within a thousand Miles of them, and when they are properly punished, I care not how soon they move their Habitations, for the Inhabitants of the Woods are the fittest Companions for them, they being more nearly allied to the Brute than to the Human Creation."[25]

When the rebellion broke out, most of Britain's troops were tied down by operations in the Antilles. Finally deployed against Pontiac, they hurried to assist forts already under siege for many months. Detroit was in trouble, and the troops at Fort Pitts (once Fort Duquesne and the future Pittsburgh) were laid low by smallpox.

Amherst entrusted Colonel Henry Bouquet and 460 soldiers with the job of freeing Fort Pitts. An American lawyer knowledgeable about First Nations law, Peter d'Errico, at the University of Pennsylvania, describes the flurry of letters between Amherst and his subalterns as "filled with comments that indicate a genocidal intent."[26]

These include Bouquet's June 25, 1763, declaration to Amherst that the Indian "Vermine . . . has forfeited all claim to the rights of humanity." And again, the same day: "I would rather choose the liberty to kill any Savage. . . ." On July 9, Amherst pressured Indian agent Sir William Johnson to take measures "as would Bring about the Total Extirpation of those Indian Nations." On August 7 he hammers away at the same theme to Johnson's aide, George Croghan: "their Total Extirpation is scarce sufficient Attonement." And yet again, August 27, once more to Johnson: "put a most Effectual Stop to their very Being."

Did Amherst actually try to do this? In particular, did he condone the use of the smallpox virus to wipe them out? Until recently the matter was undecided. It was celebrated historian Francis Parkman who first published, in his 1886 book about Pontiac, Amherst's letter to Bouquet demanding the use of germ warfare: "Could it not be contrived to send the Small Pox among those disaffected tribes of Indians? We must on this occasion use every stratagem in our power to reduce them."[27]

But Parkman drew no conclusions, apart from noting that in the spring of 1764 an Englishman arrived in Fort Pitts with the news that smallpox was raging among the Indians. Historians have been divided as to whether the diabolical plan was abandoned, or put into practice without Amherst's explicit approval. However, d'Errico has recently settled the matter while studying microfilms kept in the U.S. Library of Congress.[28] They include Bouquet's letter to Amherst of July 13, 1763, where the matter of smallpox-infected blankets was first proposed:

> I will try to inoculate the Indians by means of Blankets that
> may fall in their hands taking care however not to get the
> disease myself.
> As it is a pity to oppose good men against them, I wish we
> could make use of the Spaniard's method, and hunt them down
> with English dogs, supported by Rangers and from Light Horse,[29]
> who would, I think, effectively extirpate or remove that vermine.

On July 16 Amherst approved the plan: "You will Do well to try to inoculate the Indians by means of Blankets, as well as to try Every other method that can serve to extirpate this execrable Race. I should be very glad your Scheme for hunting them Down by Dogs could take effect. . . ."

"All your Directions will be observed," replied Bouquet, now charged with the underhanded execution of this criminal plan. Ten days later Amherst especially applauds the "Spanish method" of running the Indians to ground, lamenting only the shortage of dogs.

Captain Ecuyer, a British officer at Fort Pitts, took measures in 1763 to deliver infected blankets to the Delaware, Shawnee, and Mingo who besieged the fort. By August the siege was lifted. And the Shawnee, it appears, carried the smallpox virus into the southwest, where peaceable tribes were infected.

Pontiac's uprising dissolved of its own accord by the end of the autumn, as the allied tribes slipped away for the annual hunting season. By October there was further bad news from the commander of the French fort of Chartres in Illinois: a peace treaty has been signed.

Still, Pontiac persists. The following April, spring of 1764, he appears at Chartres demanding reinforcements. But a rival chieftain, Manitou, has already persuaded the remaining warriors of the old French Alliance to lay down arms.

Robert O'Connell, a specialist in biological warfare, records that Britain's use of infected blankets set a precedent.[30] It went well beyond the old custom of catapulting diseased corpses into besieged towns. It appears the British were intimately aware of how devastating smallpox was against the feeble immune systems of Amerindians. And so the blankets were the first bioweapon to exploit an enemy's known immunodeficiency.

Amherst went to his grave in 1778 with the title of Field Marshal Baron Amherst of Montreal. His reputation was excellent. Quebec historians greatly admired the moderation of the surrender terms he imposed on Montreal, and his sympathy for Canadiens. . . .

How, then, shall we deal with the now-established fact that he set out to exterminate vulnerable native populations with a bioweapon? Is it quite normal to venerate genocide in a Montreal street name?

There was breathtaking pomp when the city celebrated the 300th anniversary of the Great Peace of Montreal, signed among the French, their allies, and the Iroquois. But it would have been more memorable had the city used the occasion to rename Amherst Street the Rue de la Grande-Paix.

ORIGINS OF THE ENGLISH
OLIGARCHY IN MONTREAL

For four years Quebec lived under martial law: September 1760 to August 1764. The British army's wagon trains groaned under the weight of profiteers and traffickers who felt perfectly entitled, by right of conquest, to the goods and the sweat of the Canadiens. Governor James Murray, Amherst's successor, wasted no time in sharing his distaste for the carpetbaggers with his London agent:

> it has not been easy to satisfy a Conquering army, a Conquered People, and a set of Merchants who have resorted to a Country where there is no money, who think themselves superior in rank and fortune to the Soldier and the Canadian, as they are pleased to deem the first Voluntary and the second born Slaves.[31]

These gentlemen will certainly make the fortune they seek. From 1770 to 1970, give or take a few years, their descendants will be in the catbird seat in Quebec. A moneyed caste.

The Canadiens were British subjects from the signing of the Treaty of Paris (1763), and their religion was protected "to the extent permitted by British law." This didn't prevent Murray from dreaming of converting them to Protestantism, a project much endangered by the pushiness and fanaticism of the monopoly-minded merchants.

> Great progress is already made; the National Antipathy is entirely got the better of on the side of the Canadians. I wish I could say as much of the British subjects, several from New England now established here are most inveterate fanaticks, a little address however may even make them of advantage, a proper contradiction of their insults will gain and strengthen the confidence of the Canadians to Governmt., which confidence being the Main Spring must be perpetually kept in order and cannot fail of perfecting the

business I charge myself with, which is no less than the reforma-
tion of the greatest part of the inhabitants of this colony.[32]

Even while working to convert the Canadiens, Murray followed a parallel path of making sure his administration got
control over the Catholic hierarchy. Monsignor Pontbriand had
died in June of 1760, leaving the Quebec church without a bishop.
The local authority had designated the Sulpician superior, Father
Mongolfier, as his successor; but Murray was bitterly opposed to
the choice of this principled and not-at-all docile clergyman.

There were other reasons to question the choice, but it was
very likely British opposition which decided the matter. Murray
much favoured his own friend, Quebec vicar-general Jean-Olivier
Briand. Briand would become "superintendent of the Roman
Church" after himself going to London, with the governor's blessing, to beg for the post.

And "Murray's role would have enduring consequences. For
seventy-five years, governors would intervene in both episcopal
and parish appointments. Worse even than becoming a ward of a
Protestant prince, the Quebec Church passed under the direct
authority of a Protestant governor quietly determined to control
its future."[33]

Thus the English sword dipped itself in the French holy-water
font, giving birth to an alliance which would endure into the
twentieth century.

Given that there were no Protestants at all among the Canadiens,
Murray had to find allies there or else resign himself to choosing
his administration from 300 or so francophobic profiteers. This
would have been aberrant, even under the circumstances. As
Marcel Trudel writes:

the King's instructions to Murray in 1763 and Carleton in 1768
would have proven harsh to the Canadiens had they not been
moderated in practice. The oath attached to the Test specified

by the King would have prevented Catholics from becoming court clerks, prosecutors, lawyers, apothecaries, civil servants, captains, lieutenants, sergeants, or corporals. Murray and Carleton showed sensible moderation once they realized it would be impossible to enforce English civil law or fill government posts if the Test were observed. So they allowed the Catholic hierarchy to acquit itself of its customary duties and set aside the oath where competent and necessary Canadiens were concerned. They also restored pre-Conquest civil law and permitted French trials. By the time a new government had been designed for Quebec, in 1771, the rights it officially proposed had already been accorded in fact: freedom of religion and French civil law.[34]

It's less than truthful to claim that these concessions involved magnanimity toward the Canadiens. The first British governors had little choice but to soften the royal edict if they wanted to govern the colony at all, and did so grudgingly.

The English wheeler-dealers managed to get Murray recalled, but when Carleton arrived he quickly realized that he'd have to continue Murray's policy of openness.

STORM CLOUDS ON THE HORIZON

As New France passed under British authority, discontent was spiralling out of control in the American colonies. Where was their share of Conquest spoils? The new lands, the reparations? And what was this nonsense about new taxes to pay the bills for the Seven Years War? Outraged opinion led to revolt, and London went on red alert. The British authorities were well aware of their weakness, should the American colonies demand independence; placating the Canadiens would at least assure a secure base of operations in Canada. Mad King George III was lucid enough to approve the Quebec Act in June of 1774.

It was to become effective in 1775, a mini-constitution for the province of Quebec. This was an immense relief to Carleton, who had, since becoming governor in 1766, become convinced that civil war was inevitable in North America. In his view, repressing the Canadiens would make them ripe for the plucking by France, which was already casting an eye at American instability and dreaming of winning back the continent. Far better to flatter the priests and the seigneurs, and let the minuscule British minority grumble in the corner of the room.

But the merchants weren't taking this sitting down. They never ceased pulling strings in London to ensure a continued monopoly of influence. Marcel Trudel writes: "When the matter of establishing a new government arose, they petitioned repeatedly for a legislative assembly through which, given that Catholics would be excluded, they could control to control all the country's affairs."[35]

The Quebec Act restored the old frontiers of New France, except for the loss of the Lake Champlain Valley. It also swept aside the troublesome Test in favour of a bland oath of allegiance, and restored French civil law and even the Catholic Church's traditional right to impose a tithe on its flock. Finally, the Act relegitimized the seigneurial system. It needs to be said, of course, that these concessions were linked to the fact that the seigneurs and the clergy were well and truly bought by then. Carleton's arrival from England in September of 1774 was welcomed by fifty seigneurs and the entire senior clergy. The era of the collaboration of the Canadian elites had begun . . . which gave ulcers to the English merchants, their general opinion being that the Canadiens were a degenerate race. Papists on top of everything else!

The colony was well-secured, Carleton felt. But he was wrong on several counts. The people were not at all fond of seigneurs and tithes. The nobility and clergy weren't nearly as influential as he had thought. In addition, the Canadiens didn't share his mounting anxiety, especially after February of 1775, about the unrest in the territories which would soon become the United States.

Sublime indifference comes closer to describing their feelings about what, to them, was just another Anglo-Saxon family quarrel. And in any event, the British had confiscated their firearms. Carleton didn't dare impose conscription.

On the first of May, 1775, as the Quebec Act was about to be proclaimed in Montreal, the citizenry noted with stupefaction that George III's bust had been vandalized: "Here you see the Pope of Canada and the English idiot." It was *lèse-majesté*, but with the flavour of Anglo-Protestant merchant trickery about it. Street fights broke out between Canadiens and the English.

QUARRELLING IN THE THIRTEEN COLONIES

But if the Montreal merchants were grousing, the thirteen colonies were in an uproar. Their thanks for helping undo New France was soaring taxes, the restoration of the pre-war borders, and the recognition of Catholicism. Not what they'd hoped for! Especially since these rights and favours were showered on a people whom they'd fought for a century and a half. For the American colonies, the Quebec Act was nothing less than a low blow against themselves, a *casus belli*.

"The Canadian business is more offensive, in truth, than that of Boston," thundered Alexander Hamilton, a future author of the U.S. Constitution. The War of Independence began in May of 1775.

It wasn't long before Quebec became part of the military stakes, as the Americans set out to occupy Montreal and Quebec City. The advance of 1,500 men sowed panic in the streets of Montreal, and Carleton fled north to the capital. By November 13 the assailants were in the streets of Montreal, and occupied the city all winter. Twelve hundred of their compatriots marched on Quebec City.

Here they were less successful, reduced through disorganization to a frightful state where men gnawed on boiled shoe leather. Led by the same Benedict Arnold who later betrayed his country for money, a motley 800 men showed up in front of the walls of Quebec. The rest had fled. Even with reinforcements from Montreal, Arnold's attack was a travesty: an assault in a snowstorm on the memorable night of December 31.

The survivors lasted out the winter, until spring thaw brought British reinforcements down the Saint Lawrence and sent them fleeing.

Although the Americans had denounced the papist French and the Quebec Act with equal scorn, they now set about, in a curious reversal, the task of recruiting Quebec as an ally. But the Canadiens were suspicious. The wind was changing direction too frequently, and so they settled into sullen neutrality while the Anglo-Saxons settled their differences among themselves.

It must be said the Americans weren't outstanding as occupiers. David Wooster, their senior officer in Montreal, forbade the celebration of Midnight Mass. And after a promising beginning, where they paid for supplies with silver, came an abrupt shift to worthless paper money.

The U.S. Congress sent Benjamin Franklin to negotiate a solution. He soon grasped that nothing would bring the Canadiens into the American fold. His own advisor, a Catholic priest who had accompanied him, pointed out that the Catholic Canadiens already had everything they could desire, thanks to the Quebec Act.

With the Americans vanquished, Carleton ordered a commission of inquiry to find out how many Canadiens had collaborated with the invaders. He was prepared to overlook the regular wartime dealing which people did in order to survive. But there were also true traitors, and they were found mostly among the Anglo-Montreal traders, like Thomas Walker, who had exchanged intelligence with the Americans. Walkers' letters were full of the poor-me, look-how-the-French-oppress-us tone familiar to anybody who listens to today's Quebec anglophones complain to the Americans about us marginalizing them. Consistently self-interested, Walker and his friends also underlined to the Americans that they couldn't afford entirely to break with Great

Britain, since that would mean Paris taking control of Quebec's trade once again.

By 1783 the Americans had their independence, but had done nothing to free Montreal's English from the clutches of the French. Nothing direct, that is; by chasing the city's Loyalists north to Quebec they inadvertently boosted the fortunes of Quebec's beleaguered English minority. These Loyalists were the most royalist, reactionary, blinkered crowd of undemocratic Catholic-haters you could find anywhere. They wasted no time forging an alliance with the resident British war profiteers, to the future misery of the French majority.

2

"BRITISH LIBERTIES," 1791–1811

Throughout our history we've been spoon-fed the words "British liberties" on every possible occasion. Pick any date and you'll find "Canadian" politicians and their French-speaking sidekicks, from Wilfrid Laurier to Stéphane Dion, not forgetting Pierre Trudeau, telling us how terribly grateful we ought to be not only for the British gift of democracy, but also for the splendid cultural blossoming we've known beneath the Union Jack.

These liberties, even in Britain itself, were always the perquisite of a tiny, ennobled minority. In the New World even that wasn't quite the case. Over here, the object of British policy and the local dominant Anglo-Saxon clique was always to England-ize Quebec by assimilating the Canadiens as rapidly as possible. Even today this policy toward those who, once "Canadiens," were soon identified as "French Canadians," has not been abandoned.

So how have we survived? Through endless political combat, fierce and nonstop struggle, bitter determination. We haven't had any gifts from London or Ottawa, federal propaganda to the contrary. Consider Laurier, who in his youth was certain that Confederation would mean the end of the French Canadians. As prime minister he presided over the elimination of francophone rights outside of Quebec, a subject to which we will return.

TOWARD A PARLIAMENT OF LOWER CANADA

The thousands of post-revolutionary Loyalist refugees who streamed into Canada were a mixed blessing for the British colonial administration. Their loyalty to the Crown had cost them everything. But the authorities understood right away that they could alter the demographic preponderance of francophones in the former New France. The 5,000 who settled in the "province of Quebec" upped the population by 9 per cent. It was an enormous change, equivalent in quantity and quality (so to speak) to welcoming three million white South Africans to today's Canada. They received their own territory on the South Shore of the St. Lawrence, the so-called "Townships" (les Cantons de l'Est). This created a useful buffer zone separating the "French" from the influence of French and American agents who courted them and kept them informed of events south of the forty-fifth parallel.

From 1783 to 1789 both French- and English-speaking Quebec subjects petitioned the Crown for a legislative assembly in the province. For both English and American immigrants it meant a familiar form of government and one to which, moreover, they felt entitled, because of the privations they had undergone. For the Canadiens it meant a counterweight to the power of the anglophone minority.

It might also have broken the political logjam which then existed, where the Legislative Council (Conseil législatif) was divided between the French Party (representing 13,000 Canadiens) and the British Party (representing the 6,000 English who controlled the economy).

Scottish and English merchants had already crystallized into the arrogant business caste which would dominate Montreal's economy until the end of the twentieth century. The British Party was certain it could "manipulate any new political institution in its own interests,"[1] believing as it did that the French and their representatives were bumpkins unable to contest true political control.

Its fingers burnt by the American revolution, and its confidence further shaken by the revolution underway in France since 1789, the British government was lukewarm to any proposal that meant going beyond the terms of the Quebec Act. But it felt bound nonetheless to look into a new form of administration which might satisfy the English minority. The dossier ended up on the desk of Pitt the Younger, the prime minister. Lord Grenville, the Colonial Office secretary, who was a partitionist before the word was invented, let Pitt know that he thought Quebec should be divided along ethnic lines.

As throughout our history, the British invoked democracy only where it served their interests. Thus was created Upper Canada, a safe refuge for British-born would-be Loyalist aristocrats from the noisily aggrieved francophone majority. Ontario was created from ethnic politics and the profound English conviction of their own superiority. Safe from "French power" in Lower Canada, the English Protestants were now, so to speak, "maîtres chez eux." The Canadiens would be confined to the St. Lawrence Valley in the hope that a steadily growing ethnic British population in the surrounding regions would lead to their disappearance.

THE CANADIENS ARE HAPPY, BUT NOT THE ENGLISH . . .

The creation of Ontario pleased the English of Upper Canada and many of the French of Quebec who – it's only fair to acknowledge – had effective majority representation for the first time in their history. But Quebec's merchants were fuming. Bad enough that they were now outnumbered by a throng of peasants and a thin bourgeoisie of lawyers and priests; still more insufferable, the new constitution was copied from that of Britain, where landowners dominated the parliamentary system to such an extent that Louis-Joseph Papineau later described the British monarchy as little more than "a tool of the noblemen, a shiny bauble which their charlatans would occasionally bring out to dazzle the mob."[2]

A landowner's franchise in the colony provoked immediate opposition from the English merchants because land ownership there was much more widespread than in England. In Albion, voters were a minuscule minority. But in Quebec one person out of eight was a landowner, now entitled to vote! For that period of history, it was unheard of.

The high rate of land ownership in Quebec was an artifact of the seigneurial system. And now anybody who paid a poll tax (property tax) would be included on the voters' list. In the towns, not only landlords but also tenants could vote. The English minority quickly sensed the dangers of the new electoral system, which would overturn the institutional control it relied on for power.

Adam Lymburner, one of Montreal's English merchants, was sent to London to convince the authorities that the Upper Canada/Lower Canada partition would harm the crown's long-term interests. He argued that the hoard of capital held by the English merchants ought to count as heavily as the land-hoard of the Canadien seigneurs. Here is his statement to Parliament:

> There are now, among the Mercantile Gentlemen in the province,
> those whose moveable fortunes are perhaps equal, if not superior
> to any of the Seigneurial estates; and who, from the Employment
> and Support they give to thousands of people, have infinitely
> more influence in the country than the Seigneur. . . . This
> Honourable House must perceive, from the very small value of
> the landed fortune, that the only means of accumulation in that
> country must be by the operation of Trade and Commerce. . . .
> That it is more probable in twenty years, perhaps in ten years, a
> new set of men may come forward, who may have acquired and
> realized fortunes much superior to any now in that country; and

it is natural to suppose, will possess a proportional degree of
Political Power and Influence.[3]

His intentions were clear: the profiteers who had appropriated the
fur trade and our forests for the mizzenmasts of the British navy,
the McGills, Molsons, Frobishers, and MacTavishs, will claim political control in addition to the wealth built by Canadien labour.

The eighteenth century hasn't yet drawn to a close, and they
have already invented the economic arguments still used today:
since they employ the ignorant and uncultured francophone
masses, clearly they should rule them as well. A familiar melody,
but older than we might have imagined. . . .

But the British nobles turned a deaf ear to these admonitions,
coming as they did from the ill-regarded and (in England) all-too
numerous class of Scottish merchants. The gentry simply could
not imagine a Parliament ruled by middle-class businessmen. But
their inflexibility toward the English-Canadian bourgeois will
inadvertently bring forth a French-Canadian bourgeoisie from the
liberal professions, and that elite will little by little come to dominate the Assembly.

As for the seigneurs, their day has passed. A new elite has taken
their place. June 10, 1791: George III, in a fit of sanity, finally
accepts Grenville's plan. The next year, during June and July, elections will be held. But watch out: the elected Assembly is still
under the thumb of the Legislative Council, and the Council is
composed of men hand-picked by the governor.

THE FIRST ELECTIONS

By 1792 it was necessary to divide Lower Canada into fifty electoral ridings. Rapid growth had brought the population to 160,000
inhabitants.

British-style elections involved voters declaring their preference in a loud voice in front of a riding officer. Polls were open

from 8 a.m. to 6 p.m. But if no vote had been cast for an hour, any citizen on the voting rolls could demand that the votes be counted and a winner proclaimed before the polls officially closed.

On the other hand, elections could continue for several days. But it frequently happened that goons in the pay of a particular candidate blocked the voting booth and forced it to close.

In Lower Canada's first election, however, nothing of this sort occurred. And the results were revealing. The English won fifteen of the fifty seats, about a third. But remarkable, to say the least, since they made up only 18 per cent of the population. Historian John Hare explains this surprising result: "British success was due in good part to group solidarity. English-speaking voters quite simply supported candidates from their group, while the Canadiens were more inclined to vote for the best candidate, regardless of origin."[4]

As early as these first Quebec elections, English-speakers were ethnocentric in their electoral behaviour – as they remain. Language is always their first consideration in voting, a statistical and historic reality. Nothing changes in Quebec, and that suits them very well.

But in spite of block voting, there were still thirty-five Canadien members of this first Parliament, including Louis-Joseph Papineau's father Joseph. As for Adam Lymburner, who presented himself in the Quebec Lower Town riding, he bit the dust, and the English Party candidate, Robert Lester (no relation!), was elected.

EARLY DIFFICULTIES

The first election, then, was a success, notwithstanding the partisan voting of the English. But the ethnic rivalry quickly re-established itself in the new Parliament, and over a major issue.

A novice parliamentarian's first chance to debate was often over the choice of Assembly president (or *orateur*, as he is called in French). Quebec Upper Town deputy Jean-Antoine Panet was rejected by the English minority, on the supposed grounds that the president must speak English so as to address the governor general in "the language of the Empire." The Canadien delegates had no time for this, and elected Panet.

The English could not stomach the loss. Haughtiness had led them to believe they could manipulate simple Habitant delegates at will. Now, for the first time ever, they understood that they were a political minority.

By the time Parliament closed in 1793 they had developed a strategy. They would limit Canadien ambition by naming certain of their leaders to the powerful Executive Council (Conseil exécutif), which could overturn the votes of the Assembly.

It was a sly idea, and it proved itself with one of their first choices, the seigneur Pierre-Amable De Bonne. During the first Parliament, De Bonne had championed the Canadien cause. But once on the executive, he saw where his interests lay, and for twenty years fought as fiercely against Canadien interests as he once had to defend them. Our first turncoat! But only the first in a lengthy procession of renegades and swine who sold out to the English.

The politico-ethnic cleavage between the English-dominated Council and the popularly elected Assembly was instant and enduring. But it was put under wraps in the first month of 1793 by the shocking execution of Louis XVI and the spread of the Terror through France. Priests who refused to submit to the Revolutionary authority fled to Quebec.

It was no coincidence that London encouraged these priests to take ship in the direction of Quebec. Owing their lives to British clemency, they arrived in the colony and quickly set about convincing the indigenous clergy that submission to this generous Crown was the best possible choice.

At the same time, England declared war on the Revolutionary regime. Bourbon France no longer existed, and the Canadiens who had been inspired by it were now forced to rely on themselves. Lacking other options, they set about building political power within British parliamentary institutions which, ironically, had been established in Quebec to undermine them.

BRITISH PARANOIA ON PARADE

English suspicion about French Canadians – most of them Québécois today – has been constant throughout our history. Colonial minorities normally feel themselves a target of unfriendly machinations. And never more so than at this particular moment of history.

A small number of revolutionary emissaries from France managed to get into Lower Canada through the United States to preach revolt. Whether these agitators were effective or not, the colonial authorities were prepared to blame them for any kind of unrest. So it was that two routine protests between 1794 and 1797 – one against an Assembly vote on taxes, the other against an Assembly order concerning possible military mobilization – led some English officials to imagine, absurdly, that a French invasion was likely. Everyday politics had them on the edge of their seats.

By October 1797 they were ready to believe wild rumours about the appearance of a French flotilla in the Saint Lawrence . . . and that the local French majority might feel this was good news. Here is William Osgoode, chief justice of the colony: "The exultation on the late appearance of a French fleet in the Gulf was manifested but too evidently. The ignorance of the people is beyond conception, and they firmly believe that, either on French or American government, they should be exempted from the payments of both tythes and rent."[5]

Here we see ignorance used as an analytical tool for understanding the Canadiens. How mad is it, in reasonable terms, to wish to be free of the Church's tithe and the seigneur's toll? But it's an approach we see again and again in English discourse throughout Quebec's history: the Canadiens (or Québécois) are too stupid to understand the political stakes of the game they're caught in.

In 1797 the authorities decided to make an example of an American, David McLane, who was happy to tell anyone who'd listen that he was a French secret agent. Some felt he was a simpleton, but he was made to appear before a kangaroo court in Quebec City, and was hanged and dismembered. The hangman cut out his heart and entrails for burning, and exhibited his head to the transfixed crowd.

This was wantonly cruel and seriously barbaric, even for the period. How odd we don't have a "Heritage Minute" about it. But you can be sure it got the attention of all those supposedly seditious Canadiens: you don't toy with English freedom!

THE SPARK

The first decade of the 1800s was one of epic struggles. The local English obsessed over the possibility that Napoleon's empire was hatching all manner of plots against them. Ethnic relations kept going downhill, to the point where a trivial dispute was enough to ignite the powder keg between French and English in Lower Canada.

It began with the decision to replace the Montreal prison. Its walls were in ruins, escapes were frequent, and the prisoners lived in conditions often compared to those of animals. Things were scarcely better in Quebec City. Beginning in 1796, the authorities lobbied for eight years to have new prisons built.

By 1805 the Assembly, which had never debated the point, finally resolved that construction begin. But how to finance it? The Canadien majority wanted a tax on imports, which left the merchant minority aghast. The merchants in their turn called for a land tax, which left the land-owning Canadiens furious.

Toward the end of February, the Canadien majority called for a vote on the import duty. The vote split on ethnic lines, with the exception of a single English delegate who decided in favour of the import tax. It happened he was a major property owner.

It was an important victory for the French-speaking farmers, many of whom were tenants and would have seen their rents and feudal duties increase.

The merchants reflexively lobbied the Legislative Council to block the law, but it voted unanimously in its favour on March 16. Nine days later, Lieutenant-Governor Sir Robert Shores Milnes ratified the new tax.

The English merchants had once again learned that economic power would fail against the political weight of the majority. But did they pause to wonder whether democracy ought to be respected? For them, it was simply absurd that they, the conquerors who had brought British freedoms to these place, should not be left to run it according to their class interest.

ESCALATION

Their thoughts were expressed in the April 1 edition of the Montreal *Gazette*, already the house organ of the business minority. It described a banquet given for the British Party and published the various toasts offered to:

The British Empire, may the people of this province be impressed
with a grateful sense of happiness and advantages they derive
from being part of it;

The Honourable Members of the Legislative Council, who were
friendly to the constitutional taxation, as proposed by our worthy
members in the House of Assembly;

May our representatives be actuated by a patriotic spirit, for the
good of the province as dependent of the British Empire, and be
disvested of local prejudices;

May the commercial interest of this province have its due
influence on the administration of its government.[6]

Clearly, these gentlemen felt that only the mean-spirited could find fault with their heaping up monopoly profits. And so they carried their lament to London, explaining what a dead weight the new duties would be on colonial trade, not to mention how they would encourage black-market trade.

They lost again. George III, between hallucinations, approved the new tax, on the recommendation of the House of Lords. The result was unprecedented anti-French rhetoric in the English newspapers, with the *Quebec Mercury* arguing for an English monopoly on political participation:

> What can we do? Remove privileges which, some say, are too rare,
> but which in truth are far too numerous and lead to immoderate
> rejoicing among the conquered. And restore an English-language
> public administration for the English and those who share their
> principles. This would be the first, and by far the most
> efficacious, step toward the anglicizing of the province.[7]

From the English point of view, their language and customs were the only effective remedy for the defective speech and religion from which the Canadiens suffered. British liberties belonged to the British (and friends). *Le Canadien* responded moderately to an attack essentially racist:

> Is loyalty then a function of similar language? Or is it to be
> found in similarity of principles, which does not require the de-
> Frenchifying of Canada? What essential difference exists
> between English and Canadien subjects? And if it exists, why
> then did the Americans, speaking, worshipping, and living as
> the English, withdraw from them while crying for the French to
> come to their aid?[8]

Le Canadien had been founded in Montreal (like *Le Courrier* in Quebec) in reaction to the escalating English-supremacist attacks in *The Quebec Mercury* and the Montreal *Gazette*. Both were edited by members of the Parti canadien, especially the renowned lawyer Pierre Bédard, an authority on the Constitution Act of 1791.

A new governor was named at this moment of tension and mistrust: the authoritarian and intransigent James Craig.

Craig surrounded himself with a coterie of bigots, who repeated the caricatures of the French which he could also read daily in the *Gazette* and *Quebec Mercury*: "Totally void of both information and judgment, fore the purpose of being nose led by designing and interested demagogues, who are the great abettors and supporters of such a voice."[9]

Notable among these feared "demagogues" was Pierre Bédard, leader of the Parti canadien. He was, in Craig's view, "by far the most dangerous. . . . Those who know him best . . . give it as their opinion that there are no lengths to which he is not capable of going."[10]

The episcopate sided with its English masters. This was not a difficult choice, since the Church at the time was chary of all democratic change and depended on an ignorant and submissive population. It particularly detested the secular ideas which had become widespread among the new elite of lawyers and notaries. In 1810 Monsignor Plessis denounced the Parti canadien, instead supporting "all necessary measures to rip out this accursed race of men whose subtle and lying stratagems dishonour and besmirch the Canadien nation. . . . It is past time to purge the province and make sure these unseemly creatures no longer drag the people of the country into a hideous labyrinth."[11]

The Church could not abide the Parti canadien's wish to represent the majority. This, the church leaders perceived, would one day give it a more legitimate claim to social leadership than the Church could possess. And this new French class's chief instrument was the Assembly.

Thanks to men like Pierre Bédard and Joseph Papineau, the Canadiens had figured out the Assembly's mechanism and how to make it work for them. That's what the English abhorred and the clergy dreaded.

BRITISH LIBERTIES IN ACTION

Between 1808 and 1810, Governor Craig suspended the Assembly three times and announced new elections in the hope that the francophone representatives would be turfed out. But each time they bounced back and took up the fight again. Which shows, in passing, that it's not true that Canadiens were always on their knees before temporal and spiritual authority.

At last, in 1810, Craig was reduced to the measure of detaining without trial (or charge) Bédard and other Parti canadien leaders, even as he dissolved the Assembly for the third time. For good measure he shut down *Le Canadien* as well.

Back in 1806 the Parti canadien had tried to force the publisher of the *Gazette* to defend a scurrilous article in front of the Assembly. The *Quebec Mercury* took this as an opportunity to denounce the French and their congenital inability to understand political freedom:

> In the *Secret History of Europe*, an old and scarce book, we have
> read some remarks by which it would seem that the French
> nation supported the same character formerly as the present.
> "T'is observable," says the writer, "that wherever the French are
> concerned, they are very uneasy at the liberty of free states." . . .
> This needs no comment. . . .
>   It is certain that nothing could be more gratifying to our arch-
> enemy and the French nation, than a prohibition of our press.[12]

But now, four years later, the arbitrary jailing of Bédard and the theft of his printing press by the government did not seem to trouble a hair on the head of these ardent defenders of British liberties. Freedom of the press belonged to the English owners of the *Gazette* and *Quebec Mercury*, not to the conquered people.

By the beginning of May 1810, Governor Craig[13] had been per-suaded to send London a dispatch on the situation. It included measures that would effectively end the democratic rights of the French-speaking majority. These included, in the words of Mason Wade, "the necessity of anglicizing the province if it were to remain British; a recourse to massive American immigration to swamp the French Canadians; the establishment of high property restrictions upon the franchise; . . . [and] the union of Upper and Lower Canada for more prompt anglicization."[14]

Craig got his ideas from Jonathan Sewell, an imperialist whose hatred of the French would be rewarded with the position of chief jurist in Lower Canada from 1808 to 1838! Out of these ideas came Craig's advocacy of a return to the draconian measures of 1763, which had been judged excessive even then. It was, he said, an inexcusable blunder to have bestowed British liberties on the French Canadians,

> To a People circumstanced as I have described these to be, igno-rant and credulous in the extreme, having no one common tie of affection or union, viewing us with Jealousy, mistrust and hatred, having separate & distinct Interests, it has been thought proper to give a share in the Government of the Country, by a House of Representatives in which they must ever have the Majority.[15]

What especially dumbfounded Craig was the Canadien refusal to become English, their obstinate belief that they were already a people: "Indeed it seems to be a favorite object with them to be considered as [a] separate Nation; La Nation canadienne is their constant expression."[16]

It's important to remember that throughout this period, right up to the end of the nineteenth century, in fact, the English in no way felt themselves to be Canadians. They proudly called them-selves Britons, and belonged to no place except the British nation. The term "Canadians" was detested and reserved for French-speakers, while the idea of a "Canadian nation" attracted the haughtiest contempt. It was only after Confederation, rummaging around for an identity, that they laid hands on the word "Canadien." The French, stripped of their old name, had to call themselves French Canadians and eventually Québécois.

Craig jailed the leaders of the Parti canadien without proof of sedition: he was anticipating what would much later be called, in October 1970, an "apprehended insurrection." But Craig would not succeed in destroying the Parti canadien, any more than Trudeau was able to eliminate the Parti Québécois.

He did succeed in keeping Bédard in jail for thirteen months, refusing the man's requests to be charged with something, and setting him free in 1811 with no explanation.

The Bédard who walked out of prison was a broken and infirm man. Penniless, he agreed to live with his family in Trois-Rivières and accept a position as magistrate. This might not seem harsh, but magistrates were not allowed to leave their district or to sit in the Assembly (a wise measure which Bédard himself had supported). It was internal exile. Craig, who was terminally ill, would soon return to England to die. His loss was lamented by the *Quebec Mercury*, whose administration, it claimed, was "marked throughout by pure intentions and successful results. This noble, generous human being, whose reigning passion was to perform his duty completely and conscientiously . . ."[17]

In spite of Craig's efforts to turn back the clock as far as political rights were concerned, the authorities in London continued to support the liberal Constitution of 1791. As American historian Mason Wade says: "The growing prospect of war with the United States discouraged the adoption of any measures which might arouse unrest in Canada; and once again the French Canadians won concessions affecting their survival from the British government, lest Canada should join the lost American colonies."[18]

The Parti canadien was leaderless. The war clouds of 1812 were already gathering on the horizon. Canadiens would soon be sent to fight on the Chateauguay River, south of Montreal, against an American army outnumbering them ten to one. Montreal's

English took the opportunity to flee north to Quebec, but, against all odds, Salaberry secured a decisive victory.

The English of Lower Canada were indignant that the mother country had accorded the conquered people of the Saint Lawrence Valley rights equal to their own. Being a minority in no way disturbed their sense of entitlement. As racists, nothing could persuade them that the Canadiens were able either to understand democracy or (in the case of the hardened bigots among them) to practise it. At the same time, innocent of the irony, they used the most contorted stratagems to undermine that democracy – a situation which hasn't changed much.

3

THE BRITISH ASSASSINATE FREEDOM IN LOWER CANADA, 1820–1838

On entering the town there was little quarter. Almost every man was put to death, in fact, they fought too long before thinking of flight. Many were burned alive in the barns and houses, which were fired, as they would not surrender. Gun-barrels, and powder-flasks were exploded all night in the burning houses, and the picture that presented itself the following morning to my eyes was terrible. A number of swine got loose, and were eating the roasted bodies of the enemy who were burned in the barns and killed in the streets; those brutes were afterwards shot.

The loss of the rebels was great. Their position was strong, and they defended it with desperation, but they were totally routed, and received a lesson that they are not likely ever to forget. We took twenty-eight prisoners, destroyed a great quantity of arms and ammunition, spiked their two guns, and sunk them in the river. We burned every house from whence a shot was fired, turned the priest's house into an hospital, and the church into a barrack.[1]

This sounds a lot like Vercors in 1944, where Nazi units attacked French partisans, showing no mercy. But it actually happened at Saint-Charles, a few kilometres south of Montreal, on November 25, 1837. The British army was at the time the strongest on earth. It had just defeated a handful of insurgent peasants in the Richelieu Valley. George Bell, whom I have quoted, was one of the officers of the regiment responsible for these atrocities.

It's hard to estimate the Canadien losses, since some were drowned while trying to cross the Richelieu, others were burned beyond recognition, and some of them – not to dwell on the matter – became pig feed; but the numbers vary between 56 and 152. The British lost 3.

Also blurring the record is the fact that none of these men was accorded a Christian burial. Jean-Jacques Lartigue, Catholic bishop of Montreal and cleric in the service of the British sabre, excommunicated them for taking up arms. The episcopate had once again made itself an accomplice of the British.

The Patriotes of 1837 were liberals, and their demands were the foreshadowing of the great liberal movement which would shake Europe itself in 1848 and 1849. With the wholehearted support of the French bishops, judges, and seigneurs, the British army cruelly extinguished the cry for liberty.

THE STRUGGLE FOR RESPONSIBLE GOVERNMENT

Whatever possessed these peasants to risk the salvation of their souls in the quest for democratic rights? We have already seen that the numerous French countryfolk experienced "British liberties" in a fashion rather different from the English-speaking minority. This privileged few believed that every Frenchman should wish to become English; and if he didn't, it was because he had chosen to stagnate in the old French seigneurial system. Why then trouble them with their fair share of power in the Assembly, the Legislative Council, and indeed the economy itself?

Meanwhile, the French, influenced by new liberal ideals, had decided to use their Parti patriote (Patriot Party) to turn the Assembly into the true voice of the people. This certainly annoyed the English, much as it did the traditional seigneurial elite. And the English, in addition, had adopted what historian Murray Greenwood calls a "garrison mentality," a feeling that, being only 10 per cent of the population, they were eternally under siege.

The prejudices which they developed against Quebec's native-born (French) population weren't much different from the reflex prejudices demonstrated by WASP minorities elsewhere in the world.

The English–French tensions which had been unleashed by the war of 1812–14 led directly to the confrontation of 1837–38. Unelected British officials and their friends among the French made it their business to oppose the elected French representatives. The prejudice, verging on contempt, which the English had developed toward the French so coloured their feelings that the thought of democracy itself in the colony could only be shocking and disagreeable. Their belief in the natural superiority of the British over all other peoples was so strong that they could never accept British citizens being subject to French voters.

To prevent this dreadful day from dawning they adopted Craig's idea of uniting Upper and Lower Canada. There was no other way for the chosen people to immediately submerge the French in an English-speaking majority.

To this end, the British of Lower Canada petitioned the king to put an end to their scandalous situation. How could His Majesty's loyal Britannic subjects be left to the whims of the French Catholic mob!

For many years our proportion of representatives has scarcely amounted to a quarter of the Assembly and, at the present hour, a mere ten of Lower Canada's fifty representatives are English. One might say that this branch of the government is entirely in the hands of illiterate peasants under the influence of a certain few of their compatriots whose personal importance depends on the continuation of the present system, to the detriment of the country in general. . . .

Your Majesty's petitioners cannot remain silent about the excessively generous political rights which have been conferred on this population, to the cost of his co-subjects of British origin; and these political rights, together with the general sentiment they should be enlarged, has also given birth in the popular imagination to the dream of a distinct nation, under the name of the "Canadian nation". . . .

The French inhabitants of Lower Canada, today separated from their co-subjects by their particularities and national prejudices, and evidently animated by the desire to become, thanks to the present state of things, a distinct people, would be gradually assimilated into the British population, melting together with them into a people of British character and sentiment.[2]

Even at the dawn of the nineteenth century the phrase "distinct society" was already giving the British the jitters! Among those who inspired the above text were John Molson and Peter McGill, future president of the Bank of Montreal. Both men today are part of the myth of "great Montrealers," and it's worth reflecting on the opinion they held of French Canadians: illiterates standing in the way of a healthy British government!

Even worse, the habitants were the pawns of a self-interested political elite which sprung up to take advantage of them. Molson and McGill, seconded by the Scots/English business clique, were in their own eyes the saviours and protectors of French-Canadian hopes and aspirations.

This sturdy rhetoric is still with us 175 years later, regularly popping up in the Montreal *Gazette* and the *National Post*. The "Canadians," it seems, can't let go of a dismissive and lordly attitude toward the Québécois. Take, for instance, the infamous

Diane Francis. Her incendiary little book, *Fighting for Canada*, describes separatists as a clutch of demagogues lording it over six million straw-chewing hayseeds.

Canada never changes. Nor will it, so long as this little distinct society sits like a grain of sand in its oyster belly.

The pressure paid off: in 1822 London proposed the union of Quebec and Ontario into a single, English-dominated province. But the project was abandoned by the colonial secretary a year later. There were many reasons for the rapid about-face, not the least being the appearance in London of an exceedingly persuasive new figure: Louis-Joseph Papineau.

LOUIS-JOSEPH PAPINEAU AND THE PARTI PATRIOTE

Papineau was by this time president of the Assembly so disdained by the English. He was a lawyer, son of a well-to-do notary who had been given the seigneury of Petite Nation, in the Ottawa Valley, by the Sulpician fathers, for whom he had worked. The same elder Papineau was also one of the first political men in Lower Canada: he triumphed in the very first elections, in 1792.

His son Louis-Joseph inherited both the estate and the taste for politics. In particular his ardent campaign against the English oligarchs in Montreal and the Château Clique in Quebec captured the hearts of the French population.

At the outset, the younger Papineau shared with many men of his generation a genuine admiration for the British parliamentary system. All his life he was proud to have defended Canada against the American invasion of 1812–14. By the time he became chief of the venerable Parti canadien, it had changed its name to the Parti patriote. This change occurred in 1826, at a moment when the struggle took a radical turn. In the words of historian Allan Greer, the members of the Parti patriote by 1830 had become

fiercely secular and given to adopting positions that were steadily more anticlerical. Their vision of government was essentially negative, and they proposed to protect citizens against the state's administrative authority, and against the officers of any other "irresponsible" authority. One means of guaranteeing individual liberty is to submit public authority to the people's approval, directly or through their elected representatives . . . the Patriotes believed that religion was a thing apart from electoral suffrage, so much so that they accorded the vote to Lower Canada's Jewish population in 1831.[3]

So the Patriotes were secular democrats, caught up in the same historical current which gave birth to liberation movements in Latin American and Europe. They favoured individual freedom and free trade, and opposed state intervention in commerce; they were even against chartered banks.

They were also civic nationalists. Our enemies insist on calling them backward-looking reactionaries, but in fact they were honest representatives of the liberal democratic spirit then flowering throughout the world. They were true believers in British rights and English "fair play." They just wanted the rules to be respected.

Poor fellows. It would cost them dearly. Canada's history is a tedious tale of rule-breaking on the part of the English and their francophone flunkies, except where the rules suited them. Where changing circumstances threatened their control, the rulebook was easily modified, suspended, or simply dispensed with. True in 1830, true in 1970, true today.

THE NINETY-TWO RESOLUTIONS

Throughout the 1820s the Assembly was paralyzed by a permanent struggle between the Anglo-Saxon clan and the tribunes of the French majority. Liberals also demanded greater power in Upper Canada and Nova Scotia, but they did not have to contend with the ethnic dichotomy which undermined Lower Canada's liberals in the Assembly. Almost everybody in favour of liberal democracy was French, and almost everybody who longed to see the colonial order upheld was English (or a French collaborator).

At the beginning of 1834 the Parti patriote controlled the Assembly, and went on the offensive by adopting the Ninety-two Resolutions. Too numerous to detail here, they were written by Papineau and those of his associates who wanted to put an end to the standoff which had undermined Lower Canada's government for nearly forty years.

The authors of these resolutions began by underlining francophone loyalty to the Crown, and quickly moved to their major demands: control of tax revenue and the Legislative Council. The Council was an urgent matter because its congeries of British merchants and officials, with a leavening of French courtiers, blocked any Assembly move which they judged inimical to their interests. Finally, the authors proclaimed the permanence of the French character of Lower Canada and asked London to do likewise, in the interests of allowing the French-speaking majority to live in dignity.

The resolutions concluded by observing that the loyalty of the Canadiens had been sorely tried since the Conquest and it would be unfortunate to continue to delay action on its just and judicious demands.

The document's references to American democracy were perceived by the English-Canadians as a veiled threat. But its demand for control of the budget was, in their view, a simple outrage. If granted, their hegemony was finished. . . . The petition was sent to London.

MOUNTING TENSIONS

No sooner were the contents of the Ninety-two Resolutions made public, than the English community in Montreal went on red alert. Some of them founded the British Rifle Corps, a gang of overexcited fanatics looking to wipe the French off the face of the earth. Not long after, those opposed to the Patriotes joined together generally under the name of the Constitutionals, as if this word, in spite of its miserable history in Canada, could magically transform vice into virtue.

Adam Thom, one of the party's founders, was an extreme supremacist whose newspaper, the *Montreal Herald*, called on the English to take up arms against the audacious Canadiens: "Low submission to the French faction and its Frenchified government would make of the province's English inhabitants the vilest of cowards; worse, it would mark them as traitors to the first among sovereigns, the first among empires, and to the best of constitutions."[4]

Nothing but obsessional hatred of all things French can explain such excesses. What, after all, were the Patriotes demanding, except a greater degree of democracy within the constitutional structure of the British Empire? Ludger Duvernay of the Patriote newspaper *La Minerve* answered Thom's attacks by attending the founding banquet of a new mutual aid society in June 1834. It was to be called the Société Saint-Jean-Baptiste.

The Patriotes called public assemblies to promote their arguments, and collected 24,000 signatures for the Ninety-two Resolutions. At this point the English understood that they were no longer in control of the situation.

The Patriotes' high-water mark was the election of December 1834, when they won seventy-seven of the Assembly's eighty-eight seats. The split in the popular vote was even more dramatic: 483,739 votes against 28,278 for the oligarchs' Constitutional Party. As soon as the new parliament sat, in February 1835, it locked horns with Governor Aylmer's administration.

Aylmer had little use for French Canadians, and loudly proclaimed that most of them would be little interested in the high-flown rhetoric of the Ninety-two Resolutions. He was in a rage with these peasants, whose vote had been a repudiation of his government. With his approval, the Legislative Council blocked every Assembly initiative. In retaliation, the Assembly refused to vote a budget. The English sought to buy time while preparing a devastating counterattack.

COMMISSION OF INQUIRY

In Canada, setting up a commission to study a contentious issue has always been the best way of stalling, when stalling is called for. Thus it was that in 1835, London solemnly asked Lord Gosford to replace Aylmer as governor, with a particular mandate to look into the political deadlock. One of Gosford's first correspondents was that exalted bigot, Adam Thom, whose newspaper's favourite bon mot was "We are the conquerors, not the conquered."

> Your Lordship may have been led to believe that the
> Constitutional Party's threat to resist growing French domination
> is an empty one. But the members of this party have not forgotten
> that the glory of Crécy, Poitiers, Agincourt, and Minden was
> seized by "miserable" English minorities battling vast French
> majorities.[5]

By 1836 the Assembly decided to shut itself down until London granted the province an elected Legislative Council. London's reply was Gosford's report, in which he rejected any form of responsible government for the colony. By God, one simply does not allow the defeated, most particularly the defeated French, to sing out the orders in His Majesty's colonies, does one?

By 1837, London had considered the resolutions for three years and made no reply. In the colony, the English prepared for armed battle. Nobody can say that the Patriotes were impatient.

Finally Lord Russell of the Colonial Office submitted his proposal that the French Canadians be suppressed once and for all. The Russell Resolutions took their tone from Gosford's report, most particularly in their insistence that the Governor hereafter control finances without reference to the Assembly.

London understood that stripping away an existing right was a provocation. Two regiments of the British army, quartered in New Brunswick, were dispatched to Lower Canada.

The Montreal *Gazette*, then as now the "voice of English mercantile interests," concluded that the Patriotes' various manoeuvres were aimed ultimately at political independence:

> What is and what has always been the leading object of the
> leading demagogues of the unwary people of this province? A
> complete severance from the Mother Country. It is true that they
> have not yet dared to give utterance to the ungrateful and disloyal
> sentiments; but it is in their hearts and on their lips; and nothing
> but their wretched impotency of moral and physical courage, pre-
> vents them from proclaiming their independence.[6]

For years the *Gazette* had warned readers that the Patriotes meant to found "a French Canadian dominion and a French Canadian nationality in America . . . a French republic in the heart of British American provinces."[7] Their secret object, bleated the newspaper, was to ensure that the majority of the province's inhabitants controlled its government! Could anything be more repugnant to this imperialist rag than democracy?

But at least people back then weren't hypocrites. It was common to hear them say the Canadiens would already have been assimilated if the Proclamation of 1763 had been applied. And the *Gazette* couldn't find words strong enough to condemn the 1774 Quebec Act and "the uncontrolled exercise of all those usages and habits, manners and language which tended to conserve them as a distinct and separate people."[8]

The worse things got, the richer the harvest of bile in the pages of the *Gazette*. You'd think an avatar of Diane Francis was loose in the newsroom! These "stupid and ungrateful" French Canadians "have never left the barbarous condition in which we found them in 1759; and no earthly power shall ever convince them to leave their condition of ignorance or to abandon their deep-rooted prejudices."[9] Like all the racist pamphlets, whether today's or yesteryear's, the *Gazette* solemnly intoned that the Canadiens were "deaf and blind to their own true interests." Ah! If only they'd take advice from Albion's small but sturdy local detachment of two-faced profiteers, happiness would be theirs!

And it's remarkable how much the *Gazette*'s letters-to-the-editor page back then was full of the same francophobia we see today: "A French Republican government . . . would rule with despotic oppression and keep their constituents the slaves of their tyranny, and bring them with a yoke, from which they could never free themselves."[10] And, oh, the *Gazette*'s knack for portraying the merchant-plutocrats as an oppressed class! Their situation "is more like that of the serfs of Poland beaten down by Russian despotism, than the free and honoured victors, enjoying the reward of their gallantry and bravery."[11] These Canadiens – the ones who lost the battle – talk about ingrates! Can't their betters enjoy the fruits of victory without this endless racket about democratic rights?

At this moment in history the *Gazette* dreamed of eternal marriage between Great Britain and her colonies. A steady influx of British immigrants was meant to perpetuate the bond, while the Mother Country extended its hegemony to the ends of the earth. Even poor Ireland, in this roseate imperial fantasy, could be an example to the French; had Ireland not, since 1800, added "to the glory, unity or prosperity of this great empire. . . . She is equally free and independent as Great Britain, of which she forms not a federation, but an incorporated portion, a tie which cannot be now legally dissolved by either party"?[12]

One of the delightful benefits of Ireland's annexation, a surprise arranged by the English gentry, was the great famine of the 1840s. So durable was British affection that it took the Irish 121 years to break the embrace and declare independence. In Ulster today there are still benevolent Orangemen who want nothing but happiness for the Irish. Graceless Paddies, can't you manage a thank-you?

Today there's no shortage of editorial writers telling Ottawa to take a hard line with Quebec. No concessions! The tone was set back in the 1830s when the local English called for firmness, declaring that "further concession would become a virtual admission of French Canadian independence."[13] The *Gazette* called upon the government to intervene against the Patriotes lest the Anglo-Montrealers take matters into their own hands. Violence, it argued, was the best answer to Patriote-style democracy: "we promise them that it will be neither with impunity nor without a mortal struggle that will be as memorable as any portion of history."[14]

To Montreal's English, the French were so distasteful that even Yankee rule was better. "True and loyal subjects of the Crown," reported the *Gazette*, "would prefer even the Democracy of the United States to the complete degradation of all forms of Government which would exist in Canada if Papineau held the reins of Government."[15] One reader wrote that he would instantly prefer the American guardian angel "instead of the hideous wrinkled hag of 'nationalité' which has fastened with vampire ferocity on the vitals of the land. . . ."[16] You can easily find similar sentiments in today's *Gazette*, 160 years later. Same paper, same readers, same wild-eyed fanaticism. Fascinating.

French Canadians drove the English minority into such a frenzy that imperialists like Adam Thom were even capable of proclaiming that "Lower Canada must be English at the expense, if necessary, of not being British," a phrase which Lord Durham noted in his famed report.

This obsession with not being contaminated by lesser peoples was general throughout the British Empire. It can be seen once again in the white Rhodesians who, learning that the country's black majority was to gain independence, declared their own little White English Rhodesia in the heart of Africa. It wasn't whimsical of René Lévesque to compare Anglo-Montrealers to "White Rhodesians."

In 1836 the English thought of another way to rid themselves of the French vermin. Partition! A movement sprang up with the idea of attaching the island of Montreal and Vaudreuil County to Upper Canada. The folks in the Eastern Townships, afraid of being left behind, cried: "We too, we too!"

Our interests, however, are interwoven with those of the
Constitutionalists of Montreal, and should they become emanci-
pated from their state of political thraldom, by the easy-course of
connecting themselves with Upper Canada, the Eastern
Townships must be included in the compact. We must not be cast
off a prey to the tyrants of a foreign race. The dismemberment of
our forces would entail ruin upon us. We are ready at any moment
to fight the battle of independence with the loyalists of Montreal.
They must not therefore forsake us.[17]

There was by then an armed Anglo-Montreal militia, the Doric
Club (a sort of Alliance Quebec before its time), that certainly
didn't intend abandoning the Townshippers. They "have strenu-
ously co-operated with the inhabitants of Montreal in their efforts
to obtain deliverance from the withering domination of an illiterate, anti-commercial and anti-British faction."[18]

PUBLIC MEETINGS AND GENERAL HULLABALOO

From May 1837, the Patriotes held assemblies where local and
national representatives explained London's reaction to their
demands in the Montreal region and the Richelieu Valley. The
Patriotes also suggested measures of resistance, including a
boycott of British imports. Magistrates and local notables were
asked to resign from their positions. Militia captains were to
return their commission by way of protest.

Most of them did resign, in a massive groundswell of patriotism so widespread that some officials had to return to their posts
when the government couldn't find any local replacements with
a shred of authority.

In Deux-Montagnes, a riding north of Montreal, they practised
charivari. Captains and magistrates excessively attached to their
emoluments suddenly found their bedrooms invaded by masked
men who gloomily suggested they consider the alternatives.
Wild rumours crackled through the overheated atmosphere.

Collaborators and traitors found it difficult to whistle while they worked: "Certain timid bureaucrats have fled to Montreal on trembling legs. The governor is awash in petitions against 'incendiary assassins,' 'pillagers,' and 'bands of cutthroats.' The governor has been made to understand that there will be 'reprisals and horrible vengeance' if he fails to dispatch troops against the miscreants."[19] All that summer the English removed magistrates suspected of sympathy or contact with the Patriotes.

And yet the unrest was not general. Outside of Montreal and the Richelieu region, people adopted a wait-and-see attitude, even in Quebec City.

But in the village of Saint-Charles in the Richelieu Valley, late that October, 5,000 people attended the largest political rally of the era. They had come to hear Louis-Joseph Papineau and local notable Dr. Wolfred Nelson of Saint-Denis. The orators succeeded each other in rolling waves of rhetoric, ranging from the bellicose to the prudent and legal-minded. Papineau was in the latter camp, but by then it was becoming clear that the moderate Patriotes had lost the contest to the radicals, and would be dragged along into violence.

The same day, October 23, the Constitutionals assembled in an English neighbourhood of Montreal, at the Place d'Armes. Orators assured a grim reckoning for any Canadien who continued to flirt with dreams of liberty.

The following day the clergy, determined to prevent any form of democratic power from evolving, sided with the English. Protestants were bad, but a secular laity was worse! That was certainly the feeling of Montreal's Roman Catholic bishop, Jean-Jacques Lartigue, as he defended his privileges from republican revolutionaries. In this pastoral letter, he issues a warning to the French faithful which doubles as a threaten to those of wavering loyalty:

"Let every soul be subject unto the higher power," sayeth Saint
Paul in his letter to the Romans. And "Whosoever . . . resisteth
the power, resisteth the ordinance of God: and they that resist

shall receive to themselves damnation" [Romans 13:1–2].

Is not the prince the minister of God's beneficence? And yet he
must also be the arm of God's anger against the wicked.
Therefore submit, not out of fear of just punishment, but rather
from the prickings of your own conscience. . . . Understand also
that we must not fail to guide you away from a dangerous choice,
lest we betray our duty and endanger our own souls.[20]

A letter to rejoice the English heart, full of servility, not to
mention sophistries which will excuse the impending death,
destruction, and excommunications. The Church can always be
counted on to provide a peaceable flock. It had certainly never failed
to sing the praises of loyalty to British power.

Perhaps theology did have something to do with it. But not
nearly as much as the comfortable life of clerics accustomed to
living on the farmer's obligatory tithe, one of the first things the
British promised them the morning after the Conquest. . . .

But Lartigue's admonitions didn't work. By November, the militants had seized control of events from the Patriotes. His sermo-
nizing might have been more effective with the Protestants. We'll
never know! Because nothing like it was heard from their own
clergy. For some reason, *these* men of the cloth saw no reason at
all to disapprove of an armed uprising.

MARCHING TO WAR

Early in November, Papineau's house in Montreal was attacked.
Peace officers stood impassively by because anyone with French
sympathies had already been removed from the force. Papineau
sought refuge in Saint-Denis.

The Fils de la liberté (Sons of Liberty), a Patriote youth group,
were attacked by thugs from the Anglo-Montreal militia, the
Doric Club. Somebody also saw to it that the offices of an English
newspaper, *The Vindicator*, which supported the Patriotes, were

turned upside down (it was especially galling to the British that a minuscule minority of anglophones, largely Catholic, were sympathetic to the Patriotes). In the face of mounting chaos, Gosford, seeing himself without any legal or political means of damming the rising tide of French national feeling, resigned. Authority passed to General John Colborne, commander of the British army in Lower Canada.

Apprehending an insurrection (that phrase again!), and fearing the loss of a good part of the territory, he decided to provoke a battle immediately. This forced the Patriotes to fight before they had even decided to do so.

The method was a series of warrants for the arrest of twenty-six politicians including Papineau and Nelson. They were issued on November 16, just after another round of removing magistrates suspected of rebel sympathies.

It wasn't much of a choice: armed resistance, or surrender to the enemies one had fought democratically for more than forty years. Montreal's English would at last have the pitched battle for which they had longed. Their name, the "Constitutionals," belied the fact that violence would serve their interests. They would make their own justice, as the *Gazette* and the *Montreal Herald* expressed it, and crush the freedom-seeking, French-speaking democrats with an iron fist.

It appears that a plot to this effect was actually hatched by General Colborne, together with Adam Thom and other extremists. Historian Gérard Filteau believes that General Colborne had advance knowledge of the attack by the Doric Club on the Fils de la liberté, and was able to dispatch troops and issue warrants for the arrest of Patriote leaders an astonishingly short time afterward.[21]

Thus began what we now call the Rebellion of 1837. It was in fact more of an improvised self-defence against a well-organized military repression which the English had been preparing for some time.

ARMED RESISTANCE

Things began to go wrong when soldiers, who had learned their trade in the Napoleonic Wars, were sent to carry out what should have been a police operation. These "peace agents," accompanied for appearances' sake by magistrates, were to execute the warrants against rebel leaders. Especially Papineau and Nelson. (A similar procedure was used by Trudeau during the crisis of October 1970, where judges trotted alongside soldiers in the streets of Montreal.)

The Patriotes were roused. By November 17 they had freed two of their arrested fellows in a skirmish at Longeuil, and organized hidden camps in Saint-Denis and Saint-Charles to conceal their hunted leaders. In Deux-Montagnes, hundreds of habitants began an armed vigil and the population hunkered down. But everywhere else a workaday calm prevailed.

THE BATTLE OF SAINT-DENIS

Under cover of darkness, Colonel Charles Gore led 500 men out of Sorel on the nights of November 22 and 23 with the aim of breaking into the Saint-Charles camp and arresting the men under warrant. They were to rendezvous there with Colonel Wetherall from Chambly.

But at 3 a.m. that night a disguised British officer, Colborne's dispatch rider George Weir, was seized by a Patriote patrol in Saint-Denis. He soon admitted that he was trying to reach Colonel Gore's forces, and was detained with his promise that he would not try to escape.

Meanwhile, a soppy wet snow enveloped Gore's soldiers, who in the darkness were bumbling back and forth on the county roads under the amused eyes of Patriote scouts. Wolfred Nelson's troops had learned from Weir that the attack would be directed against Saint-Denis, and had therefore decided to send the prisoner to Saint-Charles. Seeing his chance for escape, Weir forgot his undertaking, lunged for freedom, and was soon overtaken and shot. His body was hastily buried under a heap of rocks by the Richelieu River.

Saint-Denis put up a surprisingly stiff resistance, from the point of view of the British, who thought it undefended. A rain of home-made bullets fell on them for six hours from a fortified house, causing Gore to retreat and dishonourably abandon a cannon.

This was the victory of Saint-Denis. Hardly a bloodbath: six dead and ten wounded on the British side, twelve dead and seven wounded for the Patriotes. Papineau had moved onward to Saint-Hyacinthe.

Patriote officers decided to spare Gore's column, which retreated in disarray to Sorel. This moderation is the best evidence that they did not feel themselves to be in a rebellion, which once resolved upon must be fought without quarter. But such nuances were lost on Colborne, who was more intent on justifying the measures he now had in mind. He wrote to the governor of Upper Canada: "Civil war has now broken out in this province. I therefore entreat you to mobilize the militia of Upper Canada and hasten to send to Montreal any men who wish to volunteer at this critical moment."[22]

THE BATTLE OF SAINT-CHARLES

As Gore's soldiers left Sorel, Wetherall's 406 soldiers (together with twenty cavalry) left Chambly. They stopped at the Rouville-Campbell manor house in Saint-Hilaire for rest and provisions. There they learned of Gore's defeat. Wetherall did not know what to do, and sent to Montreal for further orders.

Colborne's reply was that he should not go to Saint-Charles, but the message was intercepted by a Patriote patrol. Wetherall, hearing nothing, told his men to resume the march to Saint-Charles.

Just outside the town the Patriotes had built barricades around the Debartzch manor house. There, two hundred men had rallied under the command of Thomas Storrow-Brown, a Catholic Irishman from Montreal. It was the morning of November 25.

Unlike Saint-Denis, the fortifications at Saint-Charles were a mere system of trenches where the men were soon pinned down. After two hours, Wetherall ordered his men to fix bayonets and charge. Resistance rapidly crumbled.

Five days later Wetherall returned in triumph to Montreal with his prisoners, who were pelted with rotten eggs by an equally sulphurous English mob. The Richelieu Valley no longer offered refuge to Patriote leaders. Papineau fled to the United States, and within a few days not a single Patriote leader remained on the south bank of the Saint Lawrence River.

On December 5 martial law was proclaimed in Montreal and the English jostled to see who could sign up first for the next punch-up. Colborne was organizing the destruction of the democrats to the north before they had properly begun to organize themselves.

SAINT-BENOIT AND SAINT-EUSTACHE

November 23, 1837: the day of the victory at Saint-Denis. The northern Patriote group at Saint-Eustache elects a Swiss immigrant, Amury Girod, as their new leader. His elected deputy is Dr. Jean-Olivier Chénier of Saint-Eustache.

Events have outraced this Patriote group: they're not ready to fight. Fortunately, with all the British troops on the south bank (even Montreal is ungarrisoned), they have little to worry about. But neither can they profit by the situation, since Girod is still looking for guns and trying to instill some discipline in his farmer militia. It's a challenge even to find food and lodging for the columns of men converging on Saint-Eustache.

And to make things worse, an attempted transaction with the natives at Oka suggests they'll get no support there. The natives in question refuse to sell a cannon and some rifles, pleading neutrality; the next day they make a gift of them to the loyalists.

Matters are grim in Saint-Eustache. Some doubt the rebellion's success, especially when stragglers from Saint-Charles arrive with tales of gloom. Not a few are tempted to lace their boots and head for home.

The rebels on opposite banks of the Saint Lawrence never managed to create a united strategy, and it's too late now. Colborne's surprise attack in the Richelieu Valley succeeded so well that he can take his time preparing the assault on the north bank. By the time he gives the order to march on Saint-Eustache, December 13, he has nearly 3,000 professional soldiers and 220 Montreal volunteers under his command. These include 60 French-Canadian collaborators calling themselves the Saint-Eustache Loyal Volunteers. Their commander is Seigneur Maximilian Globensky.

Battle is joined the following day when Globensky's men lure Chénier's troops out onto the Rivière du Chêne. What a distressing spectacle! French firing on French, while the British army snakes around Saint-Eustache and cuts it off from outside help. Two hundred rebels barricade themselves inside the village church, even as it shudders under the impact of cannonballs. Four hours later the British put it to the torch, and marksmen wait to pick off Chénier's men as they scramble out the windows, gasping from smoke inhalation. Chénier himself, lying bleeding on the ground, is finished off by British soldiers crying: "Remember Weir!" For they have found Weir's body where the rebels had hidden it near the Richelieu River.

As the church collapses into burning embers, the village is sacked, and

> the pillaging was so barbaric that Captain Joseph Swinburne of the 83rd Regiment, a veteran of the Spanish War [of Independence], declared that it "equalled and may well have surpassed that which he witnessed at the sacking of Badajozs" . . . the Patriote corpses are stripped of their garments and left naked to the snow, and someone even steals the clock which adorns the church belfry.

When the houses have been emptied to the bare walls, the soldiers fall upon the dead once again, searching them, ripping off whatever clothes remain, and leaving their nakedness to be covered by the discreet snow.

Chénier was found about six o'clock and taken to Addison's Inn where his body suffered indignities which those present called an autopsy. During the three days the body was left exposed, a witness swore he had seen it stretched out on the tavern bar: "The chest was opened and the heart hung outside it. To a passing Patriote they cried: 'Come see your Chénier's rotten heart!' . . . I noticed that rifle blows had left his head covered with clots of blood." A correspondent for *Le Canadien*, also an eyewitness, wrote in his diary: "We were in Saint-Eustache last Sunday. The dead had been left lying about. Chénier was on the counter, so badly mutilated that he was almost cut into four pieces, his heart on the outside. A sickening spectacle to witness."[23]

Patriote losses were very high, with 60 dead, 15 wounded, and 118 prisoners. The British suffered 1 dead, though 2 of their 8 wounded also eventually died. This balance sheet is sufficient proof that no civil war occurred in this region. These numbers speak eloquently of a pathetic and improvised peasant resistance. In the year 1837 in Quebec, only the English organized themselves for war. No other means presented itself, in their view, for destroying French majority before it could take root.

The day after his victory, December 15, Colborne sets out for Saint-Benoît, where there had been reports of further rebels. A citizens' delegation comes to meet him on the road and tells him the Patriote leaders have fled the village. There will be no resistance.

Bring me all your weapons, Colborne instructs them, warning them further that a single shot will suffice to ensure the pillaging of their village. The people of Saint-Benoît gratefully comply, certain they have thereby saved themselves from the horrors of Saint-Eustache. But their village is nonetheless looted. Gérard Filteau believes that murder and rape also took place. Similar scenes were enacted at Sainte-Scholastique, Saint-Hermas, and other villages through which the British regulars and volunteers marched.

Thus ended the first rebellion. The Canadiens disappeared back down the concession roads, leaderless and terrorized. The clergy hastened to tell them, in Lartigue's name, that their dead would be buried without last rites. This, apparently, was to be the fate of those who fought an army with which God himself was allied. *Dieu et mon droit.*

The loyalist volunteers had attracted the most hardened racists from Montreal's English minority. Their excesses, Benjamin Viger would later declare to Lord Durham's confidential investigator, Stewart Derbishire, "had left wounds in the minds of the Canadiens that could never be healed."[24]

It was the Protestant citizen militias, rather than the professional soldiers, who committed the bulk of the atrocities. According to estimates,

> damage amounting to 85,000 pounds had been caused in the six parishes visited by the military. They had burnt 297 buildings, including two churches, two rectories, and a convent – thus outraging the religious feelings of the people – twelve granaries, which were scarcely military objectives, and no less than eighty-nine houses at Saint-Benoît, where no resistance at all had been offered.[25]

Payback time . . .

DURHAM'S "EXTRAJUDICIAL" MANOEUVRES

As the prisoners were transferred to Montreal, the bigot Adam Thom ranted and raved in the *Montreal Herald*:

> Punishment of the leaders, however agreeable to the English population, will hardly make such a useful impression upon the

people as the sight of foreign farmers taking over every house of
every agitator in every parish. It will do the heart good to see
widows and children display their misery outside rich dwellings
which were once their own.[26]

Thom, whatever else one might say, was no hypocrite!

The Patriotes will not be sentenced for their "crimes." Lord
Durham, hastily named governor in early 1838, soon understood
that there were excellent reasons to avoid trials. The most com-
pelling was the evidence of British provocation which the
Patriotes would certainly lay out in front of a jury by way of
explaining their own actions. Only slightly less urgent was the
risk of rising ethnic tensions in a Montreal which was by that
time already more than half English.

Lord Durham soon decided that, as was the usual British
custom in times of crisis, it was necessary to stretch the law a
little out of shape. Wolfred Nelson and seven other Patriotes
agreed to plead guilty to treason in exchange for a safe passage to
Bermuda, signed by Durham. Exiled leaders, including Papineau,
learned that if they returned to Quebec they would be executed
without the courtesy of trial.

One hundred and forty prisoners were released. Affection for
the eight leaders being deported to Bermuda was caught, then and
for the ages, in a simple and affecting melody written by a student
named Antoine Gérin-Lajoie. It was called "Un Canadien errant"
(A wandering Canadien).

Durham swept aside legal requirements, decreeing deportations without trial and death sentences against exiled men in such
a way that London was horrified. His actions were publicly dis-
avowed. The English in Montreal also disapproved of him, but for
an opposite reason: they wanted to see an outright slaughter of
the French-Canadian dogs, and finding Durham spineless, they
cheered when he left.

On returning to London Durham wrote his famous report. But
he couldn't leave Montreal without giving the citizenry a foretaste

of his thoughts. This he did in his parting words on October 9, where he declared that he wanted nothing but to

> elevate the Province of Lower Canada to a thoroughly British character. . . . to raise the defective institutions of Lower Canada to the level of British civilization and freedom, to remove all impediments to the course of British enterprise in this Province, . . . [and to] touch ancient laws and habits, as well as deep-rooted abuses.[27]

> These remarks sounded all too much like the proposals of Adam Thom and the Montreal merchants, rephrased with elegance; at the prospect of national extinction many of the French-Canadian moderates joined with the extremists, and this time the clergy made no effort to check the agitation.[28]

Church collaboration with the English had aroused general indignation in the French population, so much so that the clergy finally grasped that it had gone too far. Monsignor Lartigue, fearing assassination after Patriote newspapers accused him of treason, had fled to Quebec City. By December 1838, four months after Durham left for England, he yielded to the widespread loathing of his Montreal congregation and offered his resignation to Rome. The clergy now understood that they must pretend to distance themselves from the colonial authority, if they hoped to retain even the least influence with the people.

1838: THE CALL FOR GENOCIDE AGAINST FRENCH CANADIANS

The second rebellion broke out on November 3, 1838, at the end of harvest season. The Frères chasseurs (Brotherhood of Hunters), a secret society of the Patriotes, launched an attack from bases in the United States. But Papineau, rightly suspecting that the British planted spies in the group, dissociated himself from it completely.

But Robert Nelson, Wolfred's brother, actively worked with the groups of exiles who sneaked in from the United States, welcoming them to join the small knots of local Patriotes which he led.

He had in fact gone so far, in a Napierville rally attended by thousands, as to proclaim himself president of the new republic. The event lacked something of majesty, since he was short of guns (the Americans, officially neutral, had given his troops only one cannon and two hundred muskets). At his presidential self-proclamation he was supported by only a few Patriotes and a couple of French officers with revolutionary leanings. In total his troops amounted to a few hundred men with a grab-bag of old guns augmented by picks, pitchforks, and sharpened sticks.

The regular British army and the Glengarry Volunteers made quick work of the insurgents at Beauharnois, not forgetting to put the village to the torch afterward. Elsewhere in southwest Quebec, Montreal's Protestant auxiliaries, among whom the most wild-eyed of the Orange extremists could be found, were busy tormenting countryfolk who'd had nothing to do with the uprising. Guilty enough, belonging to a disreputable race! Nothing wrong with their cattle, though, which were led out the barn gate as the torch-bearing auxiliaries went in to burn everything to the ground.

Adam Thom was still busy at the *Montreal Herald*, calling for genocide against the French:

Sunday evening all the country behind Laprairie presented the frightful spectacle of a vast sheet of living flame, and it is reported that no rebel house has been left standing. God knows what fate awaits the Canadiens, wives and families included, who did not perish, for the winter is approaching and they may expect nothing but hunger and cold. It is sad to reflect upon the terrible consequences of Rebellion, of the irreparable ruin of so many human souls, innocent and guilty alike. Nonetheless, the supremacy of the law must remain inviolate, the Empire's integrity unsullied, and the peace and prosperity of the English assured, even at the expense of all the nation of Canadiens. . . . If we wish to have tranquility, then we must have solitude; let us sweep the Canadiens from the face of the earth.[29]

As in the preceding year, the English took advantage of the chaos "to satisfy a hatred often woven together with their infamous cupidity," as Lionel Groulx expressed it.

The worst Patriote losses during this campaign were sustained at Odelltown, where fifty rebels died and as many were wounded. Nelson fled south to the United States on November 9, while the Chevalier de Lorimier was seized by the Kahnawake Mohawks during an attempted theft of their weapons, and turned over to the British.

The second rebellion had lasted for one week. Those few pitiable days, from November 3 to 11, 1838, would see twelve rebels hanged the following February. Among them was the Chevalier de Lorimier. Another fifty-eight were exiled to Australia.

THE DURHAM REPORT

Lord Durham's mandate, when named governor in January of 1838, had been to put an end to the fissures which threatened to tear the North American colonies apart. He only got to Quebec in May, and was already preparing his return to London, when the second rebellion broke out. In the middle of that brief term, on August 9, he wrote a letter to the colonial secretary detailing the irreconcilable hostility between Canadien and Englishman:

The hatred between the two peoples is not publicly avowed by one side or the other; each affirms that its attitudes are not motivated by a difference of origins. But the evidence is solid and irrefutable, and not dependant on anecdote. It refutes without difficulty the various justifications. If the opposition of these two races were at the level of principles or partisan conflict, then one would certainly find in each camp individuals of both races. In this case, apart from the rare exception which proves the rule, the English are on one side and the Canadiens on the other. At first consideration, the immediate causes of this dispute seem quite without importance. But as the disputes break out continually, apropos of everything and nothing, the majority of the Canadiens and of the English seem at all times armed and ready for battle. In addition, the tension which sets the two groups at odds is evident not only in politics, but also in the social realm, where there are no encounters of any significance between the races. Adults of the different groups frequent each other very little, not to say never, in private life; even the brawling children are prepared at a young age to separate, like their parents, into opposing groups: English and Canadien. In the schools and streets of Montreal, the province's true capital, these groupings and conflicts are the daily currency! Nor does social class threaten these divisions and collective hostilities; even if leaders and ordinary citizens, rich and poor, merchants and porters, seigneurs and peasants speak different languages in daily life, they flow together and understand each other quite well when it is time to reject or to combat the other race.[30]

Supercilious and pretentious, Durham surrounded himself with dubious characters to aid him in his mission. In Louis-Joseph Papineau's words:

To look carefully into Lord Durham's mission is to behold an incredible profusion of personal vanity. He surrounded himself with vice-ridden and perverse men who showered him with flattery. . . . Even before leaving London, he dipped into the sewers of the prisons in order to take by the hand, elevate to his level, and sit down at his table, beside his wife and daughters, two men marked by the law: the first for having seduced a child and stolen her fortune; the second for bribing his wife's sister and exchanging the one for the other.[31]

That first gentleman was Edward Gibbon Wakefield, jailed from 1827 to 1830 for corruption of a minor; the second, Thomas Turton, had been a Calcutta lawyer whose marital imbroglio had scandalized London. But neither could compare in infamy with Adam Thom, the excitable ultra-racist who, with Colborne, was almost certainly behind the provocation which led to the military crackdown; the fellow whose diary was dense with scribbled plans for the extermination of French Canadians. This is Papineau's description of Thom, counsellor and table companion of the preening aristocrat:

He was, when treating of English politics, an everyday tub-thumping fellow fuelled by strong liquor; but the merest mention of French Canadians transformed him into a raving lunatic. His hatred was then quite limitless, and exalted by bloodlust. For many years his newspaper had disgraced itself with outrageous attacks on the entire [French-speaking] nation and in particular its most popular representatives, against whom his provocations went so far as to call for their assassination. He was a regular participant in the street riots which had plagued Montreal for four years, the same riots sponsored by magistrates who disliked the popular assembly's attacks on executive authority. Were these outbursts ever reined in by the law? Have we heard of a single investigation to identify the leaders? No. Instead the magistrates' troops have left bloodshed in the streets, while interfering with the course of justice and preventing the parents of the dead from seeking justice before the courts, as is their sacred right. They have even subverted legal procedure through drumhead courts which release the guilty back into the streets.

Meanwhile, Adam Thom has organized the Doric Club expressly so that armed force may be used to wrest back from the French Canadians any powers which might accrue to them should the government grant the object of their incessant demands: an elected Legislative Council. Even as the prisons filled up with Canadiens – and only five months before Durham invited him into his council – he wrote that "special commissioners must instantly be named so as to complete the trial of this clutch of traitors currently behind bars. Why let the process drag on all winter when we must bring it to an end sooner or later?" . . . Durham's choice (of Thom) is so mad and depraved that one must wonder whether he has decided to renege on his duty of seeking reconciliation. Worse, we must wonder if his appointment was a mere smokescreen behind which last year's plan continues apace. That plan, ratified by provincial and perhaps imperial authorities, was to provoke the people to excessive behaviour which would legitimize both the violence already done to them, and that which is contemplated for the future.[32]

The news that Durham had appointed Thom left the Canadiens slack-jawed with astonishment. American historian Mason Wade observes that the Canadiens would have been even more distressed, "if they had known that Thom also acted as liaison officer between the governor and the Tory merchants."[33] This arose from Anglo merchant lobbying of Durham before he even left England: "he had scarcely arrived before getting in touch with the agents of merchants from both Quebec and Montreal, the same merchants who had made a public show of their indestructible hatred of the Canadien people."[34]

Wade writes that Durham made use of Thom to work closely with the business oligarchs of Montreal. They were apprised in secret of his political plans through a committee of seven merchants under Bank of Montreal president Peter McGill – well before even the lieutenant-governors of the Atlantic provinces knew of them.[35]

The Durham Report was made public on February 4, 1839. It was an ambitious study of British North America which left no aspect of society untouched. Its author claimed to be a liberal aristocrat, but he was nonetheless imbued with the Briton's sense of divine right and imperial mission. To Mason Wade, the report was the racist work of a well-meaning plutocrat. Durham saw the Canadien nation as being without a culture and a literature, and opined that their only escape from ignorance was assimilation. His report's scornful tone toward French Canadians is hardly surprising when one knows that it was written in close co-operation with their most implacable enemies, especially Adam Thom. In the end he gives them what they had demanded for forty years: the union of the two Canadas.

In other words, his answer to a problem created by English fanatics and racists was to assimilate the French majority into their community. It was most unlikely that a man such as Durham might have thought of advocating a democratic state where Englishmen would dwell amongst a French majority. English noblesse oblige, one supposes. And an attitude which still dominates the thinking of Anglo-Quebeckers today, even on a question such as the uniting of Montreal's small municipalities into a megacity. So that Durham's portrait of the French and English is strangely contemporary in its brushwork, excepting that today's French anger would need to be painted in darker colours.

Certainly the English back then were very paranoid where French Canadians were concerned – much as they remain today.

> [The French] brood in sullen silence over the memory of their fallen countrymen, of their burnt villages, of their ruined property, of their extinguished ascendency, and of their humbled nationality. To the Government and the English they ascribe these wrongs, and nourish against both an indiscriminating and eternal animosity. Nor have the English inhabitants forgotten in their triumph the terror with which they suddenly saw themselves surrounded by an insurgent majority, and the incidents which alone appeared to save them from the unchecked domination of their antagonists. They find themselves still a minority in the midst of a hostile and organized people; apprehensions of secret conspiracies and sanguinary designs haunt them unceasingly, and their only hope of safety is supposed to rest on systematically

terrifying and disabling the French, and in preventing a majority of that race from ever again being predominant in any portion of the legislature of the Province.[36]

Durham was emphatic that his report was untainted by racial prejudice: "Our happy immunity from any feelings of national hostility, renders it difficult for us to comprehend the intensity of the hatred which the difference of language, of laws, and of manners creates between those who inhabit the same village, and are citizens of the same state."[37] But his personal secretary, Charles Buller, had a much different view of Durham:

> I used indeed then to think that Lord Durham had too strong a feeling against the French Canadians on account of their recent insurrection. . . . he had made up his mind that no quarter should be shown to the absurd pretensions of race, and that he must throw himself upon the support of British feelings, and aim at making Canada thoroughly British.[38]

For the next four years there was no Assembly in Lower Canada. The important political leaders were in exile, with the clergy filling the vacuum of power. This delighted the English, who felt the arrangement more appropriate to the limited capabilities of the French.

It would not be until the decade of the 1960s that Patriote ideals would once again come to centre stage in Quebec politics. The English minority once again felt menaced, and trotted out their familiar intransigence toward a confident French Quebec. But they had at least managed, thanks to Colborne and his auxiliaries, to put the clergy back in the saddle for 120 years. Among the many gifts we've received from the English, being a "priest-ridden province" was one of the most difficult to enjoy. Especially since they never stopped blaming us for it.

4

MONTREAL, 1849: THE *GAZETTE* CALLS FOR A "RACIAL UPRISING"

A useful, well-controlled democracy which served their exclusive interests: that's the kind of democracy that made Montreal's anglophones great enthusiasts for the idea. And it's the kind of democracy to which they've remained faithful throughout their history. In its name, they took up torches on the night of April 25, 1849, and turned the Parliament of United Canada into a blazing bonfire. At the time situated in the old Sainte-Anne Market, you can visit the site today in the Place d'Youville of Old Montreal. It's where the Customs Building is.

Upper and Lower Canada had been united less than ten years before. The fusion, oddly enough in the light of the now-burning Parliament, had been deeply desired by the English since its stated purpose was the assimilation of the French. The Act of Union had been Lord Durham's recommendation, jubilantly celebrated by the Montreal *Gazette* because, among other things, it made English the one and only language of Parliament.

In order to Anglify the French Canadians, the process must be begun in the Legislature; and should that take effect under the authority of the Imperial Parliament, we may be assured that, notwithstanding the national and deep rooted prejudices of the French Canadians, they will discover it to be their interest gradually to submit to the fate that awaits them – of becoming English in every thing that can tend to their moral and political improvement.[1]

Adam Thom was at one with English Quebec in exulting that the Union meant the end of French numerical superiority:

The lapse of thirty years will render the French Canadians a numerical minority. Every year. . . . will physically weaken them through the immigration of men of English blood from the old country and the United States. . . . Any future history of Lower Canada will be written only in the English language, only with an English pen, only with English feelings.[2]

The "Townshippers" shared the enthusiasm, as one of their newspapers celebrated the coming demise of this insufferable race:

Since the Conquest, the Anglo-Saxon race has increased from nothing to 140,000 souls. Like a huge boa constrictor, it is twining itself around the French population, and in the end must totally destroy it. . . . It seems to us as if Providence had appointed this continent to be English, and had pronounced the fate of all opposing tongues. . . . It is a folly in the French Canadians to struggle against their destiny.[3]

In Quebec City, the same fevered anxiety to hammer the coffin shut:

you have been long fondly imagining that you could build up a new France on this continent under the wing of England. Now, my dear fellow, you must disabuse yourself of this gross delusion

without delay – totally and irrevocably. The thing is physically
and absolutely impossible; and you might as rationally expect
that the dark tribute poured from the St.-Maurice into your
mighty river would be able to retain its hue, or change the broad
current to its own tint, as that you can continue French amidst
the great Anglo-Saxon family to which you now belong.[4]

Yesterday as now, the Montreal *Gazette* is dully incapable of
grasping why the French do not wish to join the race of overlords:

Why should the miserable and selfish French Canadians so reck-
lessly spurn away from them, what every other nation on earth is
envious of, and so ardently desires to possess? Who can tell,
except on the principle, that being once slaves to the despotic
sway and tyrannical laws of France, French Canadians of the
present day, unregenerated from the ignorance and passive obedi-
ence of their ancestors, are desirous of perpetuating their moral
degradation as a people. This is the only principle on which we
can account for the aversion, which the French Canadians have
always betrayed to the introduction amongst them of British
institutions, and their blind and wilful determination to resist
every measure having a tendency to such an end.[5]

The first draft of the bill creating United Canada had stated that
the Gaspé Peninsula and the Îles de la Madeleine be given to New
Brunswick, which had the Montreal *Gazette* very nearly salivating:

We cannot help congratulating that portion of the French population of Lower Canada upon their good fortune, for, how ever disagreeable and irksome they may consider the transition at first,
we can assure them that the sooner and more completely they are
assimilated in language, laws, institutions and manners to their
fellow-subjects of British origin, the sooner will they become a
prosperous, contented and happy people.[6]

But the burial was premature. And as this distressing realization gradually dawned on the English, their anger built up toward the spillage of hatred in the streets of Montreal which forever marks the year 1849 in our minds.

The Act of Union assumed that French would quickly become a minority language in the new Parliament, even though French speakers were still an absolute majority in the new union. Some of this attitude was merely emotional, proceeding from a sense of racial superiority and from the anger left by the 1837 Rebellion. Many anglophones simply could not believe a twice-conquered people would receive equitable representation.

But there were also practical provisions ensuring that, despite the two provinces having an equal number of seats, the English province would dominate. A typical twist of this particular knife was that riding boundaries in Quebec (now Canada East) were drawn in favour of English Quebeckers. I'll restrain myself from remarking yet again on "British liberties," which so often arrange themselves comfortably with British interests.

But Durham's assimilationist project was temporarily blocked by a convergence of political interests. The reformers of Upper Canada, who didn't like the French any better than their fellow English-speakers in Lower Canada, nonetheless realized that they needed help from French reformers if their party was ever to control Parliament.

That is how, at the beginning of the fateful year 1849, a coalition of French and English from Canada East and Canada West had taken control of the new Parliament. The Tories had been evicted from power through the efforts of Louis-Hippolyte Lafontaine, who had survived the Rebellion of 1837, and of Robert Baldwin, a Toronto reformer.

These two popular leaders were at odds with Montreal's mercantile clique (and the governors which supported it) because in the previous three years the merchants had begun flirting politically with the United States.

From their point of view, the merchants felt justified in such seditious behaviour. Had not London betrayed their interests in 1846 with new policies which removed many of the tariffs they used to protect themselves? With an influx of cheaper European goods their profit margins had been pared away.

The ease with which they then turned to the United States certainly demonstrates that these oligarchs, though they might pose as defenders of liberty, were in truth little more than the "billfold loyalists" described by Lord Elgin. This was bad enough in itself, but worse for French Canadians, who became the target of their commercial frustrations.

In 1849 the Tories, always well-equipped with extremists by English Montreal, suddenly found themselves Her Majesty's Loyal Opposition. The Reformists had been in power for a year and Baldwin had recognized Lafontaine as Parliamentary leader. This was, to put it mildly, not congenial to the oligarchs.

Here was the nightmare of "French hegemony" being re-born in front of their eyes!

INDEMNIFY THE REBELLION'S INNOCENT VICTIMS? *NEVER!*

Baldwin and Lafontaine's government felt it was urgent to come to the aid of those who had suffered from British army reprisals during the 1837 Rebellion. The first bill they proposed was called the Lower Canada Rebellion Losses Act (le Bill des indemnités). It resembled the very uncontroversial act passed by Upper Canada's Tory government to indemnify those who had suffered losses in that province's rebellion.

Lafontaine and Baldwin took care that their bill would not compensate any person convicted of sedition. Even legitimate claimants were only partially compensated. It's difficult to see what there could have been in the bill to provoke the ire of the Anglo-Montrealers. But it would lead to the most violent parliamentary debates in Canada's history, together with the worst direct attack on democracy.

The same Tories who had indemnified the English of Upper Canada three years earlier were now seething at the thought of doing likewise for French Canadians. For them, all French Canadians were guilty without further ado. Allan MacNab, who was running the Tory party after lining his pockets in questionable speculations, expressed his bitter loathing of the French as follows:

> The Union has completely failed in its purpose. It was enacted with the sole motive of reducing the French Canadians under English domination. And the contrary effect has resulted! Those that were to be crushed dominate! Those in favour of whom the Union was made are the serfs of the others! . . . I warn the ministry of peril. . . . I warn it that the course it takes is likely to throw the people of Upper Canada into despair, and to make them feel that if they are to be governed by foreigners, it would be more advantageous to be governed by a neighbouring people of the same race than by those with whom it has nothing in common, neither blood, nor language, nor interests.[7]

Could it be clearer? It is pellucid with racism and sincerity. To MacNab the Americans are blood brothers; Quebeckers are foreigners.

But he thundered in vain. Baldwin and Lafontaine's Parliament easily passed the act and awaited the approval of Lord Elgin, who had arrived from London with instructions to accommodate the responsible government. When Parliament opened in January, Elgin went so far as to give a portion of his throne speech in French, restoring its status as an official language after many unilingual years. But he didn't succeed in pleasing the English.

> The debate began on February 13; it terminated fourteen days later. There have certainly been more memorable debates in Canada's Parliament, but none of such violence. In premeditated fashion the Oppositions' orators provoked the most dangerous passions: ethnic bigotry, religious antipathy, ad hominem attacks

against members of the government. Anything which might lash
an assembly of men toward a paroxysm of rage, and make the
people in the galleries stamp their feet, was repeated with sickening indulgence. And look at the two men who have most distinguished themselves in this tawdry contest: Mr. Gugy, deputy of
Sherbrooke, and Allan MacNab, deputy of Hamilton. The first, in
orations as rambling as they were livid, denounced the "indecent
and immoral" notion of making Protestants pay for the losses of
Catholics. The second outdid the first in ardour, but aimed
higher. His targets were Lord Elgin, Lord Grey, and all of their
political station whom he generously abused. And then, as one
might have expected, MacNab also lashed out against the
immorality of the proposed law, which it pleased him to see as an
incitement to insurrection. And in all his perorations he managed
a full-tilt denunciation of French influence, while the French
Canadians were described as rebels, traitors, and even foreigners.[8]

In the grip, as always, of their unhealthy and hateful preoccupa-
tion with francophones, the Montreal English undertake a whisper
campaign to prevent the indemnity law from being proclaimed. On
February 15, 1849, the tenth anniversary (to the day) of the hanging
of de Lorimier, the *Morning Courier* proclaimed: "Responsible
government shall do us in, so long as it is controlled by our adver-
saries. It has utterly subverted the reasons for which the Union
was created; it prevents the deterioration of a foreign race; and the
voice of the people pronounces itself against us to such an extent
that such a government can never assure our well-being."[9]

In Upper Canada the Tory press was enthusiastic. Better annexation to America than the reign of the "black-hearted Frenchman!"
Members of the Orange Order organized protests in Toronto, while
in England the political and journalistic elites got their information
entirely from the Montreal *Gazette*. One can't be surprised that a
portion of the London press sympathized with the Tory agitators.

Encouraged by MacNab, the English held countless protests. By
this time, the end of the 1840s, they make up a decisive majority

in Montreal, having reduced the French to 20,000 out of 43,000 inhabitants. Their leader, George Moffat, founds the British American League on April 19. This is its manifesto:

> Inhabitants of a province ceded to England after long and glorious combat, aspiring like other dependencies of the Crown toward a virtuous emulation, and determined to be neither impeded nor thwarted by the narrow jealousy of a particular nationality, which, though entitled to perfect equality with the Imperial race, may in no way claim a pre-eminence in political power. . . . It is evident, following the known character of our race, that the British never passively submit, and never shall, to ascendancy based solely on sentiments of nationality rather than upon generous and progressive principles.[10]

Elgin waited as long as he could for the English citizens of Montreal to calm down. Finally, in spite of continuing threats from Montreal's racists, he proclaimed the law on April 25, 1849. He had run out of reasons for further delay, particularly since similar aid had been voted for Upper Canadians.

Setting aside his misgivings he proceeded – and dropped the match into the powder keg. When Elgin left the Parliament building only the lucky chance that he was in a carriage protected him from the projectiles hurled by an overwrought English mob. The *Gazette*, always exploring new frontiers in francophobia, called for an uprising which the American historian Mason Wade characterized as "racial." The special afternoon edition of April 25 is worth lingering over:

> Those who had assembled in the environs, upon learning what had occurred, burst out in screams and cries of rage and indignation against the "last governor of Canada." When Lord Elgin (no longer entitled to the rank of Excellence), left the Council Chamber and appeared in the street he was greeted by the crowd's whistles, growls, and cries of indignation. Rotten eggs

were showered on his carriage, which was soon covered with
their loathsome contents, admixed with mud, even as the savoury
liquid seeped inside to where he and his aides cowered. When the
supply of eggs was exhausted, the carriage was seen on its way in
a fusillade of stones, galloping off to the curses of his compatriots.

THE END HAS BEGUN

Anglo-Saxons, you must live for the future; your blood and your
race shall henceforth be your supreme law, if you are to be true to
yourselves. You shall be English, even if you may no longer be
Britannic. To whom do you owe your allegiance now? Let each
man respond for himself.

The star of the puppet show must be called offstage, or pushed
off, by the people's contempt.

In the words of William IV, "Canada is lost and delivered."
THE CROWD MUST ASSEMBLE AT THE PLACE D'ARMES THIS
EVENING AT EIGHT O'CLOCK.
THE MOMENT OF BATTLE HAS ARRIVED![11]

The *Courier* also called for violence:

A civil war is a great misfortune, but not the worst; and we say
without hesitation: better for the British population of Canada to
undergo twelve months of battle . . . and to lose five thousand
lives than to bend down before another ten years of the bad government introduced into this country by French domination.[12]

Remarkable that all this yelping and growling was caused by
something as innocuous as a law to compensate innocent victims
of the British army.

But the *Gazette*'s call to violence was heard far and wide.
Kindled by the paper's bellicosity, that very evening the mob – all
1,200 to 5,000 of them (depending on the report) – was ready to act.
Their anger was stoked to the point of delirium by rabid speeches.

The first speaker was the lawyer Augustus Howard, nephew

of Upper Canada's chief justice; he was followed by three other eminences, including James Moir Ferres, the *Gazette*'s editor in chief. Ferres cut his teeth at another anti-Canadien rag, the *Montreal Herald*, where he had succeeded that adept of British racial supremacy, Adam Thom. Ferres's biographer writes, in the *Dictionary of Canadian Biography*:

> He soon turned violently anti–French Canadian. . . . The sparks from the verbal "fiery cross" he promised to forward through the Anglo-Saxon community contributed immeasurably to the general Tory agitation in the city and the consequent burning of the parliament buildings in April 1849. Throughout the winter Ferres had railed against the bill as "a nefarious attempt at robbery" of the Anglo-Saxon population by "an insignificant French nationality in a corner of Canada."[13]

Crying scorn and spitting insults, the orators attacked the French Canadians. Suddenly Alfred Perry, leader of a Montreal fire brigade, shouted that the time for talking was over. Calling on the crowd to act, he led the ragged column of ruffians toward Parliament – which was in session!

This is Clayton Gray's description of the scene: "By the glow of the torches and with cries of 'To the Parliament!' the demonstrators followed narrow Notre-Dame Street and then McGill Street in the director of Sainte-Anne's market. The crowd moved like a river of fire and soon flooded all around the Parliament building."[14]

Inside the building the session was interrupted by the cries of the marchers, who approached under the leadership of the firebug fireman. Stones crashed through the windows, followed by shouted threats from the crowd. Perry's entire fire brigade was there to help him in his new incendiary identity: they lifted the great front stairs and used them as a battering ram to stave in the door of the Parliament building.

The demonstrators were soon in the Assembly hall, as deputies scampered out of the way. A hooligan, mistaking himself for Oliver

Cromwell, proclaimed the dissolution of the "French Parliament."

As the mob danced on Papineau's portrait, Perry reached the inner chamber and hurled a brick at a chandelier, smashing several burners. The fireman knew his trade! The fire tore through the building and in a matter of minutes a gigantic inferno reddened the Montreal night.

The last deputy out was none other than Sir Allan MacNab, the Tory fanatic. But this wasn't due to some particular fondness for the institution. Rather, he bent his efforts toward saving the endangered portrait of Queen Victoria.

When other fire brigades arrived, the crowd cut their hoses. The night was still young, and all of English Montreal was whooping it up: it was the night the French Parliament died!

Bravo, Montreal *Gazette*!

The French newspaper *La Minerve* reported on April 16: "People laughed . . . on street corners. By way of saving the expenditure of £90,000 in reparations, they inflicted irreparable and therefore immeasurable loss on the country. The rebel firemen gazed at the hideous conflagration with happy hearts."[15]

Full of booze and self-admiration, the English cheered as the fire leaped to the Parliamentary library and the Legislative Council.

Insatiable in the lust for destruction, some of them laid hands on the few books saved from the Library and threw them back into the fire. It was a miracle that the entire city escaped destruction. The troops did not trouble to appear until almost midnight, when there was little left for them to do but watch the embers die down.[16]

The fire brigades soaked the neighbouring houses, but not the Parliament building. Sympathetic soldiers seemed to encourage the saboteurs cutting the fires hoses, and did nothing against them apart from firing a few shots in the air. The army was on the side of the Tory faction and had been warned the day before that it was to ignore any "out of the ordinary" events.[17]

That night the barbarians of English Montreal destroyed the leading collection of history books in the country, not to mention the most complete array of law books, and the finest quality books on natural science, literature, and geography. Says Gilles Gallichan: "This fire certainly mortgaged the colony's cultural future. By ruining the best collection of books and the major depositary of public archives, it wounded the country's living memory. The loss has never fully been made up."[18]

François-Xavier Garneau would speak of "our Alexandrian catastrophe." This parliamentary library had inherited the collection of the legislative library of Lower Canada, founded in 1802 at about the same time as the Library of Congress and the library of the Chambre des députés in Paris. It was sixteen years older than the equivalent library in the British House of Commons, and Papineau, its great sponsor, had begun a program of buying books for it in France and England in 1816.

Through the Act of Union this ambitious library was ordered to merge itself with the relatively tiny political library of Upper Canada. French Canada's supposedly illiterate throngs, benighted and philistine, had somehow managed to put together the best library in the country. The true brutes emerged on that single ugly night and burned it to the ground.

Bravo, Montreal *Gazette*!

The London News, a liberal newspaper in the British metropolis, castigated the arsonists for destroying "a valuable library, together with the colony's documents. . . . [they] committed a series of actions which would have dishonoured the most ignorant population of the most depraved city in Europe."[19]

But the *auto-da-fé* had only whetted the appetite of the Anglo-Montrealers. Their rage would continue for weeks, terrorizing the town. The morning after the fire, it began with the sacking of Lafontaine's house. Only a military guard saved him from being murdered. The frustrated crowd then raced to Lafontaine's new house, which was also burned (with special attention paid to its library).

The army surrounded the Bonsecours market, where Parliament was now located. There, only three days after the fire, it adopted a resolution expressing its indignation about the events to Lord Elgin:

> When the assembly's representatives went to the Chateau de Ramezay, which served as Government House, to present this address, it was necessary to read the Riot Act and clear the streets with bayonets. Elgin was stoned as he emerged to return to his residence at Monklands. He was also expelled from membership in many of Montreal's select social organizations by the outraged English Canadians. Petitions were circulated for his recall and for disallowance of the obnoxious bill.
>
> The governor kept calm, despite all manner of provocation; he judged that "The whole row is the work of the Orange Societies, backed by the commercial men who desire annexation and the political leaders who want place."[20]

Lafontaine's intimates decided it was time for a militia to protect the government. French-Canadian and Irish subjects were armed with pistols and cutlasses. Their officer, Lafontaine's friend Colonel Étienne-Paschal Taché (a future prime minister of United Canada), had hardly begun drilling them when the order arrived to disband.

The English rioters were the masters of Montreal and their reign of terror was to continue. Any French-speaker found in the city's west end was attacked and often beaten unconscious, and the perpetrators were never brought to justice. Both the army and the police were so dominated by Orangemen that they didn't trouble to hide their sympathies.

> The French Canadians discovered to their astonishment that they were more likely than their persecutors to be the target of salvoes fired by the partisan army. Wouldn't it have been easier to let the French-Canadian neighbourhoods come in and clear the streets? . . . But Lord Elgin feared a racial war whose prologue, he

felt, had already occurred. Not an unreasonable conclusion, considering the social class of the [English] rioters. It was true that many were recruited from the dregs of the population, a class always ready for hellraising. But there were obviously many who came from a more elevated level of society. "The whole row," Elgin would say, "is the work of the Orange Societies, backed by the commercial men . . . and political leaders. . . ." The Governor spoke truly. Those haranguing the mob in the Champ de Mars and the Place d'Armes, those urging them to banditry, knew each other well from the haunts of the city's English elite. These worldly gentlemen, merchants, lawyers, journalists, and clergymen, jostled each other for the honour of hurling stones and rotten eggs at Lord Elgin. Then they chased him down the streets. . . . Those not brave enough to participate applauded in secret. Lord Elgin has left us this devastating opinion of them: "Riots, devastation, they would stop at nothing to put an end to French domination, and scarcely troubled to hide the fact."[21]

The government machinery was reduced to such chaos that Elgin's safety could no longer be assured. His residence was an armed camp, but he had to leave it from time to time, and was then pursued by frenzied Englishmen still obsessed with the money given the French victims of the Rebellion. He thought of seeking refuge at the fort on St. Helen's Island, and certainly was not seen for weeks in the government offices at the Château de Ramezay.

Four months later the English rabble still hadn't sated its anger with Lafontaine. When an armed gang tried once more to invade his home, Lafontaine was ready:

About 200 rioters appeared opposite M. Lafontaine's house, which is isolated in an orchard [in the rue de l'Aqueduc, between rue Saint-Antoine and Dorchester]. They forced the courtyard door facing the road, and then several of the boldest walked up to the house and hurled rocks at it.

M. Lafontaine was not home that evening, having left the

house under the protection of a handful of friends armed with rifles and handguns. The assailants fired first and were then repelled by a fusillade from the little garrison. They left, carrying a young man named Mason who had received a mortal wound, together with six others who had been hurt. This Mason was the son of an ironmonger in Craig Street, near Saint-Urbain. He died the next morning.

Before his death, the young man confessed that the group had planned to burn the Prime Minister's house, hang him from a tree of his own garden, and then drag the body through the streets. Another member of the group was carrying the rope they would have used.[22]

With the near-total support of the city's English population, the arsonists and agitators and bullies who attacked French Canadians were never punished. Thirty-eight years later the pyromaniac fireman Alfred Perry was still bragging about his exploits in the pages of the *Montreal Star*. Its readers were proud of him.

Even today, in Verdun's Douglas Hospital you can read an inscription honouring Perry as a valiant defender of "the blood of the Anglo-Saxon race" against "French domination."

The current head of the Société Saint-Jean-Baptiste, Guy Bouthillier, puts it this way: "It's one thing for a state to leave unpunished a criminal known to all. It is entirely another thing for a 'community' to commemorate the same criminal by carving his name on monuments and remembering it in institutions."[23]

That single day in April 1849 was the darkest moment in Canada's democratic history. But you won't find out much about it in the history books or popular media of English Canada. They do, however, find endless space to go on and on about the supposed xenophobia of the Québécois.

The year 1999 was the 150th anniversary of the pillaging of Canada's Parliament. It came and went without anybody in the English-Canadian press thinking to mention it. Can you imagine the reams of injured op-ed drivel if things had been the other way around? The *Gazette* would keep a cask of salt on hand to rub in the wound on every anniversary.

Ah, the *Gazette*. It marked the 150th anniversary of the burning of the Montreal Parliament with an article on . . . an uprising in New York City in 1849 (I'd like to thank Gaston Deschênes for his research on the articles devoted to the events of 1849).[24] This would of course be the same *Gazette* which helped instigate the attack. Just as dishonest today as it was then, but much sneakier.

"I, MARIA MONK, GOTTEN WITH CHILD BY A PRIEST AT THE HÔTEL-DIEU OF MONTREAL . . ."

Through cultural, religious, and linguistic similarities, English Canadians are always assured of a sympathetic hearing in the U.S.A. and Great Britain when they feel like vilifying Quebec. Heads nod in agreement as they recite the usual litany about the province's dictatorial and theocratic tendencies. The thoughts and feelings of francophones are turned into mean caricatures, and the policies of our government ridiculed. No lie is too gross.

It's been like this for a long time. As long as Anglo-Saxons have entertained their natural prejudices toward the French and the Catholic Church.

Consider the case of Maria Monk. A prostitute, born in Quebec City of Anglo-Protestant family, she died on September 4, 1849, in the prison at Blackwell's Island in New York. Her last known address was a bordello in that town. She was thirty-four.

She'd landed in prison after being caught going through a client's pockets. It was a long slide from her moment of glory, thirteen years earlier, when, as a tender adolescent of eighteen years, she published a shocking account of French-Canadian Catholics. It was the publishing sensation of 1836.

As one might guess from the title, *Awful Disclosures of Maria Monk, as Exhibited in a Narrative of Her Sufferings during a Residence of Five Years as a Novice, and Two Years as a Black*

Nun in the Hôtel Dieu Nunnery in Montreal, the book claims to be a true account of the licentious secret life of the nuns of the Hôtel-Dieu. Their convent was supposedly a harem for Montreal's clergy, and Maria Monk duly records being sadistically raped by more than one sweaty French-Canadian priest. She also details a group of priests sitting on a mattress to suffocate a young nun who had refused them. Then there were the subterranean tunnels between the sisters' residence and the priests' presbytery, not to mention the cave where their babies were baptized, killed, and buried. According to the Protestant press, this was a meticulously accurate account of convent life.

This malevolent fairy tale was destined to be a North American best-seller. It had six printings in 1836 and was outsold only by the Bible. According to Frederic Schwarz the book "inspired riots, looting, church burnings and countless other acts of hatred, doing for anti-Catholicism what *Protocols of the Elders of Zion* would later do for anti-Semitism."[25]

The whole thing was a fake. In it, Maria Monk claimed to have fled the Hôtel-Dieu with her child, whose father was a priest named Phelan. In reality she was a prostitute placed under the protection of an extremist Anglo-Protestant minister in Montreal, Reverend William K. Hoyt. She became his mistress.

Hoyt was director of the Canadian Benevolent Association, and saw the girl's potential use as a tool. He took her to New York and suggested she write the memoirs. Most of it would actually be dictated by another clergyman, Reverend J. J. Slocum, who also offered it for publication to Harper Brothers. The two brothers who ran the company immediately grasped both its commercial potential and its fraudulent nature. So they set up a special imprint to conceal Harper's involvement in the project.

When the book appeared, Catholic authorities refuted it line by line. Two ministers and a New York journalist were invited to Montreal to see the facts themselves. Even the habitually anti-Catholic *Montreal Herald* defended the Sisters of Charity.

The visitors from New York quickly discovered that Maria Monk was mentally ill, and that she had been a prostitute. Her mother, still a cleaner at the Château de Ramezay, told them her daughter had neither converted to Catholicism nor entered a religious community.

The group visited the Hôtel-Dieu, which was unlike its description in the book, and returned to New York convinced of the imposture. They were denounced as Jesuit agents in the Protestant press.

Soon after *Awful Disclosures* appeared, Harper Brothers and the three authors (Monk and the two clerics) started fighting over the vast sums of money the book was producing. Slocum became Monk's guardian since she was not yet twenty-one years old. Monk, in turn, did her bit in late summer of 1837 by disappearing awhile and resurfacing to claim she had been abducted by a posse of priests from Montreal. In fact she'd gone off with her latest lover, another clergyman.

By the end of the year her notoriety was such that she felt she could profit from a sequel to her "biography," which she would call *Further Disclosures of Maria Monk*. Its principal allegation was that pregnant nuns, American and Canadian alike, were sent to an island in the Saint Lawrence River. Multiple printings and heavy sales followed.

A second pregnancy the following year risked undermining her credibility. But she turned aside journalists' questions by claiming that the supposed pregnancy was just another malicious rumour spread by Catholics.

Anybody who took the trouble to look into Monk's allegations, and many did, knew full well the book was a fraud. But its popularity grew apace. "*Awful Disclosures* lost none of its appeal to the general public, and Monk's sad end did little to dent the book's popularity. It went on to become America's bestselling book until *Uncle Tom's Cabin*."[26] By the time of the Civil War, three hundred thousand copies had been sold. It has never since been out of print. Recently, an edition with pornographic engravings appeared. And lest one might imagine the book is read as a mere curiosity today, consider this: any number of English-language Internet sites still represent *Awful Disclosures* as a truthful account of nineteenth-century convent life in Quebec.

Until quite recently, even prestigious Barnes and Noble kept the book in its catalogue. It wasn't until the company was scorched by a lively protest from an American Catholic organization that its vice-president, Greg Oviatt, wrote to the organization to say: "I concur with your opinion and believe that this title is inappropriate for our catalogue," going on to promise that it would never appear there again.

Nonetheless, for the modest price of twelve dollars, Maria's fans can still procure an audio-cassette version of her travails from American evangelist Texe Marrs. If this is still too costly, there's always Early Canadiana Online, which, with the help of the Canada Council, offers the entire book, absolutely free, on its Web site, <www.canadiana.org/ECO/mtq?id=1046bf9705& doc=38886>.

Yes, friends, thanks to the Internet and the Canada Council, Maria Monk lives on a century and a half after her death, merrily spreading mockery and intolerance of French Canadians through the endless fields of cyberspace.

5

THE HANGING OF LOUIS RIEL:
A STATE CRIME

There was a torrid sunrise over the little North-West Territories village of Regina on November 16, 1885. The command post of the Mounted Police, which had quietly served as a prison since the previous July, was lately abuzz with activity. Carpenters were hammering away at the gallows that would end the life of Louis Riel. And now it was ready.

The Métis leader's lawyers have exhausted all legal avenues, and Prime Minister John A. Macdonald is about to realize his dream of a world without Louis Riel. Since 1869 this man has frustrated him at every turn, and that has been a very long time indeed. "The quarrel with Riel must come sooner or later. . . . He should be arrested for the murder of Scott and put on trial."[1]

English Canada hasn't been coy: it wants Riel dead. Orange Ontario would like to see his head on a pike. And this time Sir John A. Macdonald, member in good standing of Kingston's Orange Lodge since 1840, will not disappoint his friends as he unhappily did during Riel's first rebellion. He sweeps the desperate pleas for a pardon off the end of his desk. He falsifies a medical report to make sure the Métis millstone is never hung about his neck again.

And so, on that November 16, at about 8:15 a.m. under a brilliant Prairie sun, Louis Riel is hanged by the neck.

The body swinging in the breeze had turned forty-one less than a month earlier. At the time of his birth in 1844 the colony of Red River – it stretched over what would one day be the southern half of Manitoba – was still being administered by the Hudson's Bay Company. By 1858 the young boy's piercing intellect had come to the attention of Alexandre-Antonin Taché, the bishop of Saint-Boniface, who sent him that year to Notre-Dame College in Montreal. He would remain there until 1866, completing his studies at the Petit Séminaire.

His return to Saint-Boniface was leisurely, to say the least. It took two years. First he veered south to Chicago, and then to St. Paul in Minnesota. Arriving home in July of 1868, he already knew that the world he had left ten years earlier was under siege. The village of Fort Garry (the future Winnipeg) had sprung up beside Saint-Boniface, filled with English colonists. Almost all were Ontario Orangemen with an acquisitive glint in their eyes.

Canada is negotiating the purchase of the Hudson's Bay lands, then known as Rupert's Land. This unthinkably vast terrain stretches to British Columbia. Those who know it, the Métis, are stupefied at the way the newly arrived English strut about the place like lords. Sovereignty over the place has not yet even been transferred to Ottawa. And little do the Métis suspect that Macdonald means to shift this land, at a high mark-up, from the huge trading company which currently controls it, to a host of smaller businessmen: the railway mafia.

Nobody in Ottawa has given the least thought to the rights of the Métis, French Canadians, and Indians who make up the bulk of local residents. The 1869 law that will soon weld this territory to Canada won't devote so much as a subordinate clause to the Métis. The surveyors who appear on the prairie three months before the land-transfer act, in fact, as if they don't exist. They blithely aim their transits across the long perpendicular strips of land which ensure each family's access to a watercourse. They arrogantly presume to chop the land into "townships," as they did in the Eastern Townships of Quebec. Who cares about the decades-old cultivated fields which they see standing in front of them?

In August of that fateful year the people choose Riel to negotiate their nation's entry into Canada. Confrontation with the Canadian "expansionists" is inevitable. They are in truth a mere handful of Orangemen, but they possess enough contempt for Indians, Métis, francophones, and Catholics to equip legions of bigots. Riel's presence immediately short-circuits their assumption that they will be able simply to seize these lands. His intention is bilateral negotiation on behalf of all the established inhabitants of Red River, who he feels have the right to reasonably integrate themselves into the Federation.

Riel's National Committee of the Métis moves quickly to assert its authority. The surveyors are blocked, and William McDougall, "a snob and shabby genteel fool"[2] named by Ottawa to govern the territory, is prevented from reaching Fort Garry.

This isn't as shocking as it seems: the land has not yet been legally ceded. By November 2 the Métis have seized Fort Garry and Riel, as secretary of the national committee, invites the population to choose delegates to a convention. It will take place November 16, and is intended to have roughly equal French and English representation.

While the Métis are dreaming this democratic dream, John Schultz and lieutenant colonel J. S. Dennis are busily organizing the English settlers into an armed militia. But Ottawa is more prudent, aware that the Métis are numerous enough to act. It drags its heels on the formal annexation of the North-West Territories.

By December 1, however, McDougall is able to announce that the Territories have been joined to Canada. Five days later he offers the Métis of Red River these guarantees:

> by the authority of Her Majesty I assure you that, from the moment of the union with Canada, your civil and religious rights will be respected. Your properties are assured to you, and your

country shall continue to be administered, as in the past, by
British law and in the spirit of justice which belongs to it.
Moreover, in virtue of Her authority, I order and command those
among you still assembled and leagued together, in defiance of
the law, to disperse peacefully back to your homes, under pain of
those punishments ordained by the law in case of disobedience.
Finally I inform you that, should you disperse and obey immediately and peacefully, I shall order that no legal proceedings be
taken against those certain parties involved in said infractions
of the law.[3]

Riel and his counsellors see no reason to pay attention to this
one-sided demand to lay down arms, since they are still grappling
with aggressive Anglo-Ontarian fanatics. The council decides to
assert its authority by arresting about forty of them, including
Schultz. These men are held at Fort Garry as "political prisoners."
The following day, December 8, the National Committee of the
Métis proclaims a provisional government.

Since the day when the government we have always respected
abandoned us, transferring to a foreign power the sacred lands
entrusted to it, the people of Rupert's Land and the North-West
Territory became a free people with no further allegiance to the
said government. . . . We refuse to recognize Canada's authority,
together with its pretended right to impose upon us a government even more despotic and less respectful of our rights as
British subjects than that government to which until recently we
submitted ourselves through necessity. . . . We continue and
shall continue to oppose with all our force the establishment of
Canadian authority in this region in the form proclaimed; and,
where the Canadian government shall persist in imposing upon
us this obsequious policy through force of arms, we register in
advance our protest against such an unjust and unlawful action.
We declare the said Canadian government responsible, before the
eyes of God and man, for the innumerable calamities which may

ensue from such unjustifiable conduct. . . . We hold ourselves
ready to undertake with the Canadian government any negotiation which is favourable to good administration and the prosperity of the population.[4]

Clearly, the Métis desired to accommodate Ottawa even while
retaining mastery in their own lands. In response Ottawa sent a
delegation led by Donald Smith, the Hudson's Bay Company's
senior official and future Lord Strathcona. At this point he wished
mainly to understand the situation.

Smith persuades Riel to organize a congress of forty elected
persons, divided equally between French- and English-speakers,
who will attend a national convention from January 25 to
February 10. The convention endorses Riel's government and
decides to free the prisoners taken in December (many of whom
have already escaped, including Schultz). By February 4 it considers a proposal that Red River become a Canadian province – and
rejects it.

Even as these events unfold, Schultz and a certain Thomas
Scott have already organized the escaped prisoners in Portage la
Prairie into a militia dedicated to overthrowing Riel's representa-
tive government. Its commander is a professional officer named
Charles Boulton.

Boulton's campaign doesn't go well. On February 17, while
trying to persuade some Scots in Fort Garry to side with them, his
men are surprised and arrested by Riel's associate Ambroise
Lépine. The captives greet the reverse with ill humour, subjecting
their Métis guards to a torrent of racial abuse. Riel quietly tells
Donald Smith that he's not sure his men will remain disciplined
if the provocation continues.

The Métis government convenes a court martial to pass judgment on the captured conspirators. Boulton, the senior English
officer, is sentenced to death; but Smith intervenes to have the
sentence commuted.

The court then turns its attention to the most recalcitrant and

Métis-phobic prisoner, Thomas Scott. He has passed his time in prison shouting at the guards that he will see them executed the moment they are under Canadian jurisdiction. He has tried without success to escape.

Scott had left Northern Ireland for Canada with a single dream: to make his fortune. Fellow colonists knew him to be an inveterate racist and a congenitally violent and obtrusive fellow. He had already tried to drown his supervisor on the work gang which built the Dawson road, the most dramatic – but far from the only – incident in his criminal record.

The tribunal condemned him to death. And this time Riel refused Smith's pleas. Scott was shot on March 4, 1870.

Some days later Monsignor Taché, the bishop, returned to Red River with a federal proclamation of amnesty for all actions committed up to that date. Through his powers of persuasion he got Riel to free the remaining prisoners and send a delegation to Ottawa. Meanwhile Schultz, now in Ontario, had begun a determined campaign to see Scott's "murderers" – that is to say, the Métis whose delegation had made its way to Ottawa – arrested and indicted. The province's Orange Lodges offered their fierce support, but Manitoba's provisional government moved rapidly to defuse the situation. It agreed that Red River should become a Canadian province so long as it received the same rights as the existing ones. They wanted two senators, four members of Parliament, and a bilingual province.

On May 12 the federal government passed the law creating the Province of Manitoba, and just under six weeks later Riel's provisional government ratified it. By July 15 Manitoba was a province of Canada.

The legislation set aside 1,400,000 acres of land for the Métis. But it made no mention of amnesty.

In a sense, Riel and his loyalists had won. Here was an officially bilingual Manitoba, its Métis endowed with rights which would be defended by the Dominion and John A. Macdonald, however reluctantly.

But Macdonald also had what we would now call a "Plan B." Riel's victory was to be short-lived. Wrote Macdonald: "These impulsive half breeds have got spoilt by their émeute, and must be kept down by a strong hand until they are swamped by the influx of settlers."[5]

Nor had Protestant Ontario forgotten Thomas Scott. It would pursue Riel for the bigot's death until the end of his days. True, Riel had not participated in the court which condemned Scott; but neither had he pardoned him. Edward Blake, Liberal premier of Ontario, put a price of $5,000 on Riel's head. The pathetic person Scott had been, with his lengthy criminal record, was overnight transformed into English Canada's own martyr. Medals were struck with his profile on them, and the cry "Remember Thomas Scott" echoed through English Canada. Writes Mason Wade:

> The execution of Scott, a member of the Orange Order, was used by the expansionist "Canada First" movement in Ontario to arouse a violent agitation which exploited ethnic and religious hatred. Scott's blood was shed on many a platform, and the "traitor French priests" of the Red River were denounced, although the clergy had been Ottawa's most effective ally in quieting the Red River troubles.[6]

To pacify a still-seething Ontario, Macdonald sends a military expedition to Red River. There are 12,000 people living there, including 5,000 whites, almost all from Ontario. These racists, this "little band of disorganized and unemployed men who infested the taverns of Winnipeg," in Lieutenant-Governor Adam G. Archibald's memorable phrase, were now authorized by Ottawa to take reprisals against the abhorred half-bloods:

> This group celebrated the establishment of Canadian rule by a persecution of the French Métis which culminated in the killing of Elzéar Goulet, in which two members of the Ontario Rifles were involved. They were not brought to trial. The Ontario Rifles

organized an Orange lodge which had 200 members by 1872 and which alienated the English as well as the French Métis.

Governor Archibald reported to Macdonald on October 8, 1871, that "many of the French half-breeds have been so beaten and outraged by a small but noisy section of the people that they feel as if they were living in a state of slavery." He added that the newcomers from Ontario "seem to feel as if the French half-breeds should be wiped off the face of the globe."[7]

Elzéar Goulet was among those who were stoned and drowned at the instigation of John C. Schultz, according to Métis accusations. But the murdering of Métis and related Orange Order activities did no harm to Schultz's subsequent and distinguished career. Canada was happy to appoint the assassin to the Senate, and finally to send him back to Manitoba as lieutenant-governor from 1888 to 1895.

Riel had returned home to Saint-Vital after fleeing to the United States when the Canadian army first arrived. He knew of the racist outrages, but succeeded in greeting the new Canadian authorities with equanimity. In the fall of 1870 he and his friend Lépine even organized a Métis cavalry of 300 horsemen to discourage Fenian incursions (these were the Irish Americans who fought to free their homeland from a base in Minnesota).

The Riel–Lépine contingent actually passed in parade review before A. G. Archibald, the new lieutenant-governor of Manitoba. He thanked them feelingly for their loyalty toward Canada. The two Métis leaders, in their naïveté, believed by now that their role in the provisional government had been forgotten. But their loyal little contingent of horsemen was so much Fenian-bashing cannon fodder, as far as Ottawa was concerned, and gained them no points whatsoever against the eventual settling of accounts for Scott's death. Once the Fenian menace subsided, Riel became, once again, just a troublesome Métis. But a worrisome one, since he was capable at a moment's notice of arousing more than half the population of the new province, and seemed still to dream of one day being elected to provincial or federal office. But Prime Minister Macdonald, ever resourceful, found a simple means of removing Riel from contention. Certain sums of public money due to Riel were instead secretly routed to Monsignor Taché, who agreed to offer the money to Riel as a bribe in exchange for moving to the United States. Thus bought off with his own money, Riel began what would be a rather short exile.

RIEL AND CANADIAN DEMOCRACY

When the 1872 federal elections rolled around, Riel did indeed stand as a candidate. There were threats that, should he be chosen to represent Provencher riding, "he would be murdered if he set foot in Ottawa."[8]

This unpleasant possibility seemed averted when Riel offered the Provencher nomination to Sir George-Étienne Cartier, who had lost his own riding in Quebec. But Cartier died shortly after the election and Riel was elected by acclamation in the subsequent by-election.

By November 1873, before Riel could get to Ottawa, the Canadian Pacific Railway scandal had erupted and brought down Macdonald's government. But Riel was re-elected and finally made his way to the nation's capital – in disguise. He had barely signed the members' register when Parliament voted to expel him (the motion was introduced by the Orange fanatic and future Conservative prime minister Mackenzie Bowell).

So a third election was held in Provencher, and Riel was elected for the third time.

Throughout, he had run under the Conservative banner. This is worth remembering by way of measuring the sang-froid of John A. Macdonald, who together with his Quebec deputies would later decide to kill Riel.

As for Ambroise Lépine, he had already been arrested and sentenced to death for Scott's murder. But there was still the question of the amnesty accorded to the Métis in 1870, and in early 1875 a Royal Commission was appointed to see if the amnesty had real legal force.

It reported that the execution of Scott was the act of a de facto government accepted by the people of the Red River and recognized by the Canadian and imperial authorities; that Bishop Taché and the delegates of the provisional government believed themselves authorized to promise to the insurgents in 1870 a full and complete amnesty, on the strength of the verbal and written promises of Macdonald, Cartier, Langevin, and Howe, made with the knowledge and consent of the governor-general and the imperial government; and that Governor Archibald's appeal to Riel and Lépine in 1871 for aid against the Fenians presupposed that they were not liable to arrest and punishment for their previous actions.[9]

Within a month Ottawa had to accept the Royal Commission's decision and pardon both Riel and Lépine. But both men were forced into a five-year American exile nonetheless. In Riel's case this was because Ontario, frankly contemptuous of Ottawa's pardon, continued to put a price on his head. Bounty hunters ranged far and wide looking for him. For that reason he had prudently fled to New England even as the Royal Commission deliberated. There, the large immigrant French population welcomed him as a hero.

But the endless stress finally took a toll on his mental health. Returning to Quebec under an assumed name, he was hospitalized in Saint-Jean-de-Dieu and later at Beauport with the help of his friend Alphonse Desjardins. After two years of treatment he went to Montana, where he could be close to his native Manitoba.

There he lived a peaceful teacher's life in the mission of Saint-Pierre, became an American citizen and an active Republican, and married a Métis woman who gave him two children.

By this time anglophones made up a majority in Manitoba and set about stripping the French minority of its rights. In 1879 the Legislature abolished French as an official provincial language. Lieutenant-governor Joseph-Édouard Cauchon, who was born in Quebec, refused to ratify a clearly unconstitutional law. The English went back to the drawing board, contenting themselves for the moment with gerrymandering the electoral map to the detriment of the French population.

RIEL'S RETURN

By 1884 things were bad enough that a Métis delegation made its way to Riel's home and begged him to come back and defend their rights. Much had changed since 1870 for the province's Métis and native people. The bison, to take the most striking example, had simply disappeared, thanks to the depredations of American hunters armed with the new Winchester repeating rifles. The starving Métis then became equally easy prey for land specula-tors. Wealthy settlers lured by misleading federal advertising showed up expecting a western paradise.

In the five years after 1876 the Canadian government had signed treaties with numerous native nations, offering to supply them with food while teaching them farming, and promising to protect hunting rights for those who wished to continue the ancestral ways. The poor dupes! Before the ink was dry, the Mounties showed up to herd the signatories onto their reserves. And when it was dry, civil servants tore up the treaties without even bothering to pretend embarrassment. Here's what the *Canadian Encyclopedia* has to say about this "police force": "The NWMP helped Indians make the transition to Indian reserves . . ."[10] We have to assume the humour here is unconscious. . . .

The unhappy Amerindians became so many grade-school chil-dren, with none of an adult's rights, while Ottawa set about a cold-eyed policy of assimilation or starvation. Just as it had done with French-speakers, the government used a state policy of hidden or threatened violence under a thin veneer of legality. Yet another shameless episode from a country which today flatters itself that its treatment of natives was exemplary.

In exchange for traditional land rights, the Métis received legal documents called scrips, which entitled each to 160 acres of land. Ontario speculators quickly bought them for next to nothing. This is how the hypocrites ruined entire families while hiding behind lawyers.

Soon the Métis fled the speculative frenzy and sought refuge in the distant North-West Territories where they could join forces with related groups.

Behind this flight was a profound refusal of the new way of life offered by white settlers. The Métis were simple people, and the proposed changes were to them simply unlivable. To them, a little bit of gold in exchange for the puzzling and alien "scrip" seemed reasonable. It would let them flee the racial hell which had over-taken the ancient lands of their ancestors.

It's no exaggeration to speak of a speculative frenzy in Winnipeg. Because the Canadian Pacific Railway was snaking across the prairie, land in that forlorn Red River settlement was worth more than in Chicago! Those who had dollars could easily buy a native girl who was frantic to feed her family. Cheap booze was decimating whole tribes. In a ghastly way, Winnipeg had already become what it has remained ever since.

To the Manitoba Métis who were now living safely (or so they thought) in Saskatchewan, these horrors seemed to be taking place in another world altogether. The prairie, after all, was endless and would protect them!

But Ontario settlers were already steadily inching their way into Saskatchewan. And the Métis, both those born in Saskatchewan and those who had sought refuge there, had no title to the land they were occupying.

They knew enough by now to try to get title from the federal government, even if only for their houses and the little plot of land some had tried to cultivate. But Ottawa turned a deaf ear, and instead sent surveyors to parcel up their land. It also took care to reinforce the local Mounted Police. Only Riel could properly represent the Saskatchewan Métis against Ottawa's picked men. After all, they thought, isn't that what he did in 1869–70?

THE ANGER SPREADS TO THE NATIVES AND THE ENGLISH SETTLERS

Saskatchewan's first English-speaking colonists also had good reason to be angry with Ottawa. They had settled by the North Saskatchewan River, where the CPR line was supposed to pass through. But, in a kind of Catch-22 reasoning, the CPR instead decided to take the line through unoccupied lands farther south because it was less complicated than negotiating a right-of-way through settled areas. The abandoned northern settlers saw their future drying up and blowing away like topsoil in a dry spell. And incoming southern settlers could fume about the CPR's sweetheart deal with Ottawa, which granted it vast swathes of land along the new southern route, which it could sell dearly by way of financing railway construction.

Meanwhile, of course, the native people who had already endured eight years of famine from the collapse of the buffalo herds were humiliated by the miserable food rations and seed doled out to them by high-handed federal agents.

The railway barons in Montreal's Golden Mile weren't paying much attention to these rising tensions. By 1884 they had bigger problems to worry about: they were close to a scandalous bankruptcy in spite of the mountains of cash they'd already received from the Dominion government.

HOW SASKATCHEWAN BECAME A THEATRE OF WAR

In July of that year Riel galloped north to Batoche, the biggest town in the Saint Lawrence district on the South Saskatchewan River. He was meeting with Métis leaders and also (perhaps surprising in retrospect) with hundreds of unhappy English-speaking settlers. Both groups agreed that he write a petition in their names. It would also include Riel's personal demand to be compensated for his own lands, which had been seized from him in the Red River Valley.

The petition was sent off to Ottawa on December 16, 1884. Its twenty-five articles ranged from land rights to political representation, and a prompt response was awaited. But all that winter and spring, there was only silence.

During these crucial months Riel's support melted away. His clumsy insertion of personal demands into the general petition alienated some English colonists, though they were certainly also affected by the unending federal propaganda about the execution of Scott. And his increasingly unconventional religious ideas scandalized the local Catholic clergy and approximately half the Métis population, who were devout churchgoers. He particularly antagonized the missionary priests André and Fourmond, who were members of the federal Conservative Party.

Riel's mental condition was once again deteriorating. By February he had become prey to delusions of grandeur. Like a certain Quebec politician of a later generation, he firmly believed the hand of God was guiding his actions. He took to styling himself the Prophet of the New World, and hoped that Bourget, the ailing bishop of Montreal, might become the Pope of America.

The situation tipped into crisis when Lawrence Clarke, a federal bureaucrat, showed up in Batoche on March 15, 1885, with the news that 500 Mounties were on their way to arrest Riel. This was false, but under the circumstances nobody was checking. The community went into high alert and Riel ordered his men to seize weapons and supplies from armouries in the area.

That same evening he proclaimed himself president of a provisional government, with Gabriel Dumont as military leader. Their little army would never number more than 400 men, not all of them young, nor would their armoury consist of much more than muskets and a few Winchester carbines. Dumont was certainly a virtuoso with the Winchester, judging by the fact he finished his life as a sharpshooter in Buffalo Bill's Wild West Show! But in 1885 he was after bigger game, and quickly overcame the Mountie detachment defending Fort Carleton, just outside of Batoche.

The situation might still have been salvaged, had not a detachment of about a hundred Mounties and volunteers encountered Riel's main force eleven days later near Duck Lake. It happened entirely by chance, and the federals under Major Leif Crozier were heavily outnumbered by Riel's 300 soldiers. Crozier panicked and ordered a fusillade. In the returning fire from the massed Métis, commanded by a crucifix-bearing Riel, twelve federal soldiers were killed and eleven wounded. The Métis lost only five men.

The effect in the East was immediate and electrifying. Young men crowded into armouries begging to be enlisted. The crusade against the Western savages had begun.

TWO WRONGS MAKE A RIGHT

Macdonald, perspicacious as always, quickly saw that this was his opportunity both to get rid of Riel and find the money to finish the railway.

The latter was a pressing matter. Tens of millions in federal loans by Macdonald's government had failed to lift the Canadian Pacific out of its financial torments. And these were by now so well known in the House of Commons that he didn't dare ask for another nickel on behalf of the CPR magnates, led by William Cornelius Van Horne.

When the news of the rebellion reached Montreal, Van Horne moved quickly to put his railway at the disposition of the military. He would pay the costs of the troops who would go west to crush the rebellion!

Today we'd call it a stroke of PR genius. In one deft move Van Horne would prove that the CPR was up and running, and well worth another injection of taxpayers' money. Macdonald thought it a stunning idea, and his thickheaded militia minister Joseph Caron, who owed his position to back-room money passing under the table, enthusiastically believed whatever the prime minister believed.

Major general Frederick Middleton, a British officer in command of Canada's militia troops, was quite delighted to put his colonial experience to use against the Métis. He had suppressed Maori rebellions in New Zealand and Santhal uprisings in India. He was an old hand at getting the regiments down to the train station, and in no time they were speeding from Quebec and Ontario toward the Saskatchewan frontier.

There were, disenchantingly, some patches of unfinished track in Northern Ontario. The soldiers changed from comfortable railway cars to dog sleds and open wagons even as the temperature dropped to twenty below zero (Celsius). But Van Horne didn't lose sleep over miserable soldiers any more than he did for the Métis. The main thing was, Louis Riel was going to save the Canadian Pacific!

THE BATTLE OF BATOCHE AND RIEL'S SURRENDER

Middleton's army had its nose bloodied right away in a skirmish at L'Anse-aux-Poissons. But the quick-thinking Dumont knew that any more pitched battles would wear down the smaller Métis force, and lobbied Riel for permission to use guerrilla warfare. The Canadian expeditionary force had long and poorly defended supply lines that Dumont's "half-breed" cavalry could easily cut to pieces.

But Riel, in an excess of righteousness, would not condone such tactics. He opted instead for an obviously doomed last stand in the town of Batoche.

Among General Middleton's advisors was an ominous presage of the future of mechanized warfare, a young American officer named Howard. He was nominally attached to the Connecticut National Guard, but his true reason for journeying so far north was his connection to the manufacturers of the Gatling gun.

The American military-industrial complex had already been born. The inventors of the first operational machine gun needed battlefield testing to whet the appetites of potential purchasers. Their bulky and unproven weapon had six rotating cannons activated by a kind of windmill mechanism. It would one day ensure unprecedented mass slaughter on the battlefields of Europe in the First World War. But just now, all it required to sate its financial needs were a few easily killable guinea pigs.

And there they were, 300 unhappy Métis with not enough rifles to go around. At Riel's order they had taken up positions in Batoche, and were now facing Middleton's 900 soldiers. The skirmishes they had won up to that point were very cold comfort indeed.

Middleton had already taken the precaution of sending all his French-speaking soldiers, whom he mistrusted, back down the line to guard the railway tracks. On May 8 he laid siege to Batoche, and four days later he judged the moment right for an assault. By that time he had had intelligence from Catholic priests who had betrayed the Métis.

Long afterward Gabriel Dumont would recall the summary executions inflicted on those who surrendered at Batoche:

> The fourth day, May 12, about two o'clock in the afternoon, informed by traitors that we had no more ammunition, the soldiers advanced and our men came out of the trenches to meet them. At this time the following were killed: José Ouellet, aged 93 years; José Vandal, whose arms were broken before he was impaled on a bayonet, aged 75 years; Donald Ross, first mortally wounded and then dealt a bayonet blow, a man of advanced age; Isidore Boyer, also elderly; Michel Trottier, André Batoche, Calixte Tourond, Elzéar Tourond, John Swan, and Damase Carrière, whose leg was first broken, and who was then dragged behind a horse by a rope attached to his neck. Two Sioux natives were also killed.
>
> The final toll of these four bloody days of fighting was, on our side, three wounded and twelve dead, including a child. This child was the only victim of the famous Gatling machine gun throughout the whole campaign.[11]

Dumont's dreadful allegations were confirmed by a young soldier from Ontario, who wrote in his diary: "The rebel still coming and giving themselves up. . . . It is surprising to see so many old men, some with grey hair, and a lot of these were killed. Empty Houses were ransacked, . . . we captured over forty heads of cattle and each man has something he intends to keep as a relic: knives, saddles, beadworks."[12]

The now undefended village was subjected to an orgy of pillaging and destruction. Soldiers entered little houses by force and took everything, regardless of who owned it. There were a number of Métis loyal to the government in the town, and they watched as the uniformed thugs stripped their houses bare. After all, in time of war it's always wise to leave anybody who isn't white, Protestant, and English to shiver in the cold!

The Toronto newspaper *The Mail* sent a correspondent who reported by telegraph that soldiers had sacked Métis homes at Clarke's Crossing and l'Anse-aux-Poissons, shooting out the windows by way of entertainment. In Battleford, theft from civilians got so out of control that Lieutenant Colonel Otter was obliged to take draconian disciplinary action.

By this time Riel had gone into hiding. He negotiated for his family's safety should he surrender. This assured, he gave himself up on May 16 to a pair of Middleton's scouts (Middleton later sent a false telegram to Ottawa claiming Riel had been captured).

Riel would regret trusting the English. He should have done as Dumont did, who, before fleeing to the United States, spat out the words *"Allez au diable"* to an emissary who promised him fair treatment.

During this period of history the Montreal *Gazette* was still in fine form where pathological francophobia was concerned. Two days after Riel's surrender it was already calling for him to be hanged, insane or not. "Let us not through false sentimentality spare Riel the punishment he has deserved by his criminal folly. Let retribution be quick and remorseless. Even in conceding that there should be a regular trial, we insist that under no pretext should there be any delay in executing that which is inevitable."[13]

Only the *Gazette* could ask for a "regular trial" even while announcing the verdict in advance! But for once it was outdone by another newspaper. The *Toronto News* came up with the inventive suggestion that Riel be strangled with a French flag. "That's about all the filthy rag is good for in this country."[14]

WINNIPEG OR REGINA?

Once apprised that Riel had been "captured," militia minister Caron ordered Middleton to convey him to Winnipeg and keep him there until his trial. But a second order from Ottawa caught up with the convoy on its way to Winnipeg: it was imperative that Riel go to Regina, capital of the North-West Territories.

Why the turnabout? Ottawa had realized that in Winnipeg Riel would receive a bilingual trial in front of an independent judge. Worse, he would have the right to demand that half the jurors be French-speaking. This was just the thing Macdonald and Alexander Campbell, his justice minister, had dreaded. In a fascinating book called *The Trial of Louis Riel: Justice and Mercy Denied*, a letter of Campbell's (dated May 21, 1885) explains to Macdonald that any trial of Riel in Winnipeg will surely lead to "a miscarriage of justice."[15]

As we've seen in previous chapters, the lengthy history of Canada has been marked by Ottawa's manipulation of the judicial system for political purposes. In Riel's case, what Macdonald obviously feared was an acquittal.

Hence the desirability of Regina. It was located at the time in a territory, not a province, and its judges were fixed-term federal appointees. Without the security of permanent appointment, as was the case in the provinces, they dared not defy the government. And of course there would be no question of French-speaking jurors under territorial law.

A final bitter twist was that Riel could have only six rather than twelve jurors in Regina. And there he would be tried not under the

1868 Canadian law of treason, which did not permit capital punishment, but rather under an archaic British law dating back to Edward III's reign in 1351.

This is how far Canada was willing to go to oblige the Montreal *Gazette* and Orange Ontario. Riel had to be hanged, and if that meant accusing him of treason against the Queen, so be it!

Riel's judge, Hugh Richardson, was a Conservative appointee and a good friend of the government. He was also legal advisor to Edgar Dewdney, lieutenant-governor of the North-West Territories.

So it was decided that Canada was still a British dominion in which a medieval English law might be invoked to execute Louis Riel. It's hard to see how these men, or anybody else, could claim with a straight face that a desperate man leading a few embittered Métis intended to rock the throne of England by shooting off muskets in Batoche! But that was the accusation.

This bizarre situation was brought to the attention of Parliament by none other than Liberal leader Edward Blake . . . the same gentle fellow who put a price of $5,000 on Riel's head a decade earlier.

IT'LL BE REGINA . . .

Promptly upon arriving in Regina on May 23, Riel was locked up in the local Mounted Police post. A twenty-pound weight was chained to his ankle to ensure he didn't miss his date with destiny.

Fearing the thirst for revenge which raged throughout English Canada, Riel's friends mobilized to defend him. From as far as Fall River in New England, expatriate French Canadians urged former Quebec prime minister Adolphe Chapleau (now Secretary of State) to intervene in Riel's favour. They underlined Ottawa's years of ignoring Métis demands for justice.

Chapleau should have been the right man to approach. He had defended Ambroise Lépine against charges in Scott's death, and these same Franco-Americans had paid Lépine's legal bills at the time.

But Chapleau was now working for the English. His response to Riel's defenders was more like an indictment of the Métis people, seamed with lies: "If the Métis had serious grievances against the Canadian government, they might have petitioned as any free citizen may do. But they did not avail themselves of this remedy."[16]

Let's note in passing that Ottawa managed to ignore no less than seventy-three petitions and requests from the Métis. The proof was in a letter written by justice minister Campbell to a senator a mere four days before Chapleau wrote his letter:

> The government has received, between January 1, 1879, and March 1, 1885, many persons who take a special interest in the North-West. That would include, among others, Monsignor Grandin, bishop of Saint-Albert, and Monsignor Taché, archbishop of Saint-Boniface, together with written presentations concerning the Métis situation in the North-West and the best means of improving it.[17]

What did the federals care about the demands of mixed-bloods, French, and Catholics? They were going to kill Riel, and Chapleau would be one of the first of that eternally present and useful species, the serviceable francophone who does the dirty work.

Riel's trial began after sixty-six days of detention, on July 20, 1885. In the dark and dusty closet which passed for a courtroom in Regina he saw for the first time the judge appointed to the case – his mortal enemy – and the six jurors, entirely innocent of the French language, who would decide his fate. It's worth remembering how they were chosen: Justice Richardson put the names of thirty-six friends into a hat and chose six. Ah, Canadian justice!

Sir Hector-Louis Langevin, another French-Canadian minister, had promised Riel a regular trial by jury under perfectly impartial conditions. This weasel's name is still on the building which contains the Prime Minister's Office.

THE TRIAL OF LOUIS RIEL

Riel's lawyers immediately challenged the legality of the charges and the standing of the court. Justice Richardson, serenely certain of his own legitimacy, swatted the challenges away, and added that there was no need to allow a month for witnesses from the East Coast to arrive: surely a week would do!

The first day of hearings had barely begun when William Henry Jackson, Riel's English-speaking secretary, was declared incompetent to stand trial on grounds of "mental alienation" (mental instability). He was sent to an asylum, from which he fled to the U.S.A. with the help of federal officials. In later years Jackson repeatedly declared that he was as guilty of treason as Riel, and ought to have stood trial. This was certainly true, as Robert Rumilly indicates: "with a group of Métis, he had gone to seek out Riel in Montana in order to offer him the leadership of the group of insurrectionists. But William Henry Jackson was an English-speaking Métis, and everyone concerned was certain he was treated differently because of his race."[18]

That was the beginning of Riel's formal trial on July 28. The Crown meant to show that Riel plotted to lead the Métis and Indians into a war of extermination against the whites. It also alleged that he returned to Canada mainly in search of money owed him by the government. This made him look bad, but legally speaking was irrelevant in a trial for treason.

The defence pleaded mental illness in spite of Riel's fervid objections. Lawyers spoke of his troubled youth and his asylum stays in the 1870s. Doctors, priests, and others were summoned to testify that Riel was quite mad during the rebellion, and had no idea what he was about.

He had deliriums about the papacy and about religion which could have meant his excommunication, and throughout the Rebellion he floated about like a mystic and never actually pulled a trigger.

But Riel was furious to hear himself described this way, and persisted in claiming that he was sound of mind and wished only to be judged on the political merit of his acts: "I cannot abandon my dignity. Here I find myself obliged, in defending myself against charges of high treason, to agree to live like an animal in an asylum. An animal's life has little attraction for me if it means I may not at the same time carry on the moral existence of an intelligent being."[19]

It was thus that Riel was declared guilty. In an act highly unusual at the time, he pled for mercy. But the judge turned a deaf ear and Riel was sentenced to be hanged on September 18. Riel's last comment to the court was that it lightened his heart to know he was at last being treated as a sane man.

A DERISORY VERDICT

Quebec was stupefied by Riel's sentence. Surely he was a madman, and surely such men are not hanged in civilized countries. Was this not simply the delayed sentence for the murder of Thomas Scott fifteen years earlier? Even Confederate president Jefferson Davis, who provoked a civil war in which six hundred thousand died, was not subjected to such a humiliation. He returned from exile (in Montreal, as it happened) and lived peacefully in New Orleans to his death in 1889.

Over in Ontario, the sentence caused what can only be described as general bliss. The *Bradford Courier* described the enticing vision of Riel dancing at the end of a rope. "No clemency," cried the Peterborough *Examiner*. *The Globe* and *The Mail* in Toronto, like the Montreal *Gazette* and the *Ottawa Citizen*, found the trial impartial and the outcome equitable.[20] Nobody can claim that any of these newspapers ever allowed a moment of objectivity to mar their perfect francophobia.

Quebec newspapers found the outcome racist. If Riel's English-speaking secretary was acquitted on grounds of insanity, why not Riel himself? On August 2, *La Presse* wrote: "If insanity excuses an anglophone, surely it ought to do the same even for a Métis, even for a Riel." *L'Électeur*, another newspaper, echoed with: "Why this difference between Riel and Jackson? Because Jackson is English, and Riel is French."[21]

Riel's lawyers appealed to the Manitoba Court of Queen's Bench and to the judicial committee of the Privy Council in London. The Manitoba court rejected it, and the Privy Council washed its hands of the matter. In the Royal Military College in Kingston, Riel was hanged in effigy by the oldest serving officer, a ritual apparently repeated in military camps throughout Ontario.

Finally, on September 14, a Conservative senator named Trudel decided he'd had enough of the English-Canadian hate storm. In his newspaper *L'Étendard* he called for French-Canadian Members of Parliament to come together across political lines:

> The truth is that the English Protestant element hates the French
> and never ceases belittling them. . . . The truth is that our
> English-speaking fellow citizens are still under the illusion of
> 1763, that if they push a little harder they can suppress our
> nationality on this continent. . . . They mean for the North-West
> to be exclusively English-speaking. . . . So that's the national
> question, at least for all true patriots. And make no mistake,
> English-speaking Liberals are working just as hard as English-
> speaking Conservatives – perhaps even harder – to make sure the
> North-West becomes exclusively English.[22]

Honoré Mercier, the provincial Liberal leader, becomes the head of the crusade to save Riel. His first step is to call Chapleau to his side. But Chapleau, who was without doubt the most charismatic Quebec leader of his time, has made a cold calculation: if he takes Riel's side, and leaves Ottawa, then French influence in the federal cabinet will diminish. It's an early example of a species of French-Canadian bird we have come to know so well since then: the "it's more effective to work inside the system" parrot.

Chapleau loved the role and never outgrew it. At the end of his life he was appropriately rewarded with a silly little operetta hat and the title of lieutenant-governor of Quebec. As for Honoré Mercier, he very soon became the premier of Quebec.

SIR JOHN'S LAST GO AT PUPPETRY

Through various appeals, Riel survived his scheduled hanging on September 18. When Macdonald allowed a second delay, however, the Montreal *Gazette* became apoplectic.

For the prime minister, the political pressure was like a rope tightening around his own neck. To shift it elsewhere, he decided in October to appoint a medical commission to evaluate Riel's mental condition. Its members were Dr. Lavell, director of the Kingston Penitentiary; Dr. Jukes, doctor to the Mounted Police in Regina; and Dr. Valade, a neophyte Ottawa doctor and a friend of Militia Minister Caron. This, Macdonald was certain, would make him pliable.

Macdonald wasn't ashamed to pressure Valade and Lavell with written instructions: "You are not called upon to go behind the verdict, but your inquiry must be limited to his present mental condition."[23]

Lavell and Jukes decided, as Macdonald had hoped, that Riel was not deranged (though both found him profoundly strange). However, Valade surprised everyone with his independence of mind: he found that Riel was insane. He wired this message to John A. Macdonald: "[Riel] is not an accountable being, in that he is unable to distinguish between wrong and right on political and religious subjects which I consider well marked typical forms of a kind of insanity which he undoubtedly suffers, but on the other points I believe him to be quite sensible and can distinguish right from wrong."[24]

This could not stand! So Justice Minister Campbell dug the telegram out of a stack of government documents after Riel's death and rewrote it as follows: "[Riel] suffers under hallucinations on political and religious subjects, but on the other points I believe him to be quite sensible and can distinguish right from wrong."[25]

The medical commission was in any event just a pantomime to mask Macdonald's long-standing decision that Riel should die. His ministers met in Ottawa on November 11 to make their own final decision on the matter.

Chapleau, meanwhile, had a temporary attack of dignity and decided he would never approve the execution. But it didn't take long for him to reconsider. Surely the noose was a better idea than, good heavens, a race war.

Some of Macdonald's ministers feared the backlash in Quebec, but he knew French Canada well. At worst, he declared, it would be "a straw fire." He encouraged his ministers to buckle down and do the political arithmetic: twelve seats in Quebec, more than fifteen in Ontario and the Maritimes. Riel's fate was sealed.

Of course every newspaper in Quebec, whether Red or Blue, rained contempt on Macdonald's government for the decision. Across the political spectrum, French-speaking journalists were stunned by the depth of contempt for Quebec which was apparent in English Canada. The conservative *L'Étendard* wrote:

> The judicial murder being prepared can only serve as a signal to French Canada that no further political claim of any description from us will be tolerated in this country. Justice will be arbitrary and unjust where it pleases them. . . . There will be no limit on the provocations which may be inflicted on us. . . . Need we add that Sir John's government no longer possesses the confidence of French Canadians.

At the other end of the spectrum, the Liberal *L'Électeur* added:

> We understand very well that Riel's death is Orangeism's triumph over us. Our province has henceforth lost all influence in Ottawa. In this solemn moment, let us have the decency to abandon political squabbles. Let us unite as our fathers did when

oppression was unleashed against them. Let there be an end of Rouge and Bleu, let all Canadiens unite to block Riel's path to the scaffold, and to prevent what influence we have from being buried with his corpse.[26]

Conservative MPs in Quebec panicked. What future could they or their party have in that province? Hector Langevin made their anxiety known to Macdonald, who replied by telegram: "Remain calm and resolute: all shall be well."

Macdonald had already uttered his celebrated "Riel shall be hanged, though every dog in Quebec bark in his favour."[27] And so he was, on November 16. Another fine example of Canadian justice!

An old friend of Thomas Scott, by the name of Jack Henderson, took up the post of hangman by way of revenge. It was he who twined the rope around Riel's neck.

As for the rope, until recently it was a cherished trophy in the RCMP training centre in Regina . . .

DIAMETRICALLY OPPOSED REACTIONS

By eleven o'clock on November 16, the news reached Montreal. That day's edition of *La Presse* cried:

> Because he demanded justice for his compatriots, Riel has just now given up his life on the scaffold. . . . This patriot mounted to the gibbet because of a political crime for which no civilized nation any longer inflicts the penalty of death. This pitiful madman has been hurled into the eternal oven without so much as a review of his mental condition. . . . Riel has not died because he fought for our rights. He died because he is French.

The following day, *La Presse* went further: "Riel has broken all political bonds which were forged in the past. Henceforth we shall hear no more of Liberals and Conservatives. Let there be only

PATRIOTS and TRAITORS. Our national party is a noose party!"[28]

Israël Tarte, a brilliant journalist and opportunist who will end up in Laurier's cabinet, proclaimed in *Le Canadien*: "Blood is but a poor cement, and if Confederation has no other mastic it shall tumble down in the next gale."

How wrong he was.

Quebec's towns and settlements grieved. Commerce ceased, the death bell tolled, and Laval University students in Montreal sang the *Marseillaise*. Macdonald's associates Langevin, Caron, and Chapleau learned that their effigies were set afire along with their leader's.

None of this intimidated Ontario, which was always on the lookout for a rematch of the Plains of Abraham. Watch out, the *Globe* warned Honoré Mercier and other defenders of Riel:

> That these men glower at the current government does not shake the resolve of Upper Canada's conservatives. And if French influence succeeds in overturning the Cabinet, if this is the outcome of Mercier's machinations, then we British subjects must believe the time will have come to fight the conquest once again; and let Lower Canada know that this time there will be no treaty of 1763. This time, the conqueror shall not capitulate.[29]

Needless to say, the *Orange Sentinel* felt that total extermination of the French would be a very good idea:

> Must it be said that the rights and liberties of the English people in this English colony depend upon a foreign race? . . . The day is near when an appeal to arms will be heard in all parts of Canada. Then, certainly, our soldiers, benefiting by the lessons of the past, will complete the work they began in the North-West.[30]

Six days after Riel's death saw one of the largest and most emotional gatherings in Canada's history. Fifty thousand people came together on the Champ de Mars in Montreal where Mercier and other orators denounced the Conservatives. Among them was a young Wilfrid Laurier, making political hay on his way to taking over the federal Liberal party. "Had I been on the banks of the Saskatchewan," he bellowed to the crowd, "I should have shouldered my rifle like the others. . . . Riel was the victim of an ambush."

Ten years later, this very same Laurier will preside over the abolition of French as a legal language in the Canadian West. What a "great Canadian"! He certainly did earn his Heritage Minute.

If you want to know who gave the greatest speech that day, look to the one who doesn't have a shadow of a hope of a Heritage Minute. That would be Mercier. This great speaker brushed aside the mumblings of Macdonald's three lowlife associates and, with Laurier standing beside him, denounced every French-Canadian opportunist who ever sold his soul to the federal government:

> Our brother Riel is dead, victim of his devotion to the Métis cause which he had led, victim of bigots and traitors; of the fanaticism of Sir John and his several friends; of the treason committed by three of our own men who saw fit to sell their brother and fatten their wallets.
>
> In killing Riel, Sir John stabbed deep into the heart not only of our race but even more so into the heart of justice and humanity. For what language did not honour itself and what religion did not sanctify itself by pleading for the life of the prisoner in Regina? Our poor brother of the North-West. . . .
>
> "Here we are fifty thousand citizens gathered together under the aegis of the Constitution, in the name of all humanity crying for vengeance, in the name of two million weeping Frenchmen, to lay a curse upon the fleeing prime minister [Macdonald had left precipitately for Europe when the parliamentary session ended]. Our curse shall echo from shore to shore down the great Saint Lawrence and leap to his ears even as he passes out of sight of the country whose soil he has dishonoured with judicial murder.
>
> As for those who remain, as for the three who represented Quebec in the federal government, and who today represent mere

treason, let us bow our heads in pity for the collapse of their integrity, and for the sad fate that shall pursue them. For the bloody smears about their faces shall not be washed away, and they like Cain shall carry the mark of cowardice wherever they go.

What must we do in the face of such a crime and such a failure? Three things: come together to punish the guilty; break our representatives' political alliance with the Orangemen; and seek in a natural and unthreatening alliance the proper protection of our national interest.

Let us unite! Ah, how easily these words come to my lips! For twenty years have I called upon the nation to unite its vital forces. So long have I cried for my brothers to place upon the altar of the endangered nation the divisions which kill us, the petty hatreds which blind us! . . . The evil which we deplore has not fallen in vain upon our nation. Only through this death can the urgent need for unity make itself understood.

And I say to my fellow Liberals, let us not forget that the nation's grief for dead Riel is but little beside the gulf of pain which our Conservative brothers now know. They weep as we do for Riel, but they weep also for the failure and the treason of their leaders. Those who were so proud of Chapleau and of Langevin – and with good reason! – those who saw in the eloquence of the one and the masterfulness of the other our country's salvation, must now lower their heads and curse those men who yesterday they blessed.

Chapleau pushed aside a brother's hand in order to grasp the hand of Sir John. The howling of fanatics sounded sweeter to his ear than all the benedictions whispered by the French-Canadian nation. Death spoke to him where life did not: his own death, as well as Riel's! His career is broken as Riel's was broken. But where the one fell as a man, the other fell as a traitor.[31]

Meanwhile, in English Canada, the carnival had come to town. Riel's effigy swung in Winnipeg and in Toronto, and the Orangemen toasted sweet revenge. At the same time, the navvies' hammers rang out their silvery song and the rails of the CPR finally reached the Pacific coast: "Riel died within a week of the driving of the last spike of the transcontinental railway. CPR stocks were worth a fortune. The company's vice-president, Cornelius William Van Horne, smilingly suggested the company should erect a monument to Louis Riel. There's that Anglo-Saxon humour!"[32]

Crushing the Métis was a sound business initiative for Canadian Pacific. Jean-Guy Rens calculates that the sale of telegrams doubled in the year 1885, hitting $145,000, as the soldiers and journalists kept the lines humming back home to Montreal and Toronto.

COMMANDER-IN-CHIEF OF THE MILITIA, AND . . . HIGHWAYMAN

Middleton, the British general who led the war against the Métis, got a $20,000 bonus from a grateful federal government. This was not unlike a mercenary's dirty payday, the perfect demonstration that Riel's head was worth its weight in gold to English Canada. Middleton also became a Knight Commander of the Order of Saint Michael and Saint George.

But the saviour of English Canada soon revealed another side of his character. From the ashes of the burnt homes he stole $5,634 worth of furs from a Métis named Charles Bremner, who lived near Battleford in Saskatchewan. The Métis sued the general, but it took years before a newspaper reported the affair. By then Laurier's Liberals were ready to use it against Macdonald's government.

An MP named Day Hort MacDowall set out to defend Middleton. But his approach was maladroit, to say the least: he argued in the House of Commons that all kinds of Canadian soldiers had been looting the Métis. So far as furs and pelts were concerned, "there was hardly a single soldier who came down from Battleford who had not some furs to sell when he got to Prince Albert."[33]

Middleton himself was finally summoned before a parliamentary committee to account for his behaviour five years earlier. He put on an affronted and arrogant air: "I thought I was the ruling power up there . . . that I could do pretty much as I liked, as long as I was within reason. I did not think it was unreasonable to allow a few furs to be taken."[34] It was only the Métis, after all! Stealing from half-bloods can hardly be called stealing. The committee decided nonetheless (and unanimously) that confiscating Métis furs was "unjustifiable and illegal" and that Middleton's activities were "highly irregular." In short, he was a thief.

Middleton quit the command of the Canadian militia a few months later. "I have been a victim of politics, because I was a British soldier. I was sacrificed to please the French vote, that's the case in a nutshell."[35]

The committee's report dashed his hopes of a second career in business. He'd even dreamed of moving directly from pillage and looting to a corner office in a Montreal insurance company. Instead he returned to England, where he was named the keeper of the crown jewels. . . . As for Charles Bremner, he waited quite a while to recover the goods the light-fingered general had subtracted from him. It was 1899, in fact, when Laurier's government returned, to the penny, the $5,634 he had lost fourteen years before.

None of this is of much interest in English Canada, which still can't bring itself to admit the murder, pillaging, theft, and sundry exactions committed against the Métis by its soldiers. What we've seen instead is this kind of mealy-mouthed historical revision:

> Claims, often several years after the fact, that Canadian troops had killed helpless defenders during the storming of Batoche were more difficult to substantiate. Such acts were committed in the heat of battle and often under very confused circumstances.
>
> Throughout the North-West Rebellion of 1885, the Canadian militia acted as a disciplined military force. Soldiers obediently followed the orders given them, committed relatively few crimes, and respected the accepted rules governing warfare at the time.[36]

POLITICAL CONSEQUENCES

Within a year of Riel's death Honoré Mercier channelled popular resentment into the creation of the National Party, a political force made up of the former Liberal and ultramontane (clerical) groups. He campaigned against the Quebec Conservatives through 1886 and seized power the following year. We shall return to the subject of Mercier, who was the first true leader produced by the Quebec nation.

Federally, the Liberals went down to defeat in 1887. But there was a silver lining: Quebec loathing of Macdonald's Conservatives was such that the Liberals now found themselves with a power base there – something they could not have dreamed of before.

HISTORY LESSONS

Canadian historians, you may be interested to know, are perfectly aware of every fact cited in this chapter. They just don't talk about them. The prefer the lazy man's history: a mythic Canada of peace and compromise. Their John A. Macdonald wouldn't dream of jailing a madman, falsifying documents, and going venue-shopping with his justice minister to make sure their man choked out his life at the end of a rope. Surely the founding father wouldn't have sent 5,000 men and a machine gun to put down a pitiful mixed-blood uprising. Surely he wouldn't manipulate a rebellion to line the pockets of the railway mafia.

> Sir John Macdonald can well be considered the personification of evil in this story. . . . He certainly could not understand that the Métis were more than a group of individuals, that they had already become a tiny people, that they were in fact exactly what he habitually referred to as the New Nation, with their own national aspirations, and the determination to survive in spite of the new economical and political order which assailed them.[37]

John A. Macdonald assassinated the Métis nation. Laurier as prime minister later collaborated by endorsing the abolition of the French language throughout the West. The choice offered the Métis was to adopt the language and culture of the Ontarians, or grind out their days in a forgotten and marginal poverty.

A further consequence was that there would never be a Western francophonie to take its place beside those of Quebec and Acadia.

The assassin who arranged all this, the hardened and impudent manipulator, has been set aside in favour of the agreeable carica-ture we know today: old "brandy nose," the debonair boozer and lovable father of Confederation who winks at us from the fold of our ten-dollar bills.

George Stanley, the great English-Canadian historian, seems well aware that Riel's hanging and the subsequent uproar per-fectly illustrate Canada's invasive arrogance toward Quebec. But he prefers to evoke it by asking questions which he then delicately refrains from answering.

English and French Canadians alike demanded that justice be done. But the former cried out for Riel's blood because they under-stood justice only in the terms of Moses – an eye for an eye, a tooth for a tooth – human life for human life. The latter cried out for pardon because Justice demanded that a man whose dementia was so evident not be asked to pay the price of death for his irra-tional acts. There was more to this than the evident factors of ignorance, fanaticism, political convenience, and hysteria which lay behind the agitation of 1885 and 1886. For many English Canadians the point at issue was the question of whether British traditions and principles would triumph across Canada. For many French Canadians it was a matter of whether or not French Canada would become a dynamic force in the Canadian federa-tion, or a non-entity without influence outside Quebec itself. For both it was a matter to be settled by force. Can unity exist without domination? This is the question which both peoples asked themselves. Riel was merely the symbol of this struggle. He was not the fundamental goal in the debate. The key issue was the following: Would Canada be a unity or a federal state? Would the country's duality exist only within Quebec? Or across the land? Riel was the symbol of this duality; the symbol of the intensity of this attachment to a tiny corner of this vast land with its redoubtable distances and differences: he was the symbol of ethnic and cultural diversity within the federal structure. Here is Riel's profound significance in the history of Canada.[38]

English Canada was prepared to tolerate exactly one attitude on the part of French Quebec: total and unconditional surrender. It was true in 1885 and remains true today. And it can only be described as gross indecency that those who hanged Riel now dare to proclaim him a father of the Canadian federation. Canada has never recovered from the volcanic tensions which forced Riel into the hangman's arms.

IN CANADA, "THE ORANGE ORDER HAS BECOME A WAY OF LIFE"

Imagine the perpetual media scandal it would cause in English Canada. Imagine the indignation of the Anglo intellectuals. Imagine the reaction of René Daniel Dubois, the ecstatic delirium of Diane Francis! Imagine Quebec, its cities and villages and bucolic pastures, spilling forth tens of thousands of people who can't wait to join an extreme right-wing organization based on religious exclusivity and, by the 1930s, hardline anti-Semitism.

Even more: it's a secret organization, complete with initiation rituals and close links to a foreign hate organization that has busied itself with a religious war. That foreign organization is killing, wounding, and mutilating men, women, children, and the elderly. Little neo-Nazi groups show up at its demonstrations.

This European equivalent of the Canadian group is universally denounced by those who combat intolerance.

The Anglo-Canadian press is in a perpetual fury about this organization. Year after year it denounces the unforgivable intolerance of these Québécois and their collusion with foreign fanatics and neo-Nazis. Reporters at the Montreal *Gazette*, the *National Post*, and the *Globe and Mail* attack with gusto the job of exposing the nationalist excesses committed by the members of this organization. They lay out the blinkered, reactionary character of its Québécois militants, who will not acknowledge the endless crimes committed by the international organization. With an indignant clatter of keyboards the editorial writers and columnists of English Canada demand that these Québécois cut every link with the parent organization and its atrocities. And those who obstinately defend the organization must be denounced as the typical product of a backward and obtuse Quebec society. Why backward? Fill in the blank: *a.* Catholic, *b.* French.

Remarkably, just such an organization exists in Canada, complete with a long history of bigotry and direct links to an extremist group in Europe. But there's never a word about it in the English press because it exists in English Canada and its mother house is in Great Britain. This is the Loyal Orange Order which has for centuries persecuted Catholics in Northern Ireland and throughout the British colonies.

In Canada the Orange Order busied itself through the nineteenth century with the persecution of the French, shifting focus early in the twentieth century to torment the Jewish people.

And today it maintains lodges throughout English Canada, as well as the English enclaves of Quebec. Its representatives serenely describe it as a mutual aid society, even as some rogue individuals claiming allegiance to the Order throw grenades at mothers who dare to take their children to school down Protestant streets!

The Orange Order was founded by Protestants in Northern Ireland on September 21, 1795, after a fairly meaningless skirmish with some Catholics in the village of Loughgall in County Armagh. Its organization was inspired by the Masonic lodges, with secret oaths and a hierarchy of initiation.

Of course the new order pledged loyalty to Protestantism and the British monarchy (so long as it remain Protestant, please God!). Every July 12 it organizes a sumptuous celebration of William of Orange's victory in 1690 over James II's Catholics in the Battle of the Boyne. These commemorations usually take the form of a rowdy parade in Ulster, and of smaller rowdy parades in the little, lost bigoted towns of Ontario.

Orange Lodges in North America date back to around 1800, the virus having been carried here by British soldiers and propagated in the garrison towns of York (Toronto), Kingston, Montreal, and Quebec. The Quebec lodge was particularly distinguished by the presence of Albert Hopper, sent there by the Grand Lodge of Ireland in 1804 expressly to bring the war to the land of the French papists.

But there was probably already a Montreal lodge even before Hopper's arrival. Lieutenant-Governor Hunter mentions in a letter that an "Orange Society" was meeting secretly in Montreal with the objective of "oppress[ing] Roman Catholics."[39]

In 1830 Ogle Gowan, from County Wexford, established the first North American Grand Lodge in Brockville, Ontario. The purpose was to centralize control of the existing lodges. Fiercely Tory, anti-Catholic, and anti-French, the Orangeists were the fleshly incarnation of British imperialism. Convinced of the Englishman's natural superiority, they were quite certain of a sacred mission to rule the planet. During the uprisings of 1837–38, Quebec's Orangemen were by far the most fanatic of the irregular soldiers who joined themselves to the British army. They volunteered for the dirty work, happy to burn a farm or two. Their members in Huntingdon County fought at

Odelltown, while those from Argenteuil County appointed themselves chief sackers and terrorizers of Saint-Eustache and Saint-Benoît.

The Orange Order reached its apex in Canada after 1875. Ontario's Regulation 17 and the status of Manitoba's schools were causes especially close to their hearts, as was the assassination of Louis Riel. Linguistic cleansing of Ontario and the Prairies was a top priority.

In 1885 in the North-West Territories the Tenth Royal Grenadiers of Toronto numbered 148 Orangeists out of 250 soldiers; that is, over half its soldiers were personally committed to avenge the death of their hero Thomas Scott. Another heavily Orange unit, the Midland Regiment, besieged the Métis at Batoche.

John Hughes, soon to become Grand Master of the lodges of Eastern Ontario, commanded the company of twenty-seven men who made the final assault at Batoche. This was the group which slaughtered unarmed Métis who were trying to surrender. Hughes received the General Service Medal and pin from a government grateful for his defence of Canada against the toothless grandfathers of Batoche.

The Orangeists are still celebrating all of this, even today.[40]

John A. Macdonald, father of Confederation and first prime minister, remained a member of Kingston's Orange Lodge all his life. With his death in 1891 he was succeeded by another Orangeman, John Abbott. Abbott was subsequently honoured for his ongoing commitment to the cause with the title deputy grand master of the Grand Orange Lodge of Quebec. And today Quebec's government thinks well to honour him further by naming a Cégep (post-secondary school) in Montreal after him.

How many Orangemen became prime minister? Two others, Mackenzie Bowell and John G. Diefenbaker.

Even today the Order continues to pat itself on the back for the generous measure of sectarian hatred which it brought to the building of English Canada:

No club, organization or group has produced more leaders in Canada at the federal, provincial and municipal level of government, than has the Orange Association. Orangemen in Canada make no apologies for supporting such a boastful statement. From the local school trustee to the highest position of prime minister, Canadian Orangemen have given leadership and distinguished service in every sphere of Canadian society.[41]

I simply can't understand how the *Heritage Minutes* have overlooked such a distinguished movement, a veritable beating heart of Canadian values!

If we go back to the year 1900, we find that one out of three Protestants in English Canada was also an Orangeman. That's the figure advanced at the time by Grand Secretary T. S. Sproule, who would in later life be president of the House of Commons. And it makes perfect sense, if one also remembers that Canada at the time celebrated July 12 more noisily than any place on earth excepting Northern Ireland. In 1937 it took hours for more than 200 lodges to parade through the streets of Toronto, earning the city the unlovely moniker of Canada's Belfast. Most of its mayors were also Orangemen.

In Toronto the Orange parade started, predictably enough, at Queen's Park. Overtly anti-Catholic parades and demonstrations were openly accepted in Toronto until mid-century. Today the tradition continues in out-of-the-way places. And in Newfoundland July 12 is still a bank holiday, as it is in Northern Ireland.

Today the Orange Association of Canada is still a bastion of religious fanaticism to which only Protestants may apply. At its Web site, www.orange.ca, there's a page-long listing of Grand Lodges for each province (two for Ontario), but almost nothing about Quebec apart from the notice that provincial Grand Secretary James Allan operates from Kinnears Mills in the Eastern Townships.

The Provincial Grand Orange Lodge of Ontario West has its own Web site listing eighteen county lodges and ninety-five primary lodges. The Ontario West Grand Lodge is especially proud of its continuing struggle against separate schools and anything touching the subject of bilingualism. One of its stated objectives is highly noble: "Our aim has always been to ensure that fairness and equality can be enjoyed by all, with special privileges for none." Please, every Franco-Ontarian who wants to give three big cheers for that one, line up right here at the service entrance.

In Northern Ireland there are still somewhere between eighty thousand and a hundred thousand members, closely linked to the Ulster Unionist Party. They organize thousands of July 12 events throughout Ulster, but especially enjoy the ones which parade through Catholic neighbourhoods in hopes of provoking controversy.

The Order has an extreme faction, the Spirit of Drumcree, from which comes Robert Salters, current Grand Master of the Orange Order of Ireland. Salters has accused British prime minister Tony Blair of treason and selling his birthright because his wife is Catholic. Blair, he says, would sell his soul to the devil.

Union Orangemen have been closely linked to Northern Ireland's loyalists and its fascist movement as far back as the 1920s. That's when the British Union of Fascists founded a branch in County Down, Northern Ireland, for the purpose of harassing Catholics. A decade later the Scottish fascist group, Billy Boys, made a yearly pilgrimage to Belfast every July 12, not so much for the parade as the attendant entertainments: "Catholic-smashing."[42]

Portadown in County Armagh has become a gathering place for British fascists since the Orange Order made it the site of the annual July 12 assault on Garvaghy Road. In July 1999, no less than twenty-five members of the neo-Nazi group Combat 18 showed up in Portadown; they liked it so much that two years later they showed up at Drumcree as well. The numbers 1 and 8 in Combat 18's name correspond to Adolf Hitler's initials. Their mission is the extermination of Jews, Blacks, and Catholics.

By the 1970s the Orange Order developed a secret wing called the Orange Volunteers. It quickly grew to be second in paramilitary importance only to the Ulster Defence Association. Believed to have vanished in the 1980s, it popped up in 1998 to author a series of attacks against Catholics.

On the official Grand Lodge of Ireland site there is high praise for the Canadian organization as an exemplar of true commitment to the Orange way of life. "Canada is probably the best example outside the British Isles of how Orangeism became part of a way of life." It goes on: "The structure of Government in Canada is said to be based on the Orange Model of Lodge, District, County, and Grand Lodge."[43]

6

A HALF-CENTURY OF
INFAMY, 1867–1918

None of the explanations furnished suffices to remove the
reproach which weighs heavily, and with justice, on Quebec.
This province cannot hope to adopt and follow a policy different
from that adopted and followed by the rest of Canada. French
Canadians cannot hope to be both inside and outside of
Confederation. As a people they have, in the past, been very
jealous of their rights and privileges, which they hold by virtue
of ancient guarantees. Do these rights not deserve to be
defended? Do the people of Quebec wish, in the future, to continue to enjoy these rights as a gift, preserved by the sacrifices
of others? It would be extraordinary if Quebec escaped future
censure for its present failure to do its duty.[1]

It's April 1917. The Montreal *Gazette* is flailing away at French
Canadians for their perceived lack of enthusiasm for fighting
the war then unfolding in Europe. Quebec's lukewarm support for
England looks likely to set off yet another bout of hysterical francophobia in English Canada.

French Canadians have very good reasons to see Great Britain in a different light than the rest of the country. For one thing, they actually love *Canada* rather than Great Britain.

It's true that Quebec's view of the European war is peculiar, from an anglophone standpoint. Quebeckers, for example, take an inordinate interest in the fact that all three quarrelling countries are ruled by Germans from the same family (George V in England, Nicolas II in Russia, and William II in Germany are all grandsons of Queen Victoria!). The situation is so indecent, given the waves of young Englishmen being slaughtered in Flanders, that even the aristocrats are embarrassed: the Battenbergs change their name to Mountbatten and the Saxe-Coburg-Gotha clan rebaptize themselves as the Windsors.

English Canadians also indulge in a flurry of name-changing, though this in no way affects their deep allegiance to the Empire. In Ontario, oldest daughter of England, the little town of Berlin quietly changes itself to Kitchener. But nobody, anywhere, rethinks their beliefs.

The *Gazette*'s sanctimonious criticism of French Canadians (quoted above) rests on one of those unquestioned beliefs: that the French have enjoyed the same freedoms as other Canadians, and should therefore support the war.

French-speakers had experienced the opposite in the fifty years since Confederation. Their rights had continually been held in contempt. Those unlucky enough to live outside Quebec had been treated as if they had no rights at all. Those within Quebec were never allowed to forget that they were a single province inside a "dominion" which was itself but a vassal state to Great Britain.

As always, however, English Canadians only wish to see the rosy side of things. Those backward French Canadians really ought to count themselves lucky to be ruled by such generous conquerors!

By the time Confederation was proclaimed in 1867, English-speakers had finally managed to make themselves a majority in Canada. The idealistic French-Canadian impulses of the 1840s, which tended toward progress and liberal ideals, had been replaced by a desperate struggle for cultural survival. Caught between the Canadian army and the Church, the French had learned not to trust anybody. Writes Mason Wade:

> the development of this reactionary spirit was greatly furthered by the immediate infringement and violation of Confederation's guarantees of minority rights and privileges. Confidence in the newly achieved partnership of French and English was undermined at the outset of the period, and in two decades' time the relations between the two groups had once more reached a state of major crisis.[2]

The Riel affair, as we have seen, was one of the darkest moments in a period which extended from Confederation to the end of the First World War. But not the only one. The period was marked by suppression of the French language, petty injustice, and routine attacks on civil rights, all of them stemming from an implacable distaste for francophones. The bloody day in April 1918, when soldiers from Toronto opened fire on a crowd of anticonscription demonstrators in Quebec, killing four of them, was the inevitable outcome. But of course, those who defend British liberties must be prepared to kill anybody at all!

CONFEDERATION

July 1, 1867, was a day of jubilation throughout Canada. But Britain also had reason to be pleased. By letting the colony reorganize itself, the metropolis was freed from what had become a cumbersome administrative burden.

Roman candles filled the sky with colourful lightning, the cannon boomed, and banquet tables groaned. Canada wouldn't see the like of it for another hundred years, until Dominion Day was resurrected for the great anniversary in 1967 (it was also resurrected to compete with Quebec's exuberant Fête nationale).

Be that as it may, Macdonald, George-Étienne Cartier, and George Brown had made their dream come true. Cartier's newspaper, *La Minerve*, was present at the birth:

> Canadians, let us rally around our new banner. This is a
> Constitution of peace and harmony. All rights shall be respected;
> all races treated alike; and all, French Canadians, English, Scots,
> Irish, shall be members of the same close family. We shall become
> a powerful state, able to stand strong against the influence of yet
> stronger neighbours. . . . It would be wrong for Quebec to place
> obstacles in the way of happy events and the emergence of a great
> vision. To do so would be the province's death sentence.[3]

How gloomy! And how unfortunate Cartier forgot to mention that the flag in question was Great Britain's. Nobody who read *La Minerve* that day would be around to see the Canadian flag finally unveiled in 1965. And even that tardy selection of a national symbol was little more than a response to Quebec's having designated its own flag in 1953. There were not a few bitter English Canadians who saw the new Maple Leaf as a mere concession to Quebec.

We live in a strange country. Symbolically speaking, the new flag should more logically have had a green leaf, and its borders, intended to symbolize the oceans, should have been blue. But it was more important that it be red and white. These were the colours of St. George's cross, the English banner which makes up part of the Union Jack.

English Canada is poor in national symbols. Having borrowed the colours of its flag from England, it then went and filched a few emblems from Quebec. The maple leaf and the stirring verses of *O Canada*, let's remember, had been commissioned long before by the Société Saint-Jean-Baptiste as emblems of French Canada. This by way of defying the transplanted British imperialism of their English-Canadian fellow citizens with their Red Ensign and their *God Save the King*.

La Minerve also showed undue optimism in dreaming that

French Canadians and natives would ever possess the same status as the "superior" minorities, the Scots and the Irish. Confederation was little more than the starter's pistol in the great race to steal every possible square inch of native land.

The truly privileged minority were English Quebeckers, who naturally took advantage of being a dominant minority to protect themselves against the more numerous French. The British North America Act specified that no change could occur in the dozen Quebec ridings with an English majority unless their own twelve members of Parliament approved it.

Needless to say, no riding dominated by French Canadians elsewhere in the country got any kind of protection at all. Being conquered just goes on costing and costing.

In its Confederation-day exuberance, Cartier's newspaper verged on bad taste in mentioning peace and harmony. The newborn country would soon be a troubled child with a strong suit in acrimony and suspicion toward all the non-English kids on the block. The *Globe* in Toronto was already describing a country in which anybody who wasn't white, English, and Protestant simply didn't count: "We salute the birth of a new nation. An English America united and strong in its four million inhabitants, takes its place today among the great nations of the world."[4]

It's astonishing, isn't it, that 40 per cent of this "English" country's citizens were French and native when that issue went to press? You might say Canada was born with the umbilical cord of its own contradictions tangled around its neck.

Trouble started first with the issue of education.

THE NEW BRUNSWICK SCHOOLS QUESTION

By 1871, New Brunswick was already in crisis. Its government had decided to cut off support for the Catholic schools to which the Acadians were entitled. From that day forward, all publicly financed schools would teach in English and be devoid of religious instruction.

Of course the Acadians could pay for their own schools if they wished – on top of what they were obliged to pay in public-school taxes. In effect, they would pay twice for their children's education.

This was a blatant attack on one-third of the province's people. The only relief from it, as intended, was assimilation.

And this measure was directed against the same people whose ancestors had been deported, dispossessed, and often murdered by British soldiers.

The idea came from the province's attorney general, George E. King, who would ride the anti-Acadian cause straight into the premier's office. This is historian George Stanley's description of King's campaign:

> George King, who had become premier in 1872, called an election. "Vote for the Queen against the Pope" was the premier's battle cry. It was a good one, for religious prejudice was widespread enough to give him a good majority. When the electioneering was over and the votes counted, it was found that thirty-four candidates favouring the Common Schools Act had been returned and only five supporters of separate schools. The latter all came from counties with Acadian majorities.[5]

With a crushing majority of thirty-four seats against five, King could sweep aside Acadian rights completely. The francophone delegates could only beg for Ottawa to step in and nullify the Common Schools Act.

Cartier and Macdonald's reaction was instructive. They hid themselves behind the "separation of powers" doctrine, claiming disingenuously that the federal government couldn't intervene in a provincial domain like education. If you wish to protect your civil rights, they advised Acadians, go to the courts! And so began, before the ink was dry on the BNA Act, the practice of telling the French and the Indians to defend themselves in court against vexatious laws – at a time when the courts were highly unlikely to overturn a law.

Some Acadians refused to pay the tax; at least one priest found himself thrown into jail for that reason. By 1875 unrest was so bad that two people were killed in a street riot in Caraquet. Soon the army arrived and arrested a number of citizens. The newspapers in Saint John and Fredericton quickly compared the situation with Riel's armed insurrection in the West.

The New Brunswick government backed down after the Caraquet riot and conceded a "Catholic and French" education to French children in areas where their numbers justified it. Acadians learned that their constitutional rights would be granted only after they had rioted, and in such fashion as to suggest a generous concession was being made.

The criterion of "where numbers justify" would soon be used across the country to deny services to French Canadians. In no case was such a doctrine used to restrict the rights of English Quebeckers.

CUTTING MERCIER'S THROAT

October 14, 1886, was a historic moment for Quebec. It marked the election of the first leader determined to turn the province into a national state for French Canadians. Honoré Mercier was disgusted with the vengeful anglophone assassination of Louis Riel the preceding year. He still burned with resentment against Chapleau's betrayal of Quebec. His vehicle for attaining power was the brand-new Parti national, a strange coalition of the clerical right and the liberal left; or, in the expression of the times, the "Rouges" and the "beavers." It was in some respects the ancestor of the Parti Québécois. Mercier's plan was to transform the province's municipal-type administration into a true government. He believed this was essential to protect the Constitutional division of powers, on which Ottawa was already encroaching. To this end he convoked the first meeting of provincial premiers in Quebec City in October of 1887.

Two Conservative-governed provinces, British Columbia and Prince Edward Island, boycotted the conference under pressure from Macdonald. But five attended.

Mercier's other great passion, apart from provincial rights, was the modernizing of Quebec. He wanted to see railways, bridges, a dairy industry, modern schools, and up-to-date farming methods. But to get them he had to borrow a lot of money, and this he fatefully decided to do by end-running the Anglo financiers of Montreal and seeking overseas support. New York was his first stop, and a failure. So he set off for London, where he was welcomed with faint warmth by Charles Tupper, Canada's High Commissioner. The City's financiers did not lend him a red cent. In Paris, however, the Crédit Lyonnais loaned him four million of the ten million his projects required.

Some have sought to explain this outcome in terms of the financial marketplace. But there was clearly more to it than that: "the agents of the federal government worked steadily to ensure Mercier's failure. Their methods, nearly infallible in England, were not negligible in France either. 'I have attained my objective,' wrote Sir Charles Tupper a little later. 'Mercier can not obtain any money.'"[6]

Mercier did, however, manage to have himself received as a head of state in the French capital. President Sadi Carnot anointed him a commander of the Légion d'honneur in a ceremony at the Élysée Palace. Mercier in return made endless speeches advocating a rapprochement between France and its one-time colony. In Rome the Pope gave him the title of a count palatine.

His success abroad in winning popularity and in achieving his commercial and diplomatic ends greatly strengthened his position in Quebec, which felt itself honoured through the honour paid to its premier; but Mercier's doings were entirely too French and Catholic for English-Canadian taste.

The vague fears thus aroused were strengthened by Mercier's vigorous opposition to the imperial federalism favoured by the new governor-general, Lord Stanley, and the Imperial Federation League, whose English-Canadian nucleus had been active in the suppression of the rebellion and in the persecution of the Métis.[7]

English Canada found it offensive when a premier of Quebec used the word "national" when speaking of the province and behaved overseas as if he were the leader of an independent state. But it was Mercier's anti-imperialist speeches which provoked them beyond endurance. In a speech given at Montreal's Windsor Hotel in 1888 he dared say that not a single French-Canadian life should be sacrificed on the altar of the British Empire:

It is proposed to impose upon us a political regime which through conscription could scatter our sons from the icefields of the North Pole to the burning sands of the Sahara; an odious regime which would condemn us to pay an arbitrary tax of blood and money, and tear our sons from us, in order to cast them into remote and bloody wars which we could neither prevent nor stop.[8]

To a Canada still imbued with colonial ideas, Mercier's speech could only be that of a traitor. He made things worse, especially in the eyes of Orangemen, by naming the truculent Father Labelle as deputy minister of Agriculture and Colonization. This was the first time a priest had taken on an important public post, although English Canada had often condoned Protestant ministers doing the same.

But it was the settlement Mercier imposed in the business of the Jesuit estates which made him the particular enemy of anglophones.

In June of 1888 he announced a resolution of the old quarrel about Jesuit properties confiscated by George III at the time of the Conquest. These had passed to the Canadian government and then, at Confederation, to Quebec.

But now the Jesuits, who had returned to Canada in 1842, clamoured for restitution. Mercier's solution was a lump-sum cash settlement that was dramatically less than the true value of the assets. If the Jesuits accepted, and renounced future claims, Mercier would distribute a part of their former properties among Protestant and Catholic educational institutions. Since the bishops of Quebec City and Montreal were quarrelling over their slice of the cake, Mercier suggested the Pope arbitrate the matter.

The word Pope, of course, brought out every nutter in Ontario. The *Globe*, the *Mail*, and the *World* trotted out the customary anticlerical tirades. When the Toronto *Mail* noticed that Quebec's anglophones were oddly silent on the matter (because they were first in line for a share of the loot), it popped the proverbial blood vessel:

> If Quebec's English Protestant element is not interested in its own salvation, we shall have to procure it ourselves, in our own interests. It's clear that abandoning Quebec to the Ultramontanes and the Jesuits would mean the end of our Canadian nationality. But even Ontario itself would not be safe. Our eastern gate has already been opened by the perfidious hand of a vote-chasing politician, and the French Catholic invasion is pouring through like a torrent.[9]

In a speech on June 24, 1889, Mercier answered these attacks with a call for Quebec unity:

> This province of Quebec is Catholic and French, and shall remain Catholic and French. Even as we proclaim our respect and friend-ship to representatives of other races and religions, even as we declare ourselves ready to give them their legitimate share of all and everything . . . we solemnly declare that we shall never renounce the rights guaranteed us by treaty, law, and constitu-tion. . . . We are not as strong as we should be because we are divided. And we are divided because we have not understood how dangerous our situation is. Our enemies are united in their hatred for the French fatherland; and as for us, we are divided in our love

of our dear homeland here. . . . May you henceforth adopt as your rallying cry the words from which we shall derive our strength: Abandon fratricidal strife. Let us unite.[10]

The Orange Order prepared for war. Conservative deputy William O'Brien asked Parliament to vote a resolution calling for the withdrawal of the law regarding Jesuit goods. This is how he ended his speech: "Our country must be English, and nothing but English." The motion was crushed, 118 to thirteen, leading Orange Ontario to canonize the dissenters as "the Noble Thirteen." The *Globe* struck a commemorative medal in their honour and even today the lodge in Niagara Falls is called the Loyal Orange Lodge Noble Thirteen. Francophobia isn't a weed in English Canada, it's the lawn.

Undiscouraged by the Commons vote, the Noble Thirteen and their friends continued the struggle. On April 22, 1888, D'Alton McCarthy, Grand Master of Western Ontario's lodges and an uncommonly odious racist, made a speech in Toronto demanding a referendum on the Jesuit estates question. Less than two months later he founded the Equal Rights Association, which immediately sent out a petition on the matter. It got 156,000 signatures in Ontario and another 9,000 in Quebec.

McCarthy's mission, as he saw it, was not only to abolish the French language in Canada but, if at all possible, to physically eliminate the French themselves. It's another approach to "equality," I suppose.

It is a question of who reigns over Canada, the Queen or the Pope. It is a question of whether this country will be English or French. . . . We find ourselves in a British country and the quicker we anglicize the French Canadians, the faster we teach them to speak English, the fewer will be our difficulties in the future. At the present time we must look to the voting booth to solve this grave problem. If it brings no remedy in this generation, then the next shall seek a solution at the point of a bayonet.[11]

A wave of anti-French feeling was washing over Ontario, insti-gated by Robert Sellar from the Eastern Townships. Sellar was editor of the Huntingdon *Gleaner* and a regular correspondent (under a pseudonym) of the *Mail*. In his letters he denounced the arrival of French-speaking settlers in the Townships. His complaint echoed those of Orangemen concerned about French domination in Northern and Eastern Ontario. The founding of the Université d'Ottawa by the Oblate order further incensed those who saw "French domination" making its way into English Canada. Mercier was named Public Enemy Number One in this supposed conspiracy.

> This was how the crusade against Mercier and the province of
> Quebec began, with the Lodges demonstrating and the ministers
> preaching holy war in their temples. The cold fury of this bigotry
> was astonishing, considering that, even if Ontario's rage had a
> slender rationale in Riel's execution of Thomas Scott, it had no
> imaginable connection to this [Jesuit] business, a matter entirely
> within Quebec and not able to harm anybody at all.[12]

Robert Sellar and the "Townshippers" tried to use the Jesuit issue as a lever to pry the Eastern Townships away from Quebec, with the help of Ontario's Orangemen. At all costs, they felt, the Church must be prevented from setting out parishes and collect-ing the tithe anywhere in the Townships. Even more urgent was preventing the application of Quebec's civil code in English-speaking areas, as Mercier had proposed. The *Globe* accused him of wishing to destroy Quebec's English minority.

By the summer of 1891, the campaign against Mercier took on the quality of character assassination. Federal Conservatives spread rumours of personal corruption in an attempt to under-mine his credibility. Various newspapers alleged he had taken bribes in connection with the building of a railway to the Baie des Chaleurs. Mercier in fact was not involved with the affair, but that was entirely beside the point. This was a settling of accounts with a troublesome French Canadian.

The Baie des Chaleurs affair was a typical railway scandal: Ernest Pacaud, the treasurer of the Parti national, lobbied for a generous subsidy to the contractor building the railway, who duly kicked back part of the money into Pacaud's capacious pocket.

The *Globe* demanded Mercier's resignation even though he had been overseas when the kickbacks took place and was plausibly able to deny, when he returned on September 15, any knowledge of them. Mercier dissociated himself from Pacaud, who was evidently guilty. He'd even used part of his ill-gotten $100,000 "as a deposit toward election campaigns."

A provincial commission of inquiry was set up. But in this era of rough politics the lieutenant-governor of Quebec, an Ottawa appointee named Réal-Auguste Angers, simply fired Mercier without waiting for the commission's findings. In his place he appointed a Conservative interim premier, Charles de Boucherville, and called for an election.

The campaign was little more than a public humiliation of Mercier, who was vilified even though the commission made a preliminary finding of his innocence. The Parti national went down to defeat, though Mercier held his own riding. The next day the *Montreal Star* wrote: "Quebec's historic name shall no longer be a synonym for corruption."

Many months after the election the commission of inquiry declared Mercier's innocence. But this in no way discouraged the Conservatives, who had him charged in court with any number of fictitious offences. During the long legal battles, Mercier's health declined. He died of diabetes, aged 54, in October 1894. Seventy thousand loyal followers attended his funeral.

In April of the previous year he had given a magnificent, and far-seeing, speech in Montreal:

When I say that we owe nothing to England, I speak politically. For I am convinced, and shall die convinced, that the Union of Upper and Lower Canada, together with Confederation, were imposed upon us for reasons hostile to the dreams of French

Canadians. They were based on the hope that we should one day disappear.

I have desired . . . that you should know what our country might become. I have done all in my power to open new horizons and, by showing them to you, to make you desire in your hearts the national destiny that might be ours. In the place of colonial mendicancy, I offer independence; in the place of humiliation and misery, I offer you fortune and prosperity. If you are but a colony lost and forgotten to the world, I offer you the name of a great people, known to all the free nations of the earth.

Men, women, and children alike, now you must choose. Will you remain slaves within a colony, or seek independence and freedom among those people whose ringing voices call you to the banquet of the nations?[13]

At this time, Montreal's English money men were hard at work finding a way to bring the Quebec government's finances under their control once and for all. Even a figure as charismatic as Mercier had not completely escaped their snares. Sir Donald Smith, head of the Bank of Montreal and best remembered for his association with the Canadian Pacific Railroad, had seen to that.

Mercier's successor, de Boucherville, decided that this was a fight he could not win. He agreed to subject the province's public finances to the mercantile clique of St. James Street.

The great enterprises of St. James Street were always fearful of the next nationalist escapade which might come from a French premier. De Boucherville was made to understand that any treas- urer he might name in future must be English Canadian, residing in Montreal. This person for the moment would be John Smythe Hall, a virtual designate of the Bank of Montreal.[14]

It would be seventy long years before Quebec would see a French-Canadian treasurer again. Until 1960 the Ministry of Finance was an English-speaking fiefdom. It took Jacques Parizeau to break the stranglehold of A. E. Ames & Co., the Anglo-Montreal clique that controlled Quebec's finances.

THE MANITOBA SCHOOLS QUESTION, 1891

D'Alton McCarthy worked long and hard to get the Jesuit Estates Act nullified, and failed. But he wasn't discouraged. By February 1890 he introduced an act in the federal Parliament for the abolition of the French language in the North-West Territories and Manitoba. This was no random act of hostility. It was, as McCarthy understood, the logical outcome of the attack on French Manitobans which had begun the day the province came into existence.

It was, we have to remember, McCarthy who came up with the idea of refighting the Battle of the Plains of Abraham only six days after the hanging of Louis Riel. His hardened racism was evident in his words, which he spoke from the position of Macdonald's close adviser: "It is not religion which is the centre of this affair but a racial sentiment. Don't we see today that the Canadiens are more French today than at the time of the victory of Wolfe at the Plains of Abraham? Do they melt with us or assimilate? No, they do everything as Frenchmen; I say that they are the real menace to the Confederation."[15]

Those low-down French sneaks! Didn't we beat them once already? Are they still there? Well, maybe it's not too late to finish the job.

It was in August 1890, from a platform in Portage la Prairie, that McCarthy first articulated a fateful idea: that the French schools should be abolished. Manitoba's justice minister Joseph Martin then rose to endorse the idea, promising to bring it before the next session of Parliament. The crowd, as they say, went wild.

Soon French disappeared from Manitoba government documents. Not long after, the French separate schools were shut down (I can't resist pointing out that this is the same Manitoba legislature which hollered loud and strong for the protection of Quebec's English minority in the 1987 Meech Lake agreement).

As a federal MP, McCarthy knew his next task was to prevent Ottawa from reversing these repressive measures. He eventually got an agreement that nobody would interfere in the language choices of the Alberta and Saskatchewan (then North-West Territories) legislatures. In effect, the fate of the Prairie French was in the hands of Orangemen.

John A. Macdonald had long seen McCarthy as his successor. But the man's francophobia was so obviously going to damage the Conservatives in Quebec that old Brandy Nose decided to put some distance between them. It was too little too late. McCarthy's fanaticism made the rest of the Conservatives look so lukewarm by comparison that a lot of voters outside Quebec decided the party was soft on the French, and turfed it out in 1896.

McCarthy retained his own Ontario seat with no difficulty. In fact, Simcoe North elected him for twenty years and probably would have kept on doing so had he not died in 1898. Isn't it just wrong that a man who did so much to turn Canada into the country it is today doesn't have his very own "Heritage Minute"?

The judicial killing of Riel, together with the Manitoba Schools business, and the harassing of Mercier right into his grave, instilled a loathing of Canada in many young Québécois. The new country was, for them, little more than the walking ghost of British imperialism. High time, they thought, for French independence.

The U.S.-born journalist Jules-Paul Tardivel, an ultramontane sympathizer, had introduced back in 1885 the idea of Quebec self-rule. The suppression of the schools in Manitoba crystallized his thinking. In September 1893 he wrote an article which reflected an emerging consensus among young francophones across the political spectrum.

> We are among those, more numerous than you might suppose,
> who do not "accept" Confederation. We "tolerate" it and wait for
> better days. We cannot believe the current regime is the final
> political destiny of French Canada. We hope that Providence will

one day reverse the slow annihilation of our nationality which began in 1840.

To "accept" and "conserve" Confederation is the Conservative Party policy. For many others, Confederation is merely that which must be "endured" until French Canada finds once again the autonomy it knew before the Union. That is the aspiration of the "national" element, which should not be mistaken for the "liberal" element. . . .

True Nationalists have nothing in common with annexationist Liberals, nor may they follow the Conservatives. The one offers the perils of annexation; the other, the slow and knowing destruction of our nationality in the guise of Confederation.[16]

Tardivel's program was not far from that of the Parti Québécois today. He wanted a quasi-autonomous French Canada with friendly links to English Canada and even a feeble allegiance to England.

Another journalist, a Liberal this time, and a friend of Mercier, at the same time launched a campaign against the symbols of British rule which continued to disfigure Montreal. One of Marc Sauvalle's first targets was the statue of Nelson in Jacques-Cartier Place (the earliest in the world erected in memory of a man chiefly remembered for defeating the French). Sauvalle's polemics against the statue so inspired three young law students, including Mercier's son, that they knocked it down. When betrayed by an accomplice, they were caught in possession of dynamite.

THE LAURIER–GREENWAY "COMPROMISE"

Francophone minorities outside Quebec were at first delighted by Wilfrid Laurier becoming prime minister in June of 1896. He had promised to settle the Manitoba Schools Question. And they were proud, after the unflattering sobriquets attached to Macdonald, that the new francophone prime minister was called "Silver Tongue" for his brilliant oratory in the English language.

But Laurier was, like every Liberal leader since his time, a ruthless opportunist. By late 1897, a little more than a year after taking office, he had signed a ruinous agreement with premier Thomas Greenway that settled the future of Manitoba's francophones.

The "compromise" gave official status to Joseph Martin's publicschool system. Religious instruction would be limited to thirty minutes a day, which simply erased the article of Manitoba law which had guaranteed French Catholics the right to be educated in their religion. Their language was immediately marginalized.

When Alberta and Saskatchewan finally joined Canada in 1905, Laurier betrayed the French of the far west as well. This so disgusted the young MP Henri Bourassa that he quit the Liberal government. Need we mention that English Canada today celebrates Laurier as a Canadian hero: the great maker of compromises. We'll soon see how the masters treated him when he was disobedient.

THE BOER WAR

The next litmus test to prove that Canada contained two utterly different nations was the Boer War. Once again the French were indifferent to an issue which brought out all of English Canada's ardour; and once again they would hear themselves dismissed as treacherous and mildly retarded bumpkins.

Canada's involvement in the war began in March 1899 with a plea for help from London. Toronto at that time was in the grip of a mad imperial fervour, which was articulated by Ontario premier George Ross in a speech that can only be read with embarrassment today:

> It will not suffice to send one or two contingents to the
> Transvaal. Great Britain must know that all of our men and all of
> our wealth are at the Empire's disposition. It is improper to hold
> forth about proper Parliamentary procedure when British inter-
> ests are endangered. No, we must respond to the call made
> throughout the Empire and show that, in the thoroughfare of the

West where we find ourselves, there are people ready to support Great Britain as others did in former days at Waterloo.[17]

Although English Canada's imperialism as this time was difficult to distinguish from masochism, Laurier had no trouble becoming its eloquent spokesman. He was happy to slash the tariffs on British goods without asking for the least gesture in return from London.

The people of Quebec, on the other hand, saw no reason to turn their children into cannon fodder just because the British had got it into their heads to oppress the Boers. But when Henri Bourassa asked Laurier if he had any intention of listening to Quebec before sending soldiers to Africa, Silver Tongue came up with this immortal rejoinder: "My dear Henri, the province of Quebec has no opinions, it has only sentiments."

Since English Canada seemed determined to be more imperial than Queen Victoria herself, Laurier hastily organized an expeditionary force. But it met with little enthusiasm in French Montreal, which couldn't help but notice that the Boers were a small nation of dashing and pugnacious farmers fighting for freedom against an overwhelming British force. Rang a bell, somehow.

In English Montreal, however, it was all holiday delirium in the Golden Mile when news arrived that the British garrison pinned down at Ladysmith had been relieved. It was March 1, 1900, and the McGill students decided they just had to share their high feelings with French Montreal. Sweeping English bystanders into their ranks, billowing a Union Jack over their heads, they headed for the Rue Sainte-Catherine and invaded the offices of *La Patrie*. The journalists were dragged out and forced to raise the Union Jack on the newspaper's flagpole.

Pushing tramcars off their tracks, the mob then bulled its way over to *La Presse* and the city hall. Street fights soon erupted.

In the Rue Saint-Denis the English mob spilled onto the Montreal campus of Laval University, smashing windows and repeating the flagpole business. When a Laval student had the pluck to shinny up the pole and take the flag down, the mob lost all control and sacked the campus while howling racist epithets.

Ethnic hysteria broke out again that evening as fresh crowds took to the streets with clubs and iron bars. They assaulted the Laval campus yet again, but workers from the neighbourhood had joined the students and fought back as a blinding snowstorm burst over the city. There were so many people wounded that *La Presse* headlines the next day trumpeted the words "The War of Montreal."

By then French students were ready to counterattack. Parading under France's tricolour, they stamped a British flag underfoot in Place Victoria and lustily chanted the *Marseillaise* in front of the monument to Jean-Olivier Chénier, a hero of the 1837 Rebellion.

About midnight they were attacked by anglophones. In the ensuing melee both revolvers and knives were employed, and there were many wounded. Similar events occurred in Quebec City, and the unrest continued for two days.

Never much more than an indentured servant of English interests, Laurier snapped off a telegram to the archbishop of Montreal: "Permit me to suggest that the authorities at Laval University are merely making excuses for acts of violence. . . . We have heard here that Laval students threw down a British flag. If this is true, then our reaction must be prompt."[18]

Monsignor Bruchési replied that English-speaking students had provoked the situation. Laurier's response: "Happy to learn that Laval students were not to blame. My information came from this morning's Montreal *Gazette*."[19] The *Gazette*! That never-failing font of precise and impartial reporting.

When new elections were called in 1900, the Conservatives decided to play the race card in hopes of attracting English votes. Quebec was accused of betraying the Crown in its African struggles. The *Toronto News*:

While enthusiasm rises in the hearts of English Canadians from coast to coast, Quebec blocks the road; and its representatives, to whom the mother country has accorded special privileges and concessions, cover us with shame before the entire world. . . .

Never has the Canadian heart beat so strongly in unison with the English heart; but its palpitations are constricted by French-Canadian apathy; it is the hand of Quebec which stops its palpitations. . . . Should disaster visit British power in Africa, two million French Canadians will be encouraged to follow the example of the Boers.[20]

In an editorial, the same newspaper threatened that English Canadians would find a way of "emancipating themselves from the dominance of an inferior people that peculiar circumstances have placed in authority in the Dominion."[21]
Governor-General Lord Minto was shocked by these attitudes, and wrote to his superiors in England:

The writing of the leading Opposition papers in Ontario has been positively wicked, simply aiming at stirring up hatred of French Canada. It is perfectly monstrous . . . I believe myself that the French Canadians are very much maligned as to their disloyalty. French Canada does not wish to be mixed up in imperial wars, and is lukewarm, but at home you do not call a man disloyal if he disapproves of the war. Here, if he is only lukewarm, and is a French Canadian, he must be a rebel.[22]

Laurier enjoyed power in Canada through his electoral majority in Quebec. During the 1900 campaign, on October 20, Henri Bourassa – now running as an independent – gave a speech putting British imperialism on trial, and setting out a future relationship between Canada's two nations:

British Imperialism . . . is a lust for landgrabbing and military dominion. Born of the overgrowth of British power, bred by that blatant and stupid sense of pride known as Jingoism, it delights in high-sounding formulas: – "Britannia rules the waves". . . .

"Britons never shall be slaves". . . . "Trade follows the flag". . . . "What we have, we hold!". . . ; to this last axiom, the Prime-Minister of Ontario has added: – "and what we don't have, we take" . . . which is now supplemented by public good sense by: "when we can."

In short, military contributions from the colonies to Great Britain, in men and treasure, but mainly in men, constitute British Imperialism. . . .

A mutual regard for racial sympathies on both sides, and a proper discharge of our exclusive duty to this land of ours, such is the only ground upon which it is possible for us to meet, so as to work out our national problems. There are here neither masters nor valets; there are neither conquerors nor conquered ones; there are two partners whose partnership was entered into upon fair and well defined lines. We do not ask that our English-speaking fellow-countrymen should help us to draw closer to France; but, on the other hand, they have no right to take advantage of their overwhelming majority to infringe on the treaty of alliance, and induce us to assume, however freely and spontaneously, additional burdens in defence of Great Britain.[23]

In the 1900 elections Laurier and the Liberals were once again carried to victory by the province of Quebec. The *Toronto News* stamped its inky feet in indignation: "It is intolerable for English Canadians to live thus, under French domination . . . It is infinitely deplorable that the Government remain in power thanks to the massive support of a part of the Canadian people who speak a foreign language and defend ideals quite foreign to the country's dominant race."[24]

The energetic imperialism of Anglo-Canadians at the dawn of the twentieth century was all the more peculiar in that they were already Americanized. In *Le Devoir*, Henri Bourassa took them to task for their lacklustre Englishness. Imperialism aside, "their language, their nasal pronunciation, their everyday slang, their clothes, personal tics, the Yankee literature that overspills their homes and clubs, the style of their yellow journalism, their boastful and self-important catchphrases, their noisy, narrow patriotism, the mania for gold and folding money" marked them as American.

ONTARIO'S REGULATION 17 AND THE END OF FRENCH IN KEEWATIN

The trauma of Manitoba's schools returned with a vengeance in 1912, when the remote northern territory of Keewatin was annexed to the province. Two French-speaking federal deputies tried to amend the law of annexation to protect minority rights in the territory, and were thumpingly rejected (sixty to twenty-four) by the House of Commons.

But Henri Bourassa, still optimistic about the country's future, seized on the issue to call once again for goodwill on all sides. "If Canada's constitution is to be maintained," he said in a Montreal speech,

> the growing intolerance toward minorities which we see in the
> English provinces must disappear. The original spirit of the
> alliance must be revived. We are not British by blood or language,
> only by the force of reason and of tradition. We are neither valets,
> nor dogs curled up by the armchair. We deserve better than the
> dismissive sneer: Stay in Quebec, rot away in that ignorant back-
> water, make yourselves at home there; but if you go a-calling
> elsewhere, do it in English.[25]

Charles Hazlitt Cahan, a senior Conservative official from Montreal's legal community, was present for this speech. Bourassa invited him to speak, and he said:

> You, good people of Quebec, content yourselves with listening to
> fine speeches and then going amiably back to your homes. Your
> inaction makes a mockery of the words which you applauded

with such enthusiasm. . . . If you are unable to make yourselves respected, then blame nobody but yourselves and your leaders, who don't really have your national interests at heart.[26]

With Keewatin safely anglicized, Ontario was impatient to get started with its own linguistic-cleansing project in the schools. We have already noted the concern among the Orange lodges about growing French communities in Northern and Eastern Ontario. Their vitality led to absurd paranoia to the effect they were disloyal pseudopods of Quebec.

Perhaps more reasonably, the Irish worried that these confident French communities might make them a minority in some of their own parishes. This was enough to spark a lively animosity at a time when a majority of Ontario's dioceses had Irish-born bishops who were none too friendly to the French. Especially when they started asking for bilingual priests.

> The Orangemen and the Irish had a common project in crushing the Franco-Ontarians. The Orangemen disliked their religion, and the Irish were put off by their language. So now we had the astonishing spectacle of these two antipathetic groups making common cause. The first target, the French language, could best be attacked through the children, since adults were unlikely to forget their mother tongue. So the schools were designated the front line in the coming war.[27]

Until that time Ontario had respected the Constitutional provision that there be both Catholic and public schools, the latter officially English-speaking. But the new Regulation 17 took up the Manitoba principle by ordering Franco-Ontarians to reduce language classes in their schools to one hour per day. Anglophone Protestant inspectors were imposed on these schools.

Regulation 17 had an additional twist. It provided that no new school could teach French. And this at a time when nearly

10 per cent of the province – two hundred thousand people – were French.

Things were still bearable at the French primary-school level, where Catholic parents were not obliged to pay additional taxes to support the public schools. But that stopped the moment their children reached high school. From then on it was double taxation, quite enough to discourage financially fragile families. For them the choice was assimilation or ignorance.

They fought back. "The regulation generated an increasingly divisive battle. . . . After a year of protests, walkouts by pupils, and refusals to comply,"[28] the Ministry of Education cut off funding for the schools. Some commissioners of the French-Canadian schools were even fined and imprisoned.

Parents were also jailed, their basic rights set aside. This led Franco-Ontarians to take the matter to the Privy Council in England, hoping for relief from what had become second-class citizenship. But the Privy Council sided with the province, and in 1915 Regulation 17 became law. It would take twelve years of struggle before French Ontario forced the government to abrogate it.

But the attitudes underlying Regulation 17 have not really changed. One need only think of the recent Hôpital Montfort crisis. Or the decision by the City of Ottawa, as soon as it defined its new urban status, to spit in the eye of a third of its citizens and declare itself solely English-speaking.

MONTREAL: THE CORRUPTION AND APARTHEID OF THE UITLANDERS

Montreal's French-speaking population had reached 60 per cent by the time of the First World War, but the people were so submissive that they still followed the ritual of electing alternate English- and French-speaking mayors. Henri Bourassa began to hammer away at a new idea: elect the best candidate. His newspaper, *Le Devoir*, being as principled as he was, lobbied for the English candidate in 1910, and he won. "But the French were becoming disillusioned about English fair play; for the English always claimed their right when it was their turn, and when it was not, the best man always seemed to be English."[29]

There was one circumstance where the *Gazette* and the *Montreal Star* would support a French candidate. According to American historian Mason Wade (an outsider who didn't hesitate to skewer the English when facts warranted), these newspapers were so comfortable with municipal corruption that they "were willing to support a corrupt French candidate rather than an honest English one."[30]

These newspapers were woven into the mercantile clique to such an extent that there is no record of their having blown the whistle on anglophone corporate wrongdoing.

By 1914 the supremacist mentality of the city's English community was so insufferable that Henri Bourassa finally dropped the mask of politeness and patience. In a booklet called *French and English Frictions and Misunderstandings* he noted that the French did not hesitate to elect English Protestants, but that the English community simply would not reciprocate, rather, "living in this city and province as a group of isolated Uitlanders, wealthy, self-satisfied, and self-contained, with no care for their French-speaking neighbours – except on such occasions as when French votes are needed to elect an English-speaking mayor."[31]

Happily, such attitudes are a thing of the past! In 2001, French Montreal voted to amalgamate the city's scattered municipalities. It was dizzying the way the city's anglophones leaped to embrace the new policy! The burghers of Westmount could hardly wait to take down the fences and integrate. Who says they haven't learned anything in the past hundred years! It's a smidgen disappointing, though, that the *Heritage Minutes* folks didn't have time to drop by and film them serving tarte tatine to their new French neighbours.

THE FIRST WORLD WAR

In 1914, England needed only to declare war on Germany to drag its principal North American colony into the fray. This might normally have disturbed Quebec, but in this case it was France that was under threat. So a crowd assembled at the French consulate in Montreal to sing the *Marseillaise* and applaud the local French reserve soldiers who had hurried there to register themselves.

Likewise in Quebec City, where a vast throng accompanied the first expeditionary contingent as it descended to the port and took ship for France. There was even talk of volunteer Canadien regiments offering themselves to the French army.

English Canada, not surprisingly, was in a state of imperial euphoria. Parliament voted $50 million for the war effort in less than a minute. Arthur Meighen, Prime Minister Borden's solicitor general and a future PM himself, offered up Canada's sons and riches "to the last man, to the last dollar, for the salvation of England." Of course, it wasn't his own life or considerable fortune he was talking about.

Events compelled a curious turnabout in English Canada's habitual feelings about France, which became, for the duration, a heroic friend rather than the seditious object of French-Canadian loyalty which it had been for two centuries. Hard to take, if you know first-hand how assiduously the English had worked to besmirch the name of France in Quebec since 1789!

But people will do pretty much anything to ensure a good supply of cannon fodder. "Hey, you French Canadians," proclaimed English Canada without the least embarrassment, "it's time to fight for France!"

If the federal government had been more astute, it might even have created French-speaking regiments to go overseas, the better to exploit Quebec's emotional tie with France. But Ottawa ran true to form, press-ganging young Quebeckers into regiments officered by Orange prigs who treated them like dark-skinned skirmishers.

The irony was apparent to Armand Lavergne, a celebrated journalist and nationalist. When Defence Minister Sam Hughes asked him to recruit a battalion, he pointed out how insulting the request was, given the way francophones were being treated in Canada:

> Remember that your fellow citizens, the French-speaking people
> of Ontario, are worse-treated at the present time than the people
> of Alsace-Lorraine under the Prussian boot. The sin of Franco-
> Ontarians is wanting to speak their own language. I can't find
> much enthusiasm for foreign adventures as long as this mean-
> spirited bigotry continues. Let us see about installing liberty and
> justice in this country before we go off preaching good govern
> ment to other nations.[32]

But the pull of defending France was strong, and it led another great journalist, Olivar Asselin, suddenly to reverse his antiwar stand. He said he simply could no longer resist a brawl with the Germans when the "Vieux Pays" was under assault.

Asselin did indeed go on to raise a French-speaking battalion. But the minister of defence, with that gallantry we have come to expect from Canada, sent it to Bermuda instead of France.

In this atmosphere, where Quebec's willingness to fight was undercut by bad faith, it was Henri Bourassa who finally said what needed to be said. Starting on September 9, 1914, he published a week-long series of articles in *Le Devoir* where he argued that Canada must truly imitate Great Britain by attending to its own interests even when diametrically opposed to those of the Mother Country.

This was, shall we say, an awkward moment for this kind of Cartesian logic, and English Canada reacted badly. "Right now in Europe men who say this kind of thing are being hanged as traitors," observed *Saturday Night* magazine.

As has happened so often before and since, the English-language press refused to understand Bourassa's plain words and imputed the worst motives to him. Conservative MP Charles

Hazlitt Cahan, a friend of Bourassa's, was so upset by this that he wrote a letter of complaint to several newspapers.

The Catholic Church in Quebec, following its century-old policy of kowtowing to England, attacked Bourassa in its official publication *L'Action sociale*: "What should be the measure of this cooperation? It should be that demanded by the necessity of conquering. And of this measure, in law and fact, England is the final judge, since from her derives the authority necessary to accomplish this great task, along with the burden of defending the Empire."[33]

Montreal archbishop Paul Bruchési underlined the clergy's loyalty to Britain: "England is engaged in a terrible war, which she sought to avoid at all costs. Loyal subjects, recognizing in her the protectress of our liberties, we owe her our most generous cooperation. Indifference at the present hour would be on our part a fault, and also the gravest error. Is it not evident that our fate is bound to the fate of her armies?"[34]

Bourassa was also under pressure from the French press. He defended himself by saying that Canada should indeed help both England and France. But self-respect demanded this be done within limits that would be decided by Canadians rather than foreigners. On September 23 he underlined the curious fact that Canada was already making a greater per capita war effort than England. Was not this the surest indication that England looked upon the lives and efforts of Canadians as more expendable than its own?

His arguments resonated in Quebec, but not outside, as can be seen in the fact that among the 36,000 men of the first overseas division there were only 1,200 francophones.

The reluctance of Canadiens to get killed in Flanders would become a new goad for English-Canadian rage. Certainly it didn't occur to anybody in English Canada that they might have deserved this mulishness in the light of their own shameful treatment of French Canadians.

Since 1867 there had not been a single corner of the country, excepting Quebec, where French Canadians had not been physically assaulted or seen their Constitutional rights trampled underfoot with blithe contempt. In Ontario the military recruiters were trying to call up men whose children were being punished for speaking French at school.

But here too, blithe contempt made understanding impossible.

> The recruiting figures up to the beginning of 1916 were subjected
> to a searching analysis by a prominent Conservative senator,
> General Mason, in March, 1916. General Mason based his deduc-
> tions on figures supplied him by the census authorities and the
> Ministry of Militia. According to the census of 1911 total
> Canadian-born males between the ages of eighteen to forty-five
> had been 1,112,000, of whom 667,000 were English-speaking and
> 445,000 French-speaking. General Mason estimated that only 30
> percent of the total number of recruits to date were Canadian-
> born, while the British-born constituted 63 percent and the
> foreign-born the remaining 7 percent.[35]

The majority of the recruits were British-born. It was their homeland they were defending. Nonetheless, 35,000 French Canadians would go to the front lines before the war was over, according to historian Elizabeth Armstrong.

In Quebec the army chose a chief recruiter who couldn't speak French (*en plus*, a former Methodist pastor). The defence minister also insisted on scattering the French regiments rather than allowing them to form a brigade. French officers were assigned subaltern posts.

The endless denigration of French officers and soldiers was bound to lead to trouble. It surfaced at the Valcartier camp in July 1916, where a number of Canadien officers had been unjustly discharged from the army. A lieutenant-colonel named Tancrède Pagnuelo had had enough. He told his men to desert:

> This is their vengeance against us because you are French
> Canadians and you have made some trivial errors of judgment.

You may expect to be sent to Bermuda to rot in the sun and suffer further abuse. While military discipline forbids me to say any more about these matters, I suggest you read between the lines of what I have already said. You will then know what to do. Now I'm giving everybody permission to leave the base, and you may be certain that the modest funds your friends have subscribed to the regiment will not be wasted in chasing after those who do not return.[36]

This speech cost Pagnuelo six months in prison, even though the men he had defended were acquitted by a court martial.

At virtually the same moment Pagnuelo was making the above speech to his men, the defence minister was attacking Quebec in a speech at Lindsay, Ontario: "With all due respect to Quebec, she has not done her share in fighting this great war. Nor have her young men been taken in hand by those whose duty it was to do so, those who have so long benefited from British institutions."[37]

How could a well-informed politician talk about the benefits of British institutions even as the doors of Franco-Ontarian schools were being slammed shut? But Sam Hughes's execration of the French was such that he not only refused to see the connection, but punished Senator Philippe Landry for pointing it out. The vehicle of retribution was Landry's son, an officer. Hughes made it his personal business to see the young man was not promoted.

Hughes was a clumsy politician who scattered contracts and preferment to his friends in plain view. He was such an embarrassment that Borden had to remove him from office before the war was over.

French Ontarians continued to struggle against the linguistic cleansing underway in the province:

As soon as the Toronto Court of Appeal confirmed the validity of the contested regulation (Regulation 17) on July 12, 1915, the Ontario authorities moved immediately to dissolve the Ottawa Separate School Commission. On February 3, 1916, 122 teachers in seventeen bilingual Ottawa schools went on strike, and the classes of 4,000 children were cancelled. The professors' decision was taken "due to the refusal of the government school board to pay their salaries, or to allow the city to do so." Mr. Murphy, president of the school board, stated that it would seek an injunction to force the teachers back to work. The parents of French-speaking children supported the teachers. Mothers patrolled the perimeters of the schools day and night, for fear that "government" teachers would be sent to take the strikers' place.[38]

Quebec's Société Saint-Jean-Baptiste moved to support Franco-Ontarians and defy the repression by boycotting Ontario products. Toward the end of February Toronto mayor T. L. Church had this to say about Quebec support for the striking teachers:

Quebec would do better to spend the money getting more of its young men into soldiers' uniforms. The sons of Ontario are dying in their hundreds in Old France to protect the people of New France who don't seem interested in fighting for themselves. We'll have to deal with this bilingualism question when the war is over. There should be only one language in Ontario, and it will be English. The Constitutional Act of 1791 defined Ontario as an English-speaking province.[39]

In early May that year Ernest Lapointe, a member of Parliament, joined with Senator Landry to demand that Parliament symbolically censure the Ontario government for the way it was treating its French population. Prime Minister Borden was trying to wash his hands of the matter even as a future prime minister, R. B. Bennett, was agitating for an all-English, all-the-time, British Empire.

Lapointe's motion gave Wilfrid Laurier a rare chance to get up and cry his crocodile tears for the francophone waifs of darkest Ontario. Since everybody remembered how much he'd done for the French in the West twenty years earlier, his support probably helped ensure the speedy defeat of the motion.

Even as the Ontario business ground on, Manitoba blew up again. Anybody reading the headlines in those two provinces could be forgiven for thinking French as alien a language to Canada as High German:

> Using as a pretext the suspect behavior of German and Austrian immigrants, (Manitoba's) Norris government passed a law forbidding the teaching of all foreign languages in its schools.
> Including French. Henceforth there would be only English schools in Manitoba. This became a new source of bitter indignation not only among Quebec nationalists but among Quebeckers generally. In reply the English press spat out insulting and hateful invective.[40]

In 1917 R. B. Bennett's National Service Commission decided to make an inventory of the workforce. Henri Bourassa knew right away that this was a prelude to conscription. When Bennett went to Quebec to explain his initiative, he was greeted with raspberries and shouted suggestions that he not forget to include his own name. In Sherbrooke his presence provoked a near-riot.

As the military machine ground up more and more men, recruiting standards were relaxed. The one-eyed and one-eared, together with the three-fingered and the flat-footed, not to mention the stubby fellow who couldn't quite make the five-foot mark, put on uniforms and gave the Canadian army a (shall we say) unique profile during those huge allied military parades.

Robert Borden returned from a trip to England in 1917 with a sombre and discouraging picture of the military situation. The British army needed half a million young Canadians to fill the terrible rents in the front line caused by blundering and mulish old generals who had sent hordes of men to their deaths. A generation of young Britons was dead.

On May 18 Borden finally announced that conscription would be in force by year's end. Dominion Day that summer marked Canada's fiftieth birthday. The conscription law was receiving a second reading in the Commons. The vote, everyone knew, would reveal dreadful fissures in Confederation. Debate was as acrimonious as the outcome was preordained, and early in the morning of July 6 the law was approved by a surprisingly large majority: 118 to 55.

The split was more dramatic than anybody had expected. All but three French-Canadian Conservatives had turned their backs on Borden and voted with Laurier against conscription. At the same time, most of Laurier's English-Canadian MPs abandoned party discipline and voted with Borden. Liberal and Conservative parties vanished in a puff of wind, and only Quebec versus English Canada remained.

> There were a mere ten anti-conscription votes outside Quebec, and these mainly from French-speaking members. Unless we are mistaken, this was the second time in Canada's history where the French-Canadian delegation expressed itself with such unanimity. The first was the vote in 1874 for the expulsion of Riel (demanded by Mackenzie Bowell). The *Gazette* noted, as did every newspaper, the appearance of the two blocs: "Unhappily the province of Quebec has taken itself apart from the country. . . . It is mere futility to ignore the meaning of this division into races." Ontario's "Loyalists" intended to isolate Quebec completely, cutting it off from military decision-making and giving it a virtual outlaw status.
>
> In this atmosphere Canada's fiftieth birthday arrived, and was scarcely celebrated. In London the *Saturday Review* magazine suggested that when the Canadian army returned from the front lines, there would be a settling of accounts with French Canadians.[41]

The English-language media was virtually unanimous in supporting conscription, while all but two Quebec newspapers (*La*

Patrie and *L'Événement)* were against it. The Catholic Church for once opposed the government: a precedent! The ultramontane newspaper *La Croix* came out in favour of Quebec seceding. Armand Lavergne, a nationalist writer who was still serving as an officer in the reserves, declared he would rather be shot than submit to conscription. Quebeckers who did likewise, he declared, would be acting in the spirit of the Rebellion of 1837. Speaking to an audience of 15,000 in Quebec City, he added: "If this Conscription Law is enforced, French Canadians shall decide whether they prefer to die in Europe or in Canada. So far as I am concerned, I would rather my body fall on Canadian than foreign soil."[42]

As it so often has done, the *New York Times* assumed it could get a complete picture of the situation by studying the Montreal *Gazette*. Consequently it recommended the firing squad for recalcitrant Frenchies. These brave words, as you can imagine, were all the more striking coming from a U.S. newspaper in a country that had to be dragged kicking and screaming into the European war, managing to stall until it was almost over.

Let us measure, in this murderous editorializing, the cultural and linguistic solidarity which links the United States with English Canada.

THE FEDERAL POLICE: DYNAMITERS, CONSPIRATORS, AND *AGENTS PROVOCATEURS*

On August 9, 1917, a dynamite explosion shook the residence of Hugh Graham in Cartierville. Graham, also Lord Atholstan, was an ardent conscriptionist and owner of the *Montreal Star*. Three weeks later it was the *Gazette*'s turn, as demonstrators put out the windows of a journal always solicitous on behalf of French Canadians.

The next morning the conscription bill was proclaimed, and riots broke out in Montreal. Shots rang out, soldiers were attacked, streetcars overturned. By August 30 there were fistfights between English and French in Phillips Square. By the time the police subdued the violence, the toll was: four injured policeman, one dead civilian, and numerous wounded.

Both sides were inflamed by violent speechmaking, and the agitation spread rapidly across the province. In Shawinigan a mob which had rioted for days finally broke into the recruiting office and nearly threw the senior official into the Saint-Maurice River. Gérard Filteau writes that the incident so terrified the man that he spent the rest of the war in the Quebec Citadel.

Henri Bourassa began to grow suspicious. Recalling the government provocations which had lured his grandfather and other patriots of 1837 into traps, he wondered whether Ottawa was not fanning the flames and creating an excuse to impose martial law: "Let's be clear about one thing: the day the Government decides that the violence provoked by its own agents justifies martial law will be the day that the worst bigots and enemies of French Canada will have won their victory."[43]

Meanwhile, police authorities claimed that progress was being made in identifying those who had dynamited Hugh Graham's mansion. The dynamite, part of a consignment of 350 pounds, together with a quantity of rifles used by the dynamiters, had been stolen from the cadet corps. The police arrested Élie Lalumière, who ran an electric-appliance store on the Boulevard Saint-Laurent.

Lalumière had been making incendiary anti-conscription speeches for some time. He even claimed to have trained 500 men to resist recruiting efforts. His organization, the Ligue des Constitutionnels (Constitutional League), was organized along the lines of the insurgent Sinn Féin paramilitary group in Ireland. Or at least, so said the police reports; but Lalumière's group in fact had more sedate roots. It was founded by Philippe Panneton, who wrote novels under the pen name Ringuet, and would later serve as a Canadian ambassador.

On September 2, police agents cornered two conspirators in the town of Lachute. A gun battle broke out, during which one of the men escaped, while the other shot himself to avoid capture.

Lalumière turned out to be a self-dramatizing fantasist. In front of an avid audience of policemen he spun out a huge agenda of planned attacks. His group, so he said, was poised to devastate *The Star*, the *Gazette*, the Mount Royal Club, Parliament Hill in Ottawa, the gunpowder magazine at Beloeil, and the Windsor Hotel, where Montreal's military commander, General Wilson, was lodged. And that wasn't all! For good measure they were also going to gun down Prime Minister Borden and a bagful of other Anglo notables.

The police set out to dismantle the terrorist network. They quickly rounded up eleven men, though it was disconcerting to discover that two of them were drug addicts and two others were on parole from prison. The parolees were the men who had attacked Hugh Graham's house, but their lengthy criminal record had nothing political about it. The supposed terror network was made up of lowlife bums from the back streets. "The impotent explosion, the hasty confessions of the accused, and the dubious feasibility of their grand projected adventures marked them as small-time operators in the minds of serious observers," writes Gérard Filteau.[44]

Paul-Émile Lamarche, MP for Nicolet, was certain these men were being set up in order to discredit the anticonscription movement. He forced the government to call an inquiry into the inquiry, and it was duly revealed that one of the interned men, Charles "Ti-Noir" Desjardins, had accepted his arrest with curious placidity. He turned out to be a secret agent of the Dominion Police, the organization created by John A. Macdonald in 1867 and which later (in 1920) merged with the Mounted Police. His reports had gone straight to the Dominion Police chief in Quebec City.

Learning that Desjardins and Lalumière were the co-founders of the "terror" group, Lamarche became convinced that the whole thing was orchestrated from Ottawa. He made sure that Desjardins was arrested on the same terms as the other dynamiters. But in spite of his best efforts, a good deal about this business was never brought to light.

However, when we reflect on the practised ease with which the Mounted Police set about stealing dynamite and blowing up barns in Quebec in the 1970s (by way of framing suspected Front de libération du Québec members), it's comforting to recall the activities of Desjardins and the Dominion Police. Canadian history has so many interesting threads connecting past to present! I wonder why English Canadians find it so dull?

Patriotic unrest continued in Montreal. On September 12, four more agitators were arrested after applauding the attack on Graham's mansion and advocating the independence of Quebec or its quick annexation to the United States.

CONSCRIPTION

After failing to enlist Laurier in a coalition government, Borden lured a number of Western Liberals into a new administration which called itself the Union government. Elections were called for December 17, 1917.

That October the first conscripts were called up. An enormous number demanded exemptions. It appeared that English Canadians weren't quite as keen as had been thought about being blown to bloody rags on behalf of Britain. This is Mason Wade's description of this situation as it appeared in the *Canadian Annual Review* (as quoted by Jacques Lacoursière):

> Of all the men between the ages of twenty and forty-five who had been called up, 57 per cent had asked for an exemption by November 10. The final reports at the end of the year revealed that out of 125,750 eligible men in Ontario, 118,128 had asked to be exempted. In Quebec, out of 117,104 on the list, 115,706 had also made a claim. . . . In nearly all the provinces, an equally high proportion asked for an exemption, which was granted in most cases.[45]

Once you set aside all the British-born English Canadians who volunteered early in the war, there really wasn't much difference in martial enthusiasm between Quebec and the rest of the country. According to Mason Wade, "English Canadians, regardless of political affiliation, were loud in their lipservice to conscription, if not much more willing in fact to accept it than the French Canadians, who in overwhelming majority were opposed to it."[46]

But English Canada's ill will toward Quebec, when all is said and done, has something pathological about it. Its newspapers steadily and blindly ignored the conscription statistics throughout a campaign which carried Borden to power at the head of a Union government.

At the beginning of November, six weeks before the election, Bourassa's *Le Devoir* supported Laurier and the Liberals as the lesser of two evils. This was the kiss of death for the Liberals outside of Quebec, since English Canada by now was in a paroxysm of fury toward that province. Ontario's newspapers were once again involved in a kind of tournament of turpitude with the Western newspapers to see who could invent the worst libels against French Canada. Laurier also got his dose of bitter medicine from those he had served so loyally.

The *Toronto Mail and Empire* on December 10 announced that Laurier was undoubtedly favoured by the Kaiser, and on the following day carried an election advertisement declaring that a united Quebec sought to rule Canada. On election day the *Mail and Empire* called a vote for Laurier and his followers a vote for Bourassa, a vote against the men at the front, the British connection, and the empire; and a vote for Germany, the Kaiser, Hinderburg, von Tirpitz, and the sinker of the *Lusitania*. Laurier was depicted as the hope of Quebec, a menace to Canada, and as satisfactory to the Kaiser. The *Toronto Daily News* printed on December 14 a map of Canada with Quebec in black, under the caption "The Foul Blot on Canada." Laurier was represented as having capitulated to Bourassa. On December 7 the *Manitoba Free Press* told its readers that the choice was between union and the war or Laurier and disunion. A Toronto Citizen's Union Committee filled the English press with inflammatory advertisements declaring that "Quebec Must Not Rule Canada" and that "a Laurier victory will be the first Canadian defeat." The Unionist publicity committee under Sir John Willison constantly linked Laurier, Bourassa, and Quebec, and roused ethnic feeling against French Canada. Conservative leaders warned that "Quebec was the spoiled child of Confederation," "the plague-spot of the whole Dominion," and that "if Laurier won the election Bourassa would rule Canada."[47]

On December 4 the [Manitoba] *Free Press* stated that Quebec had failed Canada and that this truth was very bitter to a Canada which had never failed Quebec.[48]

Coming from those who assassinated Louis Riel and killed the French language in the Western provinces, what nerve! And to top it all, even before the election results were known. After the election, of course, it was worse: the English press kept racing around like a rabid dog. They were after the flat-footed and the weak-lunged who didn't want to fight, but as always overlooked the thousands of shirkers who spoke their own language. It was Traitorous Quebec! and business as usual for the ink-stained wretches.

A few days before the elections N. W. Rowell, Liberal Opposition leader in Ontario, demonstrated a remarkable ignorance of Quebec by including the Catholic clergy – who had always served English Canada – in his indiscriminate jeremiad: "There is a Nationalist, clerical, and reactionary movement at work in the Province of Quebec which today dominates the political situation in that province and is using this hour of great national peril to dominate the political situation throughout the Dominion of Canada."[49]

In order to ensure an already certain victory, Borden's unionist government loaded the dice. It decided to harass even the pitiful soldiers in the trenches.

Electoral agents and partisan officers threatened to send soldiers into the line of fire the next day if they did not vote for the Unionist government. Those who voted the right way were promised leave in Paris. These facts are recounted in Hansard together with supporting evidence. Moreover, a singular provision in the electoral law permitted military votes to be counted in ridings other than those of residence. Thus a slender adverse majority in a given riding could be transformed into a minority; and this was done without hesitation.[50]

The November 17 election was a tidal wave of conservative victory, except in Quebec where Laurier's Liberals took sixty-two of sixty-five seats. To those who feared Quebec's resulting absence from Borden's Cabinet, Bourassa replied that this was not necessarily a calamity. Having Quebec ministers in the Cabinet could as easily lead to weakness as to strength. He observed that when French Canadians recruited into the federal Cabinet spoke up, their speeches generally served to cover up humiliating concessions and climb-downs; and that in any event their English colleagues slept through them.

For English Canada, the election outcome yet again demonstrated the insolence of the conquered. Toronto's *Evening Telegram* said it was time to send in the army: "We must save Quebec in spite of itself, and put it on the right road, even if that requires force." The *Ottawa Journal* hailed the election as proof of what it had always believed, that there were two kinds of people in Canada: "decent people" and Quebeckers.

Irritated by the show of hatred, Lotbinière's Liberal member, Joseph Napoléon Francoeur, moved a motion of secession in Quebec's Assembly on December 21. Premier Lomer Gouin supported the motion, which read: "This Chamber is of the opinion that the province of Quebec would be disposed to accept the breaking of the Confederation Pact of 1867 if, in the other provinces, it is believed that she [Quebec] is an obstacle to the union, progress, and development of Canada."[51] It explained that for fifty years French Canada had yielded everything possible in seeking conciliation with English Canada: "the very great majority of our people, who are tired of being treated in this manner, and who think that the time has come to stop these futile struggles or to accept their logical consequences."[52] *Le Soleil* in Quebec City supported Francoeur and affirmed that Confederation, for French Canadians, wasn't much more than a mousetrap: "We've had enough of a Canadian federation which is little more than a mask for imperialism. . . . We are tired of putting up with your impertinence, your political backstabbing, and even less your persecution of us."[53]

But on December 23, Premier Gouin decided that things had gone far enough, and asked Francoeur to withdraw the motion.

QUEBEC 1918: TORONTO SOLDIERS
OPEN FIRE ON A CROWD

By the beginning of 1918 the problem of deserters was critical, and Ottawa decided to send "spotters" to Quebec to track them down. These bounty hunters frequently were ex-convicts or police informers, and they whizzed around the countryside on the lookout for anybody who hadn't registered with authorities. If they found somebody without papers, the next step often depended on how they happened to feel.

Nobody in Ottawa cared much about legal niceties, since Quebec was held responsible for the embarrassing fact that only 32,000 men had been recruited by spring 1918.

On March 28 things went wrong. The special federal police arrested a young man who wasn't carrying his papers. It turned out his papers were in order, but by the time they discovered that, as many as two thousand men had gathered around the police station where he was held. Rocks shattered the windows and rotten eggs lacquered the woodwork.

By the next evening the rioters fell upon the local conscription office and torched it. This finally forced Borden to send a sizeable force of a thousand soldiers, including a dragoon unit. Then things calmed down for Easter Saturday and Sunday. But by the next day the violence was careering out of control once again: "On April 1 the Ontario regiments, far from being retired, were strengthened. Machine guns took up positions in the Place Jacques-Cartier. Cavalry patrols, with carbines laid across the saddle, swept down the sidewalks of the Rue Saint-Joseph and backed citizens against the walls until they proved their identity."[54]

One can imagine how the local population felt about the strait-laced soldiers from Toronto. Here was an English army in full battle dress occupying Quebec on horseback. That hadn't happened since 1759, and trouble wasn't long in brewing.

It didn't help matters that these cavalrymen were, if possible, even more unilingual than their predecessors 160 years earlier. They took to parading like conquerors. The supposedly hardened rioters savagely attacked them that night . . . with snowballs.

A senator, Philippe-Auguste Choquette, heard the voice of a Toronto officer outside his window giving the shoot-to-kill order. Clearly, for these good Ontario boys, Quebeckers were just so many enemies, like Germans. Maybe worse! After all, weren't they traitors as well? Hadn't the newspapers back home told them for years that Quebeckers understood nothing but bayonets? Maybe a machine gun would make things crystal clear. . . . Outcome: sixty-five wounded civilians, and four fatalities, ripped to pieces by machine-gun fire. Assassinated: Georges Demeule, fifteen years of age, shoe-factory employee; Édouard Tremblay, twenty-one, technical-school student; Honoré Bergeron, forty-nine, woodworker, father of six; and Alexandre Bussières, twenty-five, railway mechanic. The inquest would later show that none of them were rioters. Bergeron had stepped out to call his children; Bussières had misplaced his tool box; Tremblay was strolling with his girlfriend; and Demeule was just there.

About the inquest, Gérard Filteau notes:

[It] was marked by singular forgetfulness on the part of the soldiers. Nobody could remember who gave the order. The forensic
doctor gave disquieting evidence: the autopsy had revealed expand-
ing bullets, not unlike big-game dumdums, in the bodies of the
victims. These were outlawed for military use by [Article 23 of the
Fourth] Hague Convention. And in any event, a heavy machine
gun could chop a man in half no matter what bullets it fired.

After five days of hearings, on April 13, the Coroner held "the
military authority responsible for the deaths of four men in a riot
caused by its own tactlessness and heedless actions" . . .

The inquest had showed that the military intervention was
marked by numerous irregularities and outright breaches of law.
General Lessard had arrogated to himself the right to proclaim
martial law, even though this was the sole prerogative of the civil
authority. And even having proclaimed a state of emergency, the
soldiers had no business ignoring civil authority. The patrols had
not taken the least notice of the strict legal requirement that they
be always accompanied by a magistrate.

The government did not take long to notice that it had put its
arm into a hornet's nest. Using the 1914 War Measures Act, the
Cabinet immediately issued a special decree with retroactive
powers making all the military actions legal.[55]

Ottawa and the army simply threw out the jury's decision that
the victims' families be indemnified. This brutal extra-legal intervention meant that none of the dead men's relatives would ever
receive an apology or a nickel. After all, they were just French
Canadians. And if they hadn't deserved it, some other French
peasant did. It was all the same.

Prime Minister Borden had ordered Major General François-
Louis Lessard to restore order in Quebec City. The perfect French-
Canadian butler, Lessard would happily have spent his life
repressing citizens in His Majesty's name. According to historian
Jean Provencher, "In 1880 the workers building the Parliament in
Quebec City went on strike. Lessard commanded the troops who

opened fire and killed three of them. In 1885 he turns up again in the Canadian West, fighting Louis Riel's Métis. In 1900–1901, it was off to South Africa to batter the Boers. And there he is again, in 1918, in Quebec City."[56]

He was whisked from Halifax by a special train from which he comfortably and illegally declared martial law before arriving in Quebec City. And without so much as a by-your-leave from mayor or premier. Lessard's aplomb, if I may permit myself a bilingual pun, arose entirely from *plomb*. Especially the kind that emerges from the end of a machine gun.

Surely Lessard and his fire-breathing dragoons deserved a . . . but you're probably ahead of me on this one. That's right, no Heritage Minute for them either. And this glorious action doesn't seem to get quite the splash it deserves in regimental histories. . . .

Some citizens of Quebec City plan to raise a monument to those who fell under the fire of the Canadian army. But *Québec: Printemps 1918* will be erected without a cent from Ottawa.[57] One might think a government which secretly spent $7.2 million on *Heritage Minutes* would have the decency to pay the whole cost of the monument, not forgetting to send Heritage Minister Sheila Copps to the unveiling. There she could ask forgiveness, and perhaps bring with her the apologies of the Ontario newspapers which egged the soldiers on to violence.

Even as Bourassa denounced the rioters' behaviour in his newspaper, the *Regina Leader* (seconded by the Toronto *Globe*) demanded he be arrested. It was time for a new outburst against French Canada. John Wesley Dafoe, the bitterly anti-French editor of the Manitoba *Free Press*, set the tone for journalists across the country:

> Editorials, tendentious news items, letters or fabricated letters
> from readers built gradually to a peak of tension. The daily
> reader of the *Free Press* (that is to say, of Dafoe) felt his rage
> toward Quebec notch higher with each morning's delivery. The
> enemy was no longer in far-off Berlin, but nearby in Quebec

City: not the German, but the French Canadian; not the Kaiser, but Bourassa. The *Free Press* published letters demanding "summary measures" against Bourassa – and it was clear what kind of summary measures were desired. Other newspapers picked up the tone and accused Laurier's supporters in the Québec-Est riding of "stooping to treason, to arson, and to murder" . . . All of them naturally attacked bilingualism. In Saskatchewan, school inspector James Anderson, whose mandate was to anglicize the schools through persuasion, found that immigrants were pliable but the French Canadians were immovable. His conclusion: "We shall assimilate all of them, except these damned French Canadians." From this thought emerged a plan to destroy French under the pretext of suppressing all foreign languages. Hatred of Quebec was such that you could cut it with a dull knife. It poisoned the provincial air, and in Ottawa weighed heavily on the deliberations of the Cabinet.[58]

In spring 1918 Ottawa declared that farmers would henceforth have to serve in the army. As a result Ontario and the Prairies developed a sudden dislike of conscription, which at least gave them something in common with Quebec. Ontario's farmers pleaded for support from the same French community their leaders and newspapers had been calling traitors a couple of months earlier. Even English-language trade unions came onside.

In Calgary, the ultra-loyalist R. B. Bennett, who while an MP had headed the Commission du service national (the equivalent of today's Public Service Commission), challenged the ministerial decree by using a writ of habeas corpus to free a twenty-three-year-old conscript from an army base. One can only imagine the outcry if a Quebec lawyer had tried that. But it was R. B. Bennett, and the Alberta Superior Court was convinced. . . .

Immediately, hundreds of Albertan conscripts began legal action. And the wave spread to other provinces. In Quebec, at the request of Armand Lavergne, the Superior Court found that

Colonel Rodgers, commander of Camp Valcartier, was in contempt of court. He was given a prison sentence for refusing to let a number of petitioning conscripts leave the camp. Meanwhile in Alberta, the provincial Supreme Court ordered the arrest of Colonel Moore for likewise restraining conscripts in violation of habeas corpus.

But some camp commanders, protected by their machine guns, refused to submit to court orders. Quite serious unrest over the question broke out in the English provinces, highlighting the arrogance of these citizens who not so long before had sneered at Quebec with its street rioting.[59]

The famous Quebec indifference toward military issues had now become the general feeling in rural and working-class communities across Canada. If it were happening today, the *Gazette* and the *Globe* and the *Free Press* could run headlines reading TRAITORS 'R' US.

But, at the end of the day, the case went to the Supreme Court of Canada, which duly found in favour of the government.

The collapse of German forces put an end to the war. The Armistice was signed on November 11, 1918. But the war between French and English in Canada, which had become red-hot during the four preceding years, was just underway.

And it will continue to rage until the people of Quebec become a distinct nation.

7

ANTI-JAPANESE CRIMES

Notice to all Japanese persons and persons of Japanese racial origin.
Take notice that under Orders Nos. 21, 22, 23 and 24 of the British
Columbia Security Commission, the following areas were made
prohibited areas to all persons of the Japanese race. . . .[1]

This notice, which appeared throughout the coastal regions
of British Columbia at the beginning of 1942, marked the
beginning of the worst deportation Canada had seen since the
evacuation of the Acadians. Its Japanese victims had endured
uninterrupted discrimination since arriving in the country in
1886. The Anglo-Saxons of British Columbia felt a baleful hostility toward the "Nikkei," and Asiatic people in general, allowing
only that they had their uses as cheap labour.

In 1895, less than a decade after the first Japanese arrived, the
provincial government took the first official measure which could
be described as racist: Asian immigrants were barred from
Canadian citizenship. The press whipped up fear about the Yellow
Peril, especially the risk it presented to white English Protestants

with good jobs. Writer Ken Adachi quotes this editorial from the Victoria *Colonist* of June 18, 1905:

> the Japanese, through an evolutionary process which has been in progress for centuries is now, as we find him, a marvellous human machine, competent to perform the maximum of labour on the minimum of sustenance. He does not require to maintain a home as white men do; does not spend one 50th part of what the meanest white labourer considers absolutely necessary for clothing; lives in a hovel where a white man would sicken and die – and with it all performs . . . unskilled laborious tasks quite as efficiently as a white man, and, given the training, is equally proficient at duties requiring the exercise of some skill.[2]

In 1907 the Asiatic Exclusion League organized the first anti-Oriental street riots, egged on by the violently xenophobic British Columbia newspapers. In the first week of September 5,000 marchers gathered at City Hall to demand a "white Canada." Then they fell upon the Chinese district, smashing windows before moving on to the Japanese quarter, where shopkeepers defended themselves as they could with wooden sticks.

Both communities reacted by going on strike, forcing the factories which relied on their pennies-an-hour labour to shut down. Factory owners in turn lobbied political leaders.

Vancouver's mayor at the time was a member of the Asiatic Exclusion League, but he realized that the violence was costly and out of hand. So did Ottawa, which sent a young deputy minister of labour, a certain William Lyon Mackenzie King, to offer $9,000 in compensation to the Japanese business community. The following year King visited Japan with a heartfelt request that the government there help limit emigration to Canada to 400 people per year.

Tom MacInnes, a writer for the *Vancouver Province* and the *Vancouver Morning Star*, could serve as a textbook example of the turn-of-the-century racist reporter in English Canada. His preference was an all-British British Columbia, but he allowed that a few Northern Europeans might also be squeezed in. His career would be marked by repeated campaigns against Chinese and Japanese alike: "We must either deport them – a thing practically impossible to do – or close our ports to further immigrants, and make life impossible for those who are already here, whose work takes the bread out of the mouths of our compatriots. So they have to be encouraged to go home."[3]

From the beginning, the Japanese immigrants demonstrated a dogged loyalty to their adopted country, in spite of the spleen of native-born Canadians. A quarter of the 200 Japanese who fought for the Canadian army in France during the First World War were killed, and a further ninety-two wounded. This extraordinary demonstration of a desire to belong and to be accepted as Canadians had little effect on official and unofficial attitudes toward them. It was only in 1931 that Ottawa grudgingly allowed that the few surviving war veterans should be allowed to vote. The rest of the Japanese-Canadian community would wait until 1947.

Part of the dislike was rooted in jealousy. The Japanese were indeed capable of hard and unflagging labour. By the end of the war they controlled half the fishing permits in B.C. and prospered so well that white fishermen settled into sullen (but not silent) resentment. The government heard them well enough to pass a regulation in 1919 favouring the granting of permits to "white residents, British subjects, and Canadian Indians." In spite of the careful hypocrisy of the wording, this measure was plainly intended to harass the Japanese. In the following six years it was applied in such a way as to take back nearly a thousand fishing permits from the Japanese-born, reducing competitive pressure on the less efficient white fishermen.

The whole idea was to ensure a Canada as white, English, and Nordic as possible; but almost nobody had the honesty to say it in so many words. Typical was an unwritten 1923 "gentleman's agreement" between Ottawa and Tokyo to further reduce the 400-per-year male immigrant quota to a risible 150.

By 1941, with the beginning of the Pacific War, anti-Japanese bigotry reached a paroxysm. Back-room deals were no longer necessary: Ottawa simply made an order that no Canadians of Japanese origin would be permitted to enlist in the armed forces. A couple of months later, in March 1941, they were ordered to register themselves with the authorities. In August it became mandatory to carry a fingerprinted identity card with photograph.

From the moment Japan entered the war, there was a widespread public clamour for the removal of the "Japanese menace" from British Columbia. Every sector of society, including city politicians and the provincial government, was in favour of repressive measures.

On December 8, the morning after the attack on Pearl Harbor, officers simply came and seized 1,200 fishing boats registered to "Japanese" owners. Surprisingly, the old distinction between Canadian-born and Japanese-born citizens simply vanished: everyone with Japanese ancestors, however worthy, was subject to the sweeping language of the War Measures Act. All people of "Japanese racial descent" were stripped of their civil rights, said the decree approved by Mackenzie King's cabinet.

Canada's Japanese became "enemy aliens." The War Measures Act provided that any person so designated could be removed to a place over a hundred miles from the British Columbia coast.

The province created a Security Commission to enforce the new measures. At first it focused on men between the ages of eighteen and forty-five, who were given (in some cases) less than twenty-four hours to prepare for deportation or internment. A curfew was imposed. Shortly afterwards the order was broadened to include wives, children, and the elderly.

Certainly it was British Columbia's WASP racists who forced the federal government to act so hastily and harshly. But the official explanation was the familiar so-called "menace to national security," the bromide customarily employed to explain ignominious actions. Trudeau used it again in 1970.

If it seems unfair to blame all this on the good people of B.C., recall that documents made public after 1980 revealed that nobody in the Mounties or the army at the time had any suspicions whatsoever about Japanese Canadians. That leaves citizen pressure as the only plausible explanation.

Cold comfort to the 23,000 "persons of Japanese racial origin" (three-quarters of them born in Canada or naturalized) ordered to turn over their possessions to the Custodian of Enemy Alien Property by March of 1942.

This was purely to safeguard them, they were told. But the *New Canadian*, a Japanese newspaper in Vancouver, was under no illusions. The March 3 issue read:

> In quick order, a whole series of repressive measures, unlike any-
> thing before in the history of the nation, have been authorized. In
> effect, the new orders uproot completely without regard some
> 23,000 men, women and children; brand every person of Japanese
> origin as disloyal and traitorous; and reduce to nothing the
> concept and value of Canadian citizenship.[4]

On March 4, Muriel Kitagawa, who had received her deportation order, scribbled a letter to her brother:

> We're being deported like the Israelites. Public opinion is getting
> bloody and it's our blood it wants. They treat us like Nazis. Okay
> we move. But where? Signs up on all highways . . . JAPS KEEP
> OUT. Curfew. "My father is dying. May I have permission to go
> to his bedside?" "NO!" Like moles we burrow within after dark,
> and only dare to peek out of the window or else be thrown into
> the hoosegow with long term sentences and hard labour.
> Confiscation of radios, cameras, cars and trucks. Shutdown of all
> business. No one will buy. No agency yet set up to evaluate.

When you get a notice to report to RCMP for orders to move, you report or be interned. "Who will guard my wife and daughters?" Strong arm reply. Lord, if this was Germany you can expect such things as the normal way, but this is Canada, a Democracy![5]

On May 16, 1942, the first deportees arrived at the Hastings Park Racecourse in Vancouver, which, for the occasion, had been transformed into a detention centre (like the Vélodrome d'hiver in Paris) for Canadian citizens of Japanese origin. In a few weeks the Canadian government, to the applause of British Columbia's citizenry, had without the slightest legitimate reason simply eliminated the Japanese community. Everything that it had built in Canada amounted to nothing in the government's eyes: the *Nihonmachi* temple, the Christian churches, the schools, the co-operatives, the community newspapers, the mutual-aid societies. Nothing.

Men separated from the families were set to hard labour building roads and railway tracks, or digging and hoeing to plant sugar beets. Women, children, and elderly parents were packed off to internment camps in the province's bleak interior. And all for the crime of Japanese birth!

Anybody who dared complain about being torn from his family, or who defied the curfew, became a "dissident." This meant, in essence, reclassification. They were sent to prisoner-of-war camps at Petawawa and Angler in Ontario, where they wore shirts with the Rising Sun printed on the back.

At some point the Canadian government crossed another line. It began disposing of the seized goods. The Director of Soldier Settlement was directed to rent or sell Japanese farms, and in due course disposed of some seventy-two properties.

The government had promised us that it would take care of our property until the end of the war. We believed it, and turned everything over to it. These things were very important to us. It

then confiscated our fields, fishing boats, and cars with this inimical law called the War Measures Act. The government intended
this abuse from the beginning.[6]

As it so often does, Ottawa was simply aping American policy.
But in this case it actually managed to set a new standard for cruel
and unjustified racism. The Americans, to give one example, had
not dreamed of separating men from their families. And the
women and elderly were warehoused in such grim conditions that
the International Red Cross had to bring food to them. It's not
surprising to learn that Canadian per capita spending on these
detainees was one-third the American figure. In some of these
concentration camps the prisoners paid for their food.

Japanese Americans were still able to serve in their country's
armed forces. But in Canada no Japanese was entrusted with a
weapon in active service, although the government quite hypo-
critically used a number of them throughout the war to translate
enemy communications. The difference, evidently, is that in the
latter case there was no other source of translators.

The anti-combat policy was lifted in 1945. It was very late in
the war but, surprisingly, 150 men signed up to fight in the Far
East in the first five months of that year; and this after deportation, spoliation, and internment.

One of them was Harold Hirose. While he defended his
country overseas, his five acres outside Vancouver were sold for
$36. When he got home he received a cheque for $15: the rest
went in administrative expenses. Hirose then embarked on a
seemingly endless series of petitions to get his land back, but was
never compensated.[7]

No formal charge of treason or spying was ever brought against a
Japanese Canadian. As mentioned earlier, the RCMP never saw any
reason for the internment policy in the first place. The whole sorry
episode was driven by white racism in the "SuperNatural Province."

And since the racism didn't go away, it shouldn't be surprising
that racist measures became even worse after the war. Mackenzie

King prolonged the application of the War Measures Act because he had quietly decided to empty the Japanese population out of British Columbia. Their choice was to move to eastern Canada or be deported to Japan.

So it was that 3,965 Japanese Canadians, many with citizenship, were forced aboard ships in May of 1946 and sent to a country most of them had never seen, and whose language they did not speak.

This was little better than criminal harassment, and the Japanese community finally fought back. The newly formed Cooperative Committee on Japanese Canadians took the case to the Supreme Court, confident that it could not possibly endorse such an offensive law. But it did, using cheap pettifogging legal arguments that amounted to a shameless abdication of duty. The Supreme Court has carried the stain of having endorsed outright racism ever since.

The Court's decision redoubled the protesters' energy and within a year they had forced the government to repeal the deportation order. It took another year to finally halt the deportation machinery, which seemed to grind on of its own accord; but finally, in 1949, all deported persons were given the right to return to Canada and live anywhere in the country they chose.

Until that moment, every Japanese Canadian in the country was, legally speaking, an enemy alien. Author Peter Ward describes the dirty business as "the most dramatic expression of racism in Canadian history."[8]

It was only a half-century later, in 1988, that Brian Mulroney's government offered an official apology to the Japanese community for the loss of civil rights during the war. Among the measures of redress proposed was a symbolic payment of $21,000 to each individual who had suffered internment or deportation. All deportees were offered Canadian citizenship, even if they were not yet citizens at the time of deportation.

It seems clear that the government recognized its wrongdoing only due to the tenacious efforts of citizens like Maryka Omatsu, who devoted her lawyer's skills to a campaign on behalf of her fellow Japanese Canadians that lasted for many, many years:

for the larger part of Canada's history, for those of us who are not
of Anglo-Saxon descent, the price we had to pay for Canadian
citizenship was the brutal extirpation of our roots and unconditional immersion in the dominant culture. For my generation
assimilation meant the denial of our ethnic origins. But a stab-
bing pain persisted nonetheless. Uncomfortable in our own skins,
we secretly tried to reconcile the image we saw in the mirror
with the daily reality of the external world.[9]

For decades Ottawa's crimes against the Japanese community
were scarcely mentioned in the English-Canadian media. Journalists, commentators, and editorialists preferred to denounce (by
way of example) Stalin's deportation of the Crimean Tatars. . . .

8

ENGLISH-STYLE ANTI-SEMITISM

For the British, the burden of Empire presupposed the existence
of a divine power which had selected them for a divine mission
through the evolutionary process, through the survival of the
fittest. As Cecil Rhodes put it, "I contend that we are the first
race in the world, and the more of the world we inhabit, the
better it is for the human race."[1]

English Canada, until quite recently, shared Britain's deep conviction of racial superiority. And this in turn meant that it
postponed for a long time the task of creating its own identity.
We have only to go back to 1947, when the law on Canadian citizenship was finally proclaimed, to enter into an era when English
Canadians were perfectly happy to be British subjects.

This in turn meant they viewed the country as a private preserve for British immigrants: "the British tradition of freedom and
self-government was thought to be properly understood only by
those of Anglo-Saxon heritage."[2]

In order to attain this end, Canada by the end of the nineteenth
century had adopted the most discriminatory arrangements

possible where immigration was concerned. The criteria were religion (Protestant), homeland (Great Britain) and skin colour (to paraphrase Henry Ford, any colour you wish so long as it is white). The Orange Order, already the declared enemy of French Canada, steadily extended the reach of its disregard for the Other until it also included Jews, who were considered, in their way, to be as difficult to assimilate as the French. They, too, lacked the gift of appreciating British freedoms.

> Although the Orangemen aimed their biggest guns at their tradi-
> tional enemy, the French Canadian, they also took a strong
> stand against European immigrants who – to quote a twelfth of
> July orator – "have no knowledge of our love of civil and reli-
> gious liberty."[3]

English Canada's war against its Jewish minority was, with some exceptions, carried out in a hypocritical and underhanded fashion. Consider the eminent Toronto intellectual Goldwin Smith, who before his death in 1910 endowed the Art Gallery of Ontario and was honoured by Cornell University in New York State, where he taught for many years. Cornell named its philosophy and classics building after him.

Smith was a liberal who had supported the English-Canadian nationalist movement Canada First, but later renounced it. Driven by racist fears, he decided in mid-life that Canada must be annexed by the United States as a first step in unifying "the Anglo-Saxon race." He was the most virulent public anti-Semite produced by nineteenth-century Canada.[4]

One of his students at the University of Toronto, perhaps unsurprisingly, was William Lyon Mackenzie King. King admired Smith all his life, and became nearly as virulent an anti-Semite.

Smith regularly denounced "Jewish domination" and judged that "Jews are no good anyhow." In seminars and in his many writings he systematically supported the ancient slurs. The Jews, he believed, were "Christ-killers." They were obsessed with riches. . . .

Smith fiercely believed that the Jews were persecuted because
they deserved it, that Jews exercised a monopolistic control over
the media, and, above all, that they needed to be watched because
they constituted a danger to the nation, mankind, and the
"general progress of civilization" . . . Smith articulated his views
for almost thirty years (1878–1906) in high-profile publications
and when holding court in Toronto. The only hope for change, in
Smith's view, would be if Jews moved to Palestine, or ceased to
exhibit the characteristics of self-centered tribalism, gave up their
belief in their chosenness (sic), stopped controlling the press, and
stopped engaging in barbaric practices like circumcision.[5]

French Canadians are often criticized for their *Achat chez nous*
(Buy at Home) campaigns early in the twentieth century[6] as if such
a thing had never occurred anywhere but Quebec. The iron rule of
such criticism is never to look at what was happening elsewhere in
Canada at the same time. In the twenties, in Toronto, Jewish businesses were so severely boycotted that in 1923 the Glass family
published a remarkable advertisement in the *Toronto Star*. They
asked the public to bear in mind that their name was not Jewish,
and that no customer should refuse to do business with them on
that basis: "We beg to state that this house is strictly gentile, owned
and managed by Canadians in Canadian interests."[7]

An Orangeist newspaper like the *Toronto Telegram* made it
clear that Jews were not worthy Canadians. In 1925 it called for
restrictions on Jewish immigration in particularly offensive terms:
"An influx of Jews puts a worm next to the kernel of every fair
city where they get hold. These people have no national tradition.
[. . .] They are not the material out of which to shape a people
holding a national spirit."[8]

In the thirties the slogan "Keep Canada British" was widespread. There was intense interest in the racist theories of biology
then current, whether eugenics or a variety of theories which
could establish a biological foundation for the "Anglo-Saxon race."
More than half of Toronto's six hundred thousand inhabitants

came from England, and 80 per cent were supposedly sprung from the "Anglo-Saxon race."

Toronto was already the chief metropolis of English Canada. But what a narrow, Orangeist, Protestant, and imperialist place it was!

> Toronto was one of the largest centres of Orange strength. . . . The Order was a powerful force in the city's administration. . . . Many of Toronto's policemen and firemen were members of Orange lodges. A good number of its civic workers were also Orangemen. The mayor of Toronto and most of the aldermen were . . . Orangemen. . . . In Toronto, and elsewhere in Orange circles, the Jew was hated because he was most definitely not British.[9]

The city already contained 45,000 Jews, which was apparently 45,000 too many, and they were made to feel that way. Incredible as it now seems, posters reading "Gentiles Only" warned Jews to stay away from certain beaches and certain neighbourhoods. Holiday camps were closed to them: "No Jews or dogs allowed."[10]

Anti-Jewish bigotry was openly practised, to the extent that it shocked a young Conservative deputy from Hamilton, Argue Martin. In 1933 he proposed a private member's bill in the Ontario Legislature that would have forbidden posters and advertisements that were openly racist or hostile to a particular religion.

To fully understand the mentality of Ontario anti-Semites, it's helpful to look at the views of one of Argue Martin's supporters. The Reverend Salem Bland, who wrote in the Toronto *Daily Star* under the pen name "The Observer," agreed that anti-Jewish sentiments should not be published in public places.

Bland went on, however, to defend anti-Semitism in and of itself. Employers and landlords had every right to discriminate on racial and religious grounds, he said, so long as they didn't admit it publicly. For that reason, a law forbidding public demonstrations of racism was an excellent idea – so long as it didn't inhibit private expression of the same views!

Private expression meant that Jews could continue to be barred from golf courses and apartment buildings, just that nobody should say so out loud.

But even this peculiar form of sympathy for Jews was too much for Ontario, and Martin's proposal was voted down.[11]

In the summer of 1933, the sun's rays beat down on a Balmy Beach (in eastern Toronto) that had in previous summers been entirely Anglo-Saxon. But it was becoming steadily more popular with the Jewish community, and local residents were appalled. That summer Heil Hitler graffiti began to appear on buildings near the beach, and there were incidents of young people chasing Jews off the beach.

These youths proudly told journalists that they were members of Swastika Clubs, and the newspapers adopted the expression as shorthand to describe the confrontations on Balmy Beach. The name stuck, and in the following months what had been a made-up catchphrase turned into a national movement, The Swastika Association of Canada. It was no longer limited to Toronto, or even Ontario.

Its founder, Joseph C. Farr, had made his reputation by harassing Jews who attempted to sun themselves on Toronto's beaches. He was, it turned out, born in Northern Ireland, and was a devoted Orangeman. As Lita-Rose Betcheman observes, his views were very welcome in English Canada:

> English Canada was shocked at every reminder of Swastika Clubs and fascist parties in its midst, and persisted in regarding them as totally alien to its democratic way of life (while quite at home in Quebec). But fascism, west of the Ottawa River, was not just an import. English-speaking Canadians themselves indulged to some degree in its main component – racism.[12]

A few years later, in 1937, a huge poster was unfurled on the eastern Toronto beaches: "GREAT BRITAIN GAVE YOU JERUSALEM, FOR THE LOVE OF GOD LEAVE US THIS BEACH."[13]

THE RIOTS IN CHRISTIE PITS

Balmy Beach and its nascent Swastika Clubs were nothing compared to events taking place elsewhere in Toronto. On August 16, 1933, a Jewish baseball team, Harbour Playground, was facing off against the very WASP St. Peter club in the Christie Pits semi-finals. Things were tense because during a game two days earlier a spectator had stood up and waved a black shirt ornamented with a white swastika, howling insults at the Harbour Playground team. The following night Heil Hitler graffiti appeared in the park.

The Jewish population in the neighbourhood had been growing, and on August 16 the gathering resentment of the mainly Protestant residents finally exploded. A crowd of racists, hearing about the shirt-waving incident during the earlier game, had assembled for the semifinal game. The Jewish kids of Harbour Playground knew what was coming, and had asked friends to come along to protect them.

The softball association had asked the police to attend the game by way of forestalling violence, but the police, riddled with high-placed Orangemen, simply ignored the request. They were also influenced by a widespread belief that Jews were Communist sympathizers. All things considered, they certainly weren't going to waste a fine summer evening protecting Jews who strayed into better people's neighbourhoods!

As far back as 1928 the Toronto Police Commission had decreed that the city's police officially understood no language other than English. Any public meeting held in other languages was assumed to be seditious in nature. This order had already been enforced against Philip Halperin, who published a small Communist pamphlet in Yiddish. When he actually dared to speak Yiddish at a gathering in memory of Lenin, he was charged with causing public disorder. Chief Draper, head of the Toronto force, carefully explained to a journalist that the arresting officer, though innocent of Yiddish, was reasonably certain he had heard Halperin insulting British institutions in his speech.

This was the background to what happened that night at Christie Pits. The Jewish players, knowing there would be no police protection, undertook self-defence. As the game drew to an end a group of anti-Semites, not mollified that St. Peter was winning, unfurled a huge swastika flag and began shouting Heil Hitler. The Jewish kids raced toward them in a group, signalling the beginning of six hours of street fighting involving hundreds of combatants. Both baseball bats and iron bars were used. Some observers claimed afterward that as many as ten thousand people were involved in the fighting and subsequent looting of the Christie Pits area. Twenty-two Nazi sympathizers underwent police questioning.[14] Four local Anglo-Protestants were arrested and confessed that they wanted to prevent Jews from using their park. But a local judge dismissed all charges "on the grounds that the provocation of the Jews was intended as a joke."[15]

This was systematic anti-Semitism, and it had worked its way into the upper echelons of society. The Canadian Jewish Congress issued a report showing to what extent Jews were barred from various jobs and professions:

Few of the country's teachers and none of its school principals were Jews. Banks, insurance companies and large industrial and commercial interests reportedly excluded Jews. Major department stores avoided hiring Jews as sales personnel. Jewish doctors rarely received hospital appointments, and universities and professional schools restricted numbers of Jewish students and conspired against hiring Jewish faculty. The report also noted that Jewish nurses, architects and engineers were often forced to assume non Jewish surnames to get jobs.[16]

In 1933 Esther Einbinder did a master's thesis on attitudes toward Jews in Toronto. Her troubling discoveries included a significant willingness on the part of professionals (as many as one out of three) to deport Canada's Jewish population. Their principal fear was the evolution of a Jewish middle class. Their university-age offspring shared the same prejudices: four out of five found the idea of Jews in their clubs and associations distasteful.[17]

It goes without saying that Jews weren't allowed to join tennis and golf clubs. So they formed their own tennis club. But it, too, was caught in the net: the Tennis Club Association refused to allow it to join.

Perhaps more seriously, English Canada's elite was intent on aping everything possible about the British upper class, good and bad. So it accepted without demur the belief that Jews were to blame for every European revolution since 1789.

This is easier to understand when one recalls that even Winston Churchill propagated a genteel version of the Jewish stereotype. In the *Sunday Herald* (February 20, 1920), he began with the customary paean to the Jewish people ("No thoughtful man can doubt the fact that they are beyond all question the most formidable and the most remarkable race which has ever appeared in the world") before proceeding to the ominous, if familiar, distinction between good and bad Jews. The latter group included "international Jews":

> It has been the mainspring of every subversive movement during the Nineteenth Century; and now, at last, this band of extraordinary personalities from the underworld of the great cities of Europe and America have gripped the Russian people by the hair of their heads and have become practically the undisputed masters of that enormous empire.

He also blamed "Jewish terrorists" for the bloody unrest which broke out in many European countries after the First World War:

> And the prominent, if not indeed the principal, part in the system of terrorism applied by the Extraordinary Commissions for Combating Counter-Revolution has been taken by Jews, and in some notable cases by Jewesses. . . . Although in all these countries there are many non-Jews, every whit as bad as the worst of

the Jewish revolutionaries, the part played by the latter in proportion to their numbers in the population is astonishing.

Churchill's rhetoric could not have been more timely, since Ontario's financial oligarchy was for the first time dealing with large-scale organized labour. The unions came from the United States, but it was convenient to point the finger at Jews and Bolsheviks. George Drew, leader of the Ontario Conservatives and soon to be premier, had a musical ear for picking only Jewish-sounding names out of the lists of labour organizers. He also insisted that nearly a third of the 1,500 people in the province's Communist Party were Jewish.

The media, as usual, parroted the elitist view. On January 21, 1935, the Toronto *Globe* printed the following: "Although it cannot be said that the majority of Jews are communist, the indications are that a large percentage and probably a majority of Communists are Jews."[18]

Jews were increasingly linked, in the print media, to the idea of revolution. When J. J. Glass, a liberal MPP, dared to suggest that the legislature should pass a law to dampen the rapid spread of hate literature, he was ridiculed in a *Globe and Mail* editorial entitled "Why Be So Sensitive?" The Orange Order was quick with a sanctimonious endorsement of freedom of speech. When Glass did not back down, the *Globe and Mail* proclaimed that such a law would violate the spirit of British tradition.

Harmful, undemocratic, and un-British – who in their right mind would want to be tarred with all three brushes at the same time?[19]

Quebec's anglophones were as anti-Semitic as their fellows elsewhere. In 1901 a ten-year-old student, Jacob Pinsler, was denied a scholarship by the Montreal Protestant School Board because he was Jewish. Now it's true that Jewish children were admitted to Protestant schools (because their parents were obliged to support them with their taxes), but the schools refused to hire Jewish teachers. Nor were any Jews hired in the school board's administrative structure or named to its board of directors.

When Jews sought full political participation in the commission, the commissioners saw this as a threat and, in no uncertain terms, told the Jews they were only guests in a system that must remain Protestant. Allowing Jewish commissioners would lead to non-Christians teaching Protestant children, protested a leading commissioner, "(and) it scarcely seems necessary to characterize such an innovation as undesirable." And indeed, Jewish teachers found it nearly impossible to get a job at a Protestant school, at a time when Jewish students constituted one-third of the student body.[20]

From the 1920s through to the Second World War, McGill University placed Jews under a quota system, and made them submit to more arduous admission tests. This was the work of Sir Arthur Currie, McGill's vice-chancellor. A gymnasium still sports his name, and no Jewish organization has lobbied to have his name removed from the campus.

As a rule, Quebec's Jewish community remains discreetly silent about the racism it endured from Quebec's anglophones. Its obsessive and noisy fixation is entirely with Lionel Groulx.

If Groulx had been the categorically anti-Semitic intellectual described by certain parties, this anti-Semitism would have occupied a noteworthy proportion of his writings and activities. He would have written anti-Semitic pamphlets and organized events, preached a belligerent attitude toward Jews, and so on. He did none of these things. Were he the leading figure of an anti-Semitic movement, as some have claimed, he was certainly an exceptional one in that he scarcely ever spoke of Jews, and when he did so, generally did so in positive terms. He held up Jews as an example of solidarity and cultural pride which ought to be emulated. Seeing certain parallels in the situation of the two groups, he even went so far as to describe French Canadians as "the Jews of America."[21]

In one of his many books, Groulx even condemned anti-Semitism: "Anti-Semitism as a solution is not only un-Christian, but negative and stupid."[22] In all of Groulx's writings, says sociologist Gary Caldwell, there are exactly two quotations which might be considered hostile to Jews.[23]

Meanwhile, back in English Quebec, it was wall-to-wall anti-Semitism. Apart from harassment within the school system, says Gérard Bouchard,

> Montreal's Jews found themselves confronted with quasi-systematic exclusion throughout the whole Anglo-Quebec establishment. They were barred from financial circles, from the English legal community, prestigious clubs, recreational organizations (YMCA, YWCA), and so on. That is why the Jewish community undertook to set up a parallel institutional network (hospital, schools, community centres, etc.). What emerges from the most authoritative writings and testimonials within Quebec's English community is a diligent and effective anti-Semitism. But it had the property of making itself more discreet than French-Canadian anti-Semitism, which tended loudly to announce itself in public.[24]

FROM ORANGEISM TO FASCISM

The growth of fascism and Nazism in Europe was bound to have repercussions in English Canada, where the Orange movement had already made the leap to anti-Semitism. It would soon weave fascist ideas into its familiar imperial rhetoric.

An early influence was Mussolini, who had many admirers in the English-Canadian elite by the mid-thirties. A former president of the Ontario Magistrates' Association, the ardently imperial S. A. Jones published a book called *Is Fascism the Answer?* and spoke approvingly on the subject to Toronto's Empire Club in 1934. In Montreal, *The Star* editorialized "Could We Import

Mussolini?" while in Winnipeg some veterans of the First World War organized themselves, in Brownshirt fashion, as the Canadian Nationalist Party.

The CNP's hall was lavishly decorated with Union Jacks and its leader, a fiftyish Englishman named William Whittaker, assured members that the group's only loyalty was to the British Crown. It was, however, a fervour which expressed itself in peculiar fashion. The CNP wished first to abolish provincial legislatures in favour of a strong central government, and then turn the attention of this powerful government on Canada's communists. In CNP parlance, however, the words "Jew" and "Communist" were not far apart.

When police raided the party's headquarters they turned up a membership list which emphasized each individual's military skills. Though its leaders were Anglo-Saxon, the bulk of the members were German Mennonites associated with a church whose director was fond of printing favourite passages from Goebbels's speeches.

An offshoot of Whittaker's group, the Canadian Union of Fascists, found its inspiration in the British fascist Sir Oswald Mosley. By 1935, less than a year after its founding, the CUF had Toronto and Vancouver branches. Members of all branches sported Mosley's trademark black shirt.

The Depression was especially miserable on the Prairies, and according to historian James Gray, there were soon Nazi sympathizers in the universities, schools, and churches. "Until the outbreak of war," he wrote in *The Winter Years*, "anti-Nazism was a lost cause in Winnipeg."[25]

English Canada was once again walking in England's footsteps. That country had seen a large part of its ruling class won over to fascist ideals. As many as 200 British legislators had expressed public admiration for Mussolini. One of them, Winston Churchill, had visited Il Duce in the 1920s and rhapsodized about him to the British press: "I could not help being charmed, like so many other people have been, by Signor Mussolini's gentle and simple bearing. . . . If I had been an Italian I should have been whole-heartedly with you from start to finish."[26]

Sir Thomas Moore, a Conservative MP, felt "there cannot be any fundamental difference of outlook between Blackshirts and their parents, the Conservatives." Four Conservative deputies belonged to Oswald Mosley's January Club, and Mosley himself was an intimate of the Royal Family. It has even been stated that the abdicating King Edward VIII passed by Black House, home of the British Union of Fascists, to received a raised-arm salute before departing England.[27]

The former king then carried on a secret correspondence with Hitler. They had agreed he would serve as regent upon the German conquest of England. It should not be forgotten that the Windsors, formerly the Saxe-Coburg-Gothas, were German in origin.

It has often been wondered why Queen Elizabeth II permitted Anthony Blunt to retain his post as curator of the Queen's portrait collection even after learning that he was a Russian double agent. The answer may perhaps lie in the fact that Blunt, during the war, was in charge of a special mission which entered Berlin to seize the letters which the duke of Windsor and Hitler had exchanged. Is it possible the Queen was purchasing Blunt's silence?[28]

Documents which have recently become public have deepened our understanding of anti-Semitism in the highest circles of British society. In May 1939, MP Archibald Ramsay had founded a secret society, The Right Club, whose 335 members, many of them women, represented the English *crème de la crème*. According to the newspaper *The Independent*, "The purpose of the organization was to support fascist policies, to 'oppose and expose the activities of Organized Jewry' and to influence the British government to maintain peace with Germany. Meetings were chaired by no less a figure than the Duke of Wellington."[29]

The moment Britain went to war with Germany, Her Majesty's Secret Service promptly seized and buried the Right Club's membership list. It remained hidden in London's Wiener Library, under lock and key, and it was many years before journalists were able to

examine it. When they did they found the names of extremely pow-
erful men including the duke of Westminster, Baron Redesdale,
Lord Sempill, Lord Ronald Graham, Lord Carnegie, the count of
Galloway, Princess Blucher, Sir Alexander Walker, the writer G. K.
Chesterton, and a number of Nazi sympathizers including E. H.
Cole, chief of the English equivalent of the Ku Klux Klan.

ADRIEN ARCAND: OTTAWA SUBSIDIZES
THE ANTI-SEMITIC PRESS

Adrien Arcand was head of Canada's leading fascist political party
before the war. His name is often pronounced with pleasure by
English Canadians who seek to associate Quebec nationalism with
totalitarianism. But they've got the wrong man. Arcand was really
more a soulmate of Pierre Trudeau and Jean Chrétien, in the sense
that he bitterly opposed separatism. His loyalties were entirely to
Canada, and he was for that reason on the prime minister's payroll.

Even as a young chemical-engineering student at McGill,
Arcand found time to sign up with the Canadian militia. Something of an anglophile, he then went on to write for the *Montreal
Star* as well as *La Presse* (he was fired from the latter for trying to
organize a union). With his ally, printer Joseph Ménard, he went
on to found a series of fiercely anti-Semitic small newspapers.

Two of them, *Le Miroir* and *Le Goglu*, supported Camillien
Houde's Conservatives in the 1930 provincial elections. But the
two men quarrelled shortly afterward and Houde was later known
for intervening on behalf of Montreal's Jewish community.

Houde was far from the only Quebec nationalist who took up the
Jewish cause. Henri Bourassa, who had tended to anti-Semitism in
his youth, later denounced it in the federal Parliament and met
with representatives of the Canadian Jewish Congress. For that
reason Arcand contemptuously classified him with his grandfather Louis-Joseph Papineau, who in 1832 had promoted the famous
law which made Lower Canada's Jews the first in the British
Empire to receive the franchise.

The federal Conservatives thought they had a chance against Mackenzie King in the 1930 elections. But everything depended on winning additional seats in Quebec. Their wealthy leader, Richard Bedford Bennett, had been giving the Conservative Party's central office a monthly stipend of $2,500 (worth about $27,000 today)[30] since September 1929, for a total of over $57,000 (about $600,000 in today's money) by February of the following year.[31]

But it wasn't making a dent in Quebec, where the Conservatives dragged the ball-and-chain of hanging Riel and enforcing conscription in the First World War. This would seem to explain why one of Bennett's envoys stealthily approached Arcand and Ménard shortly before the 1930 election. Joseph Rainville, a senator, offered to finance their publications if they became pro-Conservative. The financial guarantee would initially be $25,000, with more money forthcoming if necessary. But in exchange both *Le Miroir* and *Le Goglu*, working with Arcand's political movement, the *Ordre patriotique des Goglus*, would work to ensure the Conservatives won more than twelve Quebec seats in the election.

A third publication, *Le Chameau*, appeared on March 14, 1930, and very likely also received political funding. A letter of Arcand's to Bennett, written in late May that year and marked "Confidential," refers to an earlier meeting between the two where Arcand had presented his strategy for the election: "Last week, my partner Jos. Ménard and I were honored and favored with an interview with you. Our plan of procedure and propaganda was exposed to you as well as our program of meetings throughout this province."[32]

Arcand went on to ask that the promised cash advances begin immediately because they lacked the money to repair damage caused by an arsonist's attack on their printing plant: "We thought that, for our peace of mind and working facilities, it would be fair to ask for an immediate amount of $15,000, and a little help occasionally from Mr. Rainville until our three papers are on the way of making a business success parallel to our tremendous political results."

It was at this time that Arcand's newspapers took a sudden lurch toward anti-Semitism. The inflow of Conservative Party money also paid for a vigorous campaign on Bennett's behalf. They printed thousands of Conservative Party pamphlets.

In the July 28 election Bennett's Conservatives took power with 137 members, of whom 24 came from Quebec, 16 of those being French-speakers.

It was the first time in more than twenty years that a franco-phone Conservative had been elected to the House of Commons in a general election. It was more than the total number of "strict" Conservatives Quebec had sent to Ottawa since 1891. And to make a scarcely believable outcome even more so, the Conservatives had made no particular effort to attract the Quebec vote.[33]

It's true that the economic crisis of 1929 was the true cause of the Liberals' defeat, and that the Conservatives had harvested the protest vote. But in Quebec they were happy to acknowledge Arcand and his newspapers (which alone had supported them) as the author of their success. The two fascist leaders were secretly paid $18,000 ($190,000 today) for services rendered. This was a colossal sum of money to hand over to a fascist and anti-Semite, especially at the height of an economic catastrophe. Without it, Arcand's three newspapers would almost certainly have failed.

But it wasn't enough, or so Arcand felt. His side of the deal had been to put *Le Goglu* into the service of the Conservatives and deliver twelve seats. Done! So where was the minimum of $25,000 which Senator Rainville had promised to sustain the newspapers? Surely, added the two fascists, Bennett would see that Rainville kept his word. In their letter to Bennett of January 14, 1931, they considered the prime minister "the supreme judge, and whatever will be decided by you will be law for us. Your obedient servants, . . ."

Two weeks later, using letterhead from *Le Miroir* stamped "Confidential," Arcand and Ménard detailed the expenses they had incurred during the election campaign. There was, for example, the 24,000 free copies of *Le Goglu* and *Le Miroir* they had handed out at a cost of $2,400, not to mention $1,000 for a special edition of *Le Miroir* to neutralize *La Presse*'s attack on the Conservatives' conscription policy.

Then there was the costly business of the 400 electoral meetings they'd organized at a cost of about $500 per meeting – a tidy tab of $52,000 (about $600,000 today) but altogether reasonable when you consider 400,000 people had attended.

The whole bill reached $65,900 (about $775,000). They did acknowledge the $18,000 they had already received from Rainville, but reminded Bennett that they'd had to sign a lien on all three newspapers in exchange.

It appears that this letter was greeted by six months of silence from Ottawa. So in mid-July they fired off another letter to Bennett, who was now prime minister, their "supreme judge." A debt of $50,000 (about $600,000) was slowly dragging them down. Shortly afterward they went in person to Ottawa to beg for help, without apparent success.

After another six penurious months, this letter appeared on Bennett's desk, again on *Le Miroir* letterhead: "We are near bankruptcy, and our business is on its last legs." They continued:

We will be glad and proud in our misfortune to have loyally
served our ideal, our country, the doctrin [sic] of our Party and the
God-sent man who leads our country so wisely in this hour of
great distress and who has all our admiration and confidence. . . .
If God permits that, by one way or the other, we survive for one
week or one year, you may rest assured that we will be during
that time as we have been since our first interview,
Your loyal and faithful soldiers,
[Signed] Adrien Arcand, Joseph Ménard

The federal Conservatives weren't Arcand's only financiers. Lord Sydenham, former governor of Bombay and a faithful outrider on the extreme right flank of the British Conservatives, was the proud author of a book called *The Jewish World Problem*. His unhealthy lucubrations regularly graced the pages of Arcand's newspapers.

Arcand also corresponded with the bizarre Arnold Spencer Leese, head of the Imperial Fascist League in Great Britain. Leese had authored a much-respected scholarly tome on the subject of camels. He adored them, the British Empire, and fascism as strongly as he loathed Jews. As a vegetarian, he was peculiarly fixated on the subject of kosher meat.

Sensing in R. B. Bennett an intellectual soulmate, Arcand sent him a copy of Leese's newspaper, *The Fascist*.[34]

But it was to yet another strange bird in the menagerie of British fascism that Arcand owed an idea which he quickly came to cherish. This was Henry Hamilton Beamish's captivating notion that the Jews could be transported to Madagascar.

Arcand's bigotry was by now so noisome that the two Jewish deputies in the Quebec Legislature, Peter Bercovitch and Joseph Cohen, introduced a bill to condemn him by name. In reply Arcand wrote: "We have never hidden the fact that all our sympathy is with Hitler's movement."

Notices of libel action piled up on Arcand's doorstep until he had to call on his friends, the federal Conservatives, to get him out of the mess he'd landed in. Another desperate letter went off to Ottawa in May of 1932.

Surprisingly, even at this late date, a prominent Quebec Conservative was prepared to support Arcand's case. A few weeks after Arcand's pleading letter Leslie G. Bell, Conservative representative for Saint-Antoine, wrote to Bennett that *Le Goglu*, "as you are aware, rendered us efficient and valuable service during the last election campaign. On every occasion when it was necessary to call upon their services, they responded most effectively." Bell continued: "I am quite thoroughly convinced that the proprietors of the *Goglu* are conservative in their politics and are prepared to back the Federal interests with all their strength."

John A. Sullivan, a Montreal Conservative MP, intervened on Arcand's behalf. Of *Le Goglu*, by then a grotesque anti-Semitic rag, he wrote to Bennett: "It would be a pity to see it fail, and you alone can help it in the present circumstances."

But time had run out. Overwhelmed by lawsuits, Arcand and his partner declared bankruptcy.

This did not put an end to his relationship with Bennett. In early January 1933 he wrote to the prime minister's private secretary, saying that Kurt Ludecke, Hitler's Washington envoy, earnestly desired to meet with Bennett before the end of the month. "Let me know if that is possible."

Ludecke's job was to raise money and support for the German Nazi Party in America. While it would be interesting to know if the meeting Ludecke proposed ever took place, there is no evidence that it did. Nor is there any evidence that Bennett took any measures to avoid it.

The situation in Quebec was eloquently encapsulated by a Liberal Montreal MP, S. W. Jacobs, in a letter to a friend in Baltimore. Jacobs was the head of the Canadian Jewish Congress:

> Not one person carrying on an anti-Jewish campaign in Quebec is
> a man of responsibility. Many are youths, not yet twenty. Quebec
> public men are with us. . . . We have one paper in Quebec worse
> in its attitude to Jews than any in Germany. It must be subsi-
> dized, for prior to its present campaign against Jewry, it was
> dragged through the bankruptcy courts.[35]

Jacobs was unaware that the vile newspaper's chief funder was sitting comfortably in the prime minister's chair opposite him in the House of Commons. But by now – March 1933 – R. B. Bennett was tight-lipped on the subject. It was his chief senator, Pierre-Édouard Blondin, who had quietly approached Arcand and told him it was time to shut down the three newspapers and declare bankruptcy. "Turn a new leaf," Blondin suggested, and by May of the following year Arcand will indeed have launched what would become his most infamous journal, *Le Patriote*.

Meanwhile, the anguish of the Depression was fanning the flame of fascism, especially in the wide-open Prairies. The Canadian Nationalist Party continued publishing anti-Semitic articles in spite of a 1934 Manitoba law intended to prevent such material appearing in print. In Alberta the Canadian Corps Association asked for an inquest into fascist inroads among the province's voters. Lita-Rose Betcheman, author of *The Swastika and the Maple Leaf*, points out that, "From 1933 to 1935, the western fascists were actually more numerous and better organised than Arcand's party."[36]

You might imagine that the Conservatives had by now decided to cut all ties with Arcand. But in fact they still believed he could be an electoral asset. In early 1934 Blondin wrote to Bennett that Arcand "has launched a movement which (under the name of the Christian National Party) aims simply at the debunking of all the rot in the old parties, which, when the end comes, will be found to be 'a regenerated Conservative party' in Quebec, which I think we need."[37]

The Conservatives put Arcand in charge of Quebec campaign publicity for the 1935 elections. His newspaper *Le Fasciste canadien* launched incessant and venomous attacks on Mackenzie King and touted the Conservatives as the province's only hope.

This time it didn't work. The Conservatives ended up with a sad little caucus of 5 Quebec seats, and only 76 overall. The Liberals had crushed them, marching to Ottawa with a huge majority of 174 seats.

Although the Conservatives had dawdled on giving Arcand the money he requested, he had nonetheless received $27,000 by 1936 according to a letter signed by party organizer A. W. Reid. It's a tantalizing bit of evidence from the second half of the Depression – and about all the hard evidence that remains. The RCMP apparently took the Arcand archives into its possession in 1940 and somehow "misplaced" them. Several tons of papers disappeared and have never been found.

It seems clear there were more fascist sympathizers in English than in French Canada at this point in history, but the Anglo leaders were a pallid crew. Arcand, unfortunately, became one more of those charismatic Quebec leaders who end up in the national spotlight. His affection for British imperialism, and his fluent English, made him congenial to the wheat-field Nazis and Rocky Mountain Aryans.

Had his party ever, as he had hoped, attained national power, it would have advocated closer Canadian integration into the Empire. As Lita-Rose Betcheman has written, he was so purely British in his thinking that no Legionnaire or Orangeist would have flinched when he wrote, "[W]e will fight for our King, our God, our country. Communism is a crime against God, the family, the King, the home, everything."[38]

Every meeting of Arcand's party began with a Nazi salute. Arms as rigid as the prows of sailing ships, the militants together recited this oath:

Moved by the unshakable faith in God, a profound love for Canada, ardent sentiments of patriotism and nationalism, a complete loyalty and devotion toward our Gracious Sovereign who forms the recognized principle of active authority, a complete respect for the British North America Act, for the maintenance of order, for national prosperity, for national unity, for national honour, for the progress and the happiness of a greater Canada, I pledge solemnly and explicitly to serve my party. I pledge myself to propagate the principles of its program. I pledge myself to follow its regulation. I pledge myself to obey my leaders. Hail the party! Hail our Leader![39]

If one forgets for a moment where this oath was used, it becomes strangely apparent that it would serve equally well today for any current federal political party!

Arcand was the sworn enemy of Lionel Groulx and all Quebec nationalists. For him, federalism and imperialism were a battle cry:

> Arcand insists that his organisation has no sympathy with the extreme French nationalist movement represented by the group which split from Premier Duplessis, after he was returned to power because he would not go all the way they wished. "We were the first in Quebec to fight Separatism," Arcand declares, "and we are carrying on that fight very satisfactorily, swallowing many ex-members of that failing movement."
>
> Frankly, the National Social Christian Party is aiming for Dominion power, Arcand admits, describing Dominion power as the real key to the vital problems of this country.[40]

Arcand would remain a convinced federalist to the end of his life. In May 1965 he wrote to Daniel Johnson (Sr.), head of the Union nationale, expressing his distaste for Johnson's party newspaper:

> Disgust compels me to the unhappy duty of cancelling my subscription to *Montréal Matin*, which I had received in the Auberge Saint-Pierre at Lanoraie. Everything about it – articles, opinion pieces, editorials, so-called "press dispatches" with huge headlines – tells me that your newspaper is trying to be more separatist than the separatists.[41]

Arcand's group, like other right-wing Depression-era fascist organizations, was predicated on a strong central government. *The Thunderbolt*, the newspaper of the Canadian Union of Fascists, went so far as to ask for the abolition of provincial governments and a corporatist federal government.

By 1938 there were "shock troops" working with the Ontario Nationalist Party and training several times weekly under the direction of Joseph Farr, a prominent Orangeman. They were ethnically British for the most part, and wore blue shirts with swastika armbands.

Farther west, German immigrants polished Hitler's reputation:

Indeed, nazi and fascist activity in Saskatchewan was sufficiently alarming that a large protest meeting was held in June 1938 and a deluge of letters from veterans' groups and patriotic societies expressing their concern descended upon the Minister of Justice in Ottawa. The situation continued to cause alarm. A year later, a resident of a little town not far from Saskatoon reported to CCF HQ that "this spring fascist activities here so menaced the peace of the community that the Canadian Legion found it necessary to organize a 'protect democracy drive.'" Even after the outbreak of war, the MP for Prince Albert, John Diefenbaker, was asking the government what it intended to do about nazi influence in Saskatchewan.[42]

In 1938 Arcand's Parti national social chrétien amalgamated with the Canadian Nationalist Party and the quasi-clandestine Ontario Nationalist Party (which grew out of the original Swastika Clubs). The new organization styled itself the National Unity Party of Canada – national unity, an idea as up-to-date as a PalmPilot.

The new party's symbol was a swastika rakishly dotted about with maple leaves, over which floated a beaver. Arcand, still a great admirer of Oswald Mosley's style of provocation, proposed to roll out the new symbol at a first meeting to be held that April in a Toronto Jewish neighbourhood.

The party's first official congress took place three months later, on July 4, at Toronto's Massey Hall. Its first move was to send a polite telegram to the governor general assuring him of the party's loyalty. Then the 2,500 delegates settled back to listen to Ontario's chief fascist, Joseph Farr, deliver an anti-Jewish harangue. The other provincial representatives took the platform in succession to deliver equally charming messages.

Arcand's politics were anomalous in Quebec, according to renegades who reported that he never had more than 800 followers there. Canada's extreme right, then as now, was largely English-speaking. In Toronto alone the police compiled a list of more than a thousand members of the Nazi-leaning National Unity Party of Canada. If to these overtly fascist groups one added the considerable membership of the Ku Klux Klan (popular in the Prairies) and other rival organizations, it's clear that the Québécois were never more than a sliver of the swastika.

In 1935 Germany stripped its Jewish population of citizenship and the vote. It also barred them from the public service, which may explain the Canadian government's failure to condemn the German measures: similar practices restricting Jewish employment were widespread in English Canada.

Official silence further emboldened local anti-Semites. In Toronto, a Protestant bastion already disposed to religious and racial intolerance, posters reading "Keep Jews Out/Gentiles Only" appeared with greater frequency. Jewish businesses were boycotted. Jewish lawyers found no jobs in the major law firms; Jewish doctors had no hope of major hospital appointments.

I am underlining this by way of responding to the frequent attacks on Quebec's supposed anti-Semitism. English Canada's media, to take one example, regularly remember the 1934 incident where fourteen medical interns at Hôpital Notre-Dame went on strike to protest the hiring of Samuel Rabinovitch, who had graduated with honours from the Université de Montréal medical school. These newspapers suffer total amnesia concerning a similar event that year in Regina: A hospital there refused to hire two Jewish doctors as radiologists on the pretext that this would be "unacceptable" to the hospital's staff and clientele.

Once we've done this particular tit-for-tat, it becomes difficult to find further examples in Quebec. But there's no shortage elsewhere in the country. Irving Himel, the lawyer who founded the Toronto Civil Liberties Association, went to court to strike down a Toronto ordinance forbidding the sale of land or large buildings to Jews. Himel remembers that, "In those days, Jews couldn't get jobs in places like Eaton's and Simpson's. There were quotas to keep them out of universities and deeds had clauses restricting the sale of properties to Jews, and if you looked Jewish or had a Jewish name, you were turned away from hotels and resorts."[43]

It's true that in Quebec there were Catholic clergymen – a few – who got behind Arcand's odious campaigns. But the senior clergy had nothing to do with it, for the excellent reason that Pope Pius XI had denounced Hitler for violating the 1933 Concordat with the Vatican. No important clergyman, whatever his sympathies, would defy the Pope.

In addition, so far as Quebec's nationalists were concerned, a true-blue federalist like Arcand was a very improbable figure to rally around. The Riel affair and the conscription crisis were still open wounds for them. But most critically, anti-Semitism was simply not as widespread in Quebec as in the rest of the country. According to Simon Fraser University political scientist Martin Robin – whose specialty is pre-war fascism in Canada – there was never a popular anti-Semitic movement in Quebec:

> The nationalist organizations, though tinged and tainted with anti-Semitism, did not, separately or together, comprise an anti-Semitic movement whose primary purpose was to combat and eradicate an alleged Jewish menace. Anti-Semitism of the other sort, the virulent, obsessive kind, the psychopathological species, which elevated the Jewish question to the key to the mystery of the world and served as the one true guide to social and political action, remained in Quebec the property of the marginal misshapen few; coteries of troubled men, women – and bobolinks[44] – who, as the depression deepened, descended into the gutter of Jew-bashing and Fascist politics.[45]

The absence of widespread popular support for anti-Semitism could also be read in the comfortable everyday contacts between the French and Jewish communities. "French-Canadians," writes

Professor Robin, "in their everyday contacts got along rather well, and whatever prejudice did exist, was of the superficial sort and in any event decidedly non-violent."

Certainly, nothing like the Christie Pits riots ever occurred in Quebec. And prominent members of the Quebec Jewish community, looking askance at the horrific events in Toronto, appreciated the difference. These were Israel Rabinovitch's words to a meeting of the Canadian Jewish Congress' eastern division in October 1933:

> One must not perpetuate the error of considering the French
> Canadians as irretrievably anti-Semitic. . . . Those Jews who come
> into contact with our French-Canadian neighbors, in business or
> in any other walk of life, will testify to the fact that often one can
> most excellently harmonize with them, and particularly when
> one speaks their language and when one manifests an understand-
> ing of their national sensibilities.[46]

MACKENZIE KING

No other Canadian prime minister can match Mackenzie King's longevity in power: twenty-one years! Many English Canadians consider him the greatest as well as the longest-serving of the country's leaders. It is less well known that he was a spiritualist and an anti-Semite.

On December 17, 1933, Mackenzie King summoned his parents and friends to express their best wishes on the occasion of his birthday. The people on the invitation list, however, were dead. Here's his diary entry concerning this memorable intimate fete:

> The record tonight was an amazing one. It came through very
> clear, as follows:
>   Who is there? Mother. Any message? Love!
>   Who is there? Father. Any message? Love!

Who is there? Max. Any message? Happy birthday!
Who is there? Bella. Any message? Happy birthday![47]

Here was Canada, sunk deep in the worst economic crisis of its history. And here was the prime minister, with a degree in economics. It's not a funny joke, no matter how much one might wish it was. He fled into credulous daily encounters with the spirits "rather than try to find solutions to the crisis," wrote one of his biographers, Luc Bertrand:

> In fact, from the beginning of the 1930s Mackenzie King used every possible method to communicate with the dead. He learned to read tea leaves. He consulted with mediums, people who are supposed to possess the power of communicating with spirits.
>
> Their methods varied. Once focused, the medium would begin to write rapidly on a sheet of paper to deliver to Mackenzie King the message of the deceased person. Sometimes a spirit might speak through the mouth of the medium, addressing itself directly to him. One day Mackenzie King heard a medium speak a language unknown to both of them. That sufficed to prove the medium's extraordinary power to Mackenzie King.[48]

King was also somewhat paranoid. He apparently believed the domestic staff listened at the door during these sessions, and were very much *au courant* of his secrets. This led him after some time to abandon mediums in favour of the more discreet method of the moving table.

He was particular about the social status of the spirits with whom he kept company. No casual hobnobbing for Mr. King! Even in his days as head of the Opposition he contacted nothing but the most distinguished souls for advice on career and political issues.

According to his diary he had been in touch with Leonardo da Vinci, Lorenzo de Medici, Louis Pasteur, Wilfrid Laurier, Saint

Luke, Saint John, Anne Boleyn (Henry VIII's unfortunate, headless wife), British Prime Minister Gladstone, and other luminaries of the arts, politics, and culture.

But the spooks didn't seem especially well-informed, considering their prominence while on earth and their presumed good connections afterwards. Just before the October 1935 elections, the dapper spectre of Wilfrid Laurier assured him he would win with forty-five seats. In fact his majority "was ninety-seven seats. Moreover, every important Conservative whose defeat Laurier had foretold was instead elected. It appeared once more that a mischievous spirit had interfered. . . ."[49]

On the fateful day of September 1, 1939 – when one might have expected the spirits to be extra alert – they flashed a special beyond-the-grave news bulletin to King: Hitler had been assassinated!

In fact, of course, Hitler was hale and healthy enough for Great Britain and France to declare war on him two days later.

It's not entirely for his entertainment value, however, that we're considering Mackenzie King. It's rather to compare the way his mental illness has been dealt with by the English-Canadian pundits who are so quick to impugn the mental health of Quebec's leaders.

What one notices first is the lack of seriousness. And this is surprising, considering King's troubling naïveté together with evident psycho-emotional problems (infantile attachment to his mother and fear of women, among others). But there has been little interest in psychiatric opinions of these matters, and the consequences they may have had for the country while he was running it.

A similar inclination to sweep things under the carpet is clear concerning his anti-Semitism. The two matters were related. Here's what this perspicacious prime minister had to say (to his diary) about Adolf Hitler at the dawn of the Second World War:

> I am convinced that Hitler is a spirit and that, like myself, he
> calls upon the spirits of his parents and deceased friends. I believe

that he is devoted to his mother, as I am to mine. I believe that
the world will discover in Hitler a very great man. I do not
entirely understand his thinking, nor his cruelty toward Jews, but
Hitler himself is little more than a peasant. I'd go so far as to say
that he will one day attain the same rank as Joan of Arc, as a liberator of his people and, if he is the least bit prudent, the liberator
of all Europe.[50]

In their book *None Is Too Many*, Irving Abella and Harold
Troper quote an even more deluded observation from King's diary.
He felt, according to the entry in question, that Hitler might well
become a kind of messiah: "He might come to be thought of as
one of the saviours of the world. He had the chance at Nuremberg,
but was looking to Force, to might, and to violence as means to
achieving his ends, which were, I believe at heart, the well-being
of his fellow man, not all fellow men, but those of his own race."[51]

Such thinking might well have influenced King's support for
British prime minster Neville Chamberlain's policy of appeasing
Hitler, which Chamberlain put forward at the 1937 imperial con-
ference in London. King was at this time so excited by Hitler that
he determined to visit him in person, and arranged a journey to
Germany.

Mackenzie King arrived in a Berlin where the anti-Semitic
Nuremberg laws were in full force. Jews were barred from many
professions and refused entry to hotels and holiday resorts. Signs
everywhere reminded them that they were not welcome.

One could observe, of course, that these things were equally
true in Toronto and Ottawa. Jews were barred, for example, from
one of King's favourite haunts, the Rideau Club. So he might
perhaps be excused for seeing nothing out of the ordinary in Berlin.

While there he signed a commercial treaty with Nazi Germany,
and went to the opera with Goering. He stood in the same room
with Hitler and listened to the Führer's anti-Jewish rants. His
account of these moments in his private diary reveals a bizarre
sympathy for the sentiments expressed:

I would have loathed living in Berlin with the Jews, and the way
in which they increased their numbers in the City, and were
taking possession of its more important part. He said there was
no pleasure in going to a theatre that was filled with them. Many
of them were very coarse and vulgar and assertive. They were
getting control of all the business, the finance, and had really
taken advantage of the people. It was necessary to get them out,
to have the German people control their own City and affairs. He
told me that I would have been surprised at the extent to which
life and morals had become demoralized; that Hitler had set his
face against all that kind of thing, and had tried to inspire desire
for a good life in the minds of young people.

So here is Mackenzie King, the greatest of Canada's leaders,
uttering not a syllable to contradict this monstrous interlocutor!
Nothing in his diaries indicates the least reservation about the
contemptible sentiments which Hitler expressed in front of him.
On the contrary, he wrote, "My sizing up of the man, as I sat and
talked with him, was that he is really one who truly loves his
fellow man."

One can only conclude that this was a meeting of minds, and
that Hitler's views on the Jewish people were not far from King's.

The prime minister left Berlin in the same perfect state of
woolly incomprehension that marked his arrival. "I can honestly
say that it was as enjoyable, informative and inspiring as any visit
I have had anywhere." In his view, Germany was on the mend and
the naysayers were misled: "I come away from Germany tremen-
dously relieved."

On his return to Ottawa only one MP, a Jew from Toronto
named Sam Factor, had the courage to denounce King's fraterniz-
ing with Hitler.

By March 29 of the following year King's racial ideas had gelled.
Of course this was the same man who had done everything he
could to keep Asians out of Canada thirty years earlier, but now
his thinking (as revealed in that day's diary entry) has become

systematic: "We must nevertheless seek to keep this part of the Continent free from unrest and from too great an inter-mixture of foreign strains of blood, as much the same thing as lies at the basis of the Oriental problem. I fear we would have riots if we agreed to a policy that admitted numbers of Jews."[52]

A year after the visit to Germany, King held a dinner at his summer residence at Kingsmere. Chatting after supper with guests, including the secretary of the American delegation, he reminisced affectionately about Hitler. There, he said, was a man of tenderness and sincerity. In a later account of the dinner, the American diplomat added that King became expansive on the subject, describing Hitler's face as the face of a good man, and his dreamer's temperament as being perhaps the evidence of an artistic gift.[53]

King's delusions were still intact in September 1938: "Hitler and Mussolini, although dictators, are really obliged to see to the happiness of the masses, and by so doing, are assured of their support . . . It was perhaps necessary to adopt a dictatorial manner in order to separate the privileged groups from the benefits which they had hitherto monopolized."[54]

By this time King was also saying that admitting refugees to Canada would pose a greater danger to Canada than Hitler himself. A little later, in 1939, he received a Jewish delegation and blithely informed them that Kristallnacht might well become a benediction for their people. He was speaking, of course, of what had happened on the night of November 9, 1938, when the ss and Nazi sympathizers had burnt hundreds of synagogues, businesses, and Jewish homes, and deported 30,000 Jews to concentration camps.

THE OFFICIAL POLICY OF
REFUSING JEWISH REFUGEES[55]

Canada, for reasons more connected with hypocrisy than anything else, had never set out official quotas for specific groups, as the U.S. had done. The same thing was accomplished obliquely, through "gentleman's agreements," and this had ensured a certain racial selection among immigrant candidates. The British and the Americans were preferred, of course, and their travel expenses often subsidized. Next came northern Europeans. Far, far down at the bottom of the ladder were Jews, Asians, and blacks. These were believed to be "races which could not be assimilated without social and economic losses for Canada." According to Abella and Troper, all immigrants were evaluated according to "their degree of similar 'racial characteristics' to the Anglo-Canadian majority."

The Liberals were not alone in this policy: it received the full support of the Conservative opposition. Its leader, Robert Manion, spoke often of refugees contributing to the unemployment problem, a view which received bipartisan support, especially in Ontario. The *Globe* in Toronto reiterated that the British race must maintain a majority in Canada.

Only the CCF called for a fair quota of refugee immigrants.[56]

The official who put the refugee-exclusion policy into force was named Frederick Charles Blair. He had been named head of immigration services by R. B. Bennett, Mackenzie King's predecessor.

Blair was an anti-Semitic Baptist of Scottish background, born in 1874 in the village of Carlisle in Ontario. He saw his mission as building a breastwork against the refugee tide, lest Canada be inundated with Jews. Canada, he said, would never become "the dumping ground for 800,000 Jewish refugees." And he was explicit that Jews must never "be treated as a nation or a religious group, but only as a race."

Blair went so far as to suggest Hitler should find a "solution" to his Jewish problem. With Mackenzie King's blessing, Blair would be the man in charge of executing Canada's immigration policies right up to 1943.

In any case where a Jewish and a non-Jewish candidate for immigration possessed similar qualifications, it was always the non-Jew who was preferred. Moreover, Jews were the only group which could be classified by officials according to their race rather than their citizenship. It didn't matter which country they came from. In an annual administrative report, Blair wrote: "Canada, in accord with generally accepted practice, gives more importance to race than to citizenship."[57] No German law could have expressed the matter more succinctly.

In the years immediately preceding the war, everybody knew what was taking place in Germany: the Nazis had officially undertaken the elimination of the Jewish community, and nobody could plead ignorance of the matter. President Roosevelt was so troubled that he convened a conference on July 6, 1938, at Évian in France, to consider what might be done about the two hundred thousand Jewish refugees created by Germany's forced annexation of Austria.

Knowing that the vast majority of Austrian Jews were city-dwellers, Canada's representative at the meeting flatly stated that his country could accept only farmers. Other nations made similarly obtuse statements, and Hitler heard the message loud and clear. Nobody wanted the Jews. He could do what he wanted with them.

Frederick Blair knew perfectly well that Europe's Jews were facing extinction. He suggested as much in a letter written to an Anglian pastor in Toronto, but disingenuously added that "admitting a larger number to Canada would not solve the problem."[58]

Future governor general Vincent Massey, Canada's high commissioner to London at the time, was a member of the Clivenden group. This coterie of aristocrats, led by Lord and Lady Astor, was pro-German and deeply anti-Semitic.

Massey's particular passion was to see the large numbers of Catholic Sudeten Germans who had been displaced by the Munich Accords settled in Canada. On his recommendation, and within a very few days, the Canadian government waved this group of Germans into the country. But the gate clanged shut for Jews who had been displaced by the same Munich Accords.

Lest there be any doubt about what was going on, records show that some of these rejected German Jews made a second refugee application in which they pretended to be Christians. They were authorized to enter without difficulty.

All through the war, Massey did not waver in his belief that Jewish refugees should not find asylum and safety in Canada. And after 1945 he asserted that the country had no obligations toward Holocaust survivors either.

In a long chapter of *None Is Too Many*, Abella and Troper analyze the particular case of Canada's rejection of Jewish children, some thousands of whom were rebuffed and met their end in the death camps. Frederick Blair figures in this tale. He made fun of a group of Jews who, having escaped Japan, wished to emigrate to Canada: "That reminds me of something I saw on a farm when it was time to feed the pigs. They all tried to stick their feet into the feeding trough." In early 1939 Blair turned his attention to Jews who had arrived in Canada with tourist visas, setting in motion procedures to identify and expel them.

The 907 Jews aboard the steamer *St. Louis* knew nothing of the situation in Canada when their ship left Hamburg on May 15, 1939. Their destination was Cuba. Many among them had once been wealthy, but were stripped of their assets as well as their rights.

They received a rude shock during the sea voyage, when the ship received a dispatch to the effect that their authorization to land in Havana had been revoked. The crew contacted American authorities and were refused permission to land. They then turned to Canada for mercy.

Mackenzie King was on a tour of the United States with the British king and queen when he was briefed on the *St. Louis* dilemma. Prominent Canadian Jews wasted no time in petitioning him to show compassion.

But King was adamant. This ship was not Canada's problem. He declared himself "categorically opposed to the admission of the passengers of the *St. Louis*."

His advisor on Jewish questions, Frederick Blair, proclaimed that Canada had already been overly generous to the Jews: "if these Jews were to find refuge in Canada, they would soon be followed by boatloads of others. No country can open its doors wide enough to accommodate the hundreds of thousands of Jewish persons wishing to leave Europe: one must draw the line somewhere."

The *St. Louis* therefore returned to Europe, and found a little compassion in a little country. Belgium allowed them to land and permitted some to stay, dispersing the rest to Great Britain, Holland, and France. Only those who arrived in Great Britain were saved. Most of the others were swept up by the Gestapo as Northern Europe fell to the Wehrmacht.

What is peculiar to this terrible story is that, as things got worse in Europe (with the declaration of war), the behaviour of Canadian officials did not, as one might have hoped, improve. There was no glimmer of dawning compassion. Instead the officials became more obtuse. Two thousand Canadian Jews of German origin – the community with the least possible interest in helping Nazi authorities – were rounded up and interned in the same camps as Nazi sympathizers and SS prisoners of war.

Rabbi Erwin Schild recounted this experience in *Toward a Just Society*, a documentary produced by the Canadian Council of Christians and Jews: "we were treated as German sympathizers, and nobody hated the Germans as passionately as I did, or as we did, me and my colleagues. And then to be interned as possible German sympathizers, well that's a uniquely Jewish experience. It's an absurdity."[59]

The documentary also threw light on Canada's penchant, during Mackenzie King's watch, for subjecting its citizens to the kind of persecution normally associated with the tyrannical states it was fighting: "While Canadians fought to liberate the people of the world from the tyranny of fascism, enslavement, and genocide, at home, Canada subjected some of its own citizens to the same kind of ethnic persecution practiced by the Axis powers."[60]

THE QUIET ANTI-SEMITISM OF
THE PROTESTANT CHURCHES

Since the Catholic church is so often vilified by "Canadian" commentators, because of its association with francophones, any fair-minded person would also want to take a look at the record of the Protestant churches. Where the wartime persecution of Jews is concerned, it is a fruitful comparison.

Alan Davies, a United Church minister and University of Toronto professor, together with Marilyn Nefsky, a sociologist at the University of Lethbridge, have rigorously analyzed official documents of the Protestant churches to find out how they reacted to the embargo on Jewish refugees. It appears there was no protest whatever against Ottawa's "none is too many" policy. Davies and Nefsky suggest that Canadian Protestantism possessed a subterranean current of anti-Semitism nourished by Anglo-British chauvinism.[61]

The United Church, by far the largest Protestant denomination, did deplore Germany's treatment of the Jews. Claris Silcox, one of its most liberal ministers, also favoured Jewish immigration. But even in the most liberal quarters there were limits: Silcox wanted to see quotas of Jewish medical students in Canadian universities.

Davies and Nefsky found consistently anti-Semitic reflexes among the Anglican clergy. Bishop A. C. Headlam, head of the Anglican council for foreign relations, condemned violence against Jews but usually found a way to blame the victims. Jews, he said, had provoked the violence of Soviet Communism, and their intellectuals had defamed the Christian faith.

Theologically speaking, Anglicans and United Church adherents alike believed that Jews could and should escape anti-Semitism by converting to Christianity.

The outcome of such attitudes was that, on an official level, the Anglican church condemned anti-Semitism and its excesses. But it nonetheless continued to prefer white Protestant immigration to Canada.

Mackenzie King was a Presbyterian. Here was another tactless sect. After Kristallnacht, Reverend John Inkster informed the powerful congregation of Knox Presbyterian Church in Toronto that the Jews could have avoided such unpleasantness by converting to Christianity.[62] Similar sentiments were heard from luminaries of the Baptist faith.

Lutherans were also notably silent on Nazi crimes. Many were of German or Scandinavian origin. The Mennonites, however, managed at least to condemn the cruelty of German anti-Semitism, though their principal reason for doing so was that it impeded their missionary efforts among Germany's Jews. Davies and Nefsky finally judge the Mennonites as harshly as the others, suggesting that they were fascinated by Nazi ideology and contaminated by an extreme anti-Semitism which held Jews responsible for all the major problems of the human race.

What a pretty society to presume to judge French Canada. Complacent, without even a decent trace of self-awareness, English Canada criticized the motes of dust dancing in the air of Quebec's Catholic Church, while blissfully unaware of the great slab of lumber stuck in its own eye.

ROOSEVELT'S PLAN TO SETTLE THE MATTER OF FRENCH CANADIANS AND JEWS

In 1942, in a letter to Mackenzie King, President Roosevelt proposed that Canada and the United States work together to assimilate the Jewish and French-speaking populations. It was essential that the agreed policy be carried out in secret. Roosevelt also confided to King that he hoped after the war to disperse the Jewish and Italian communities in New York, which in his view had grown too large and influential in a city emblematic of America.

When I was a boy in the "nineties," I used to see a good many French Canadians who had rather recently come into the New Bedford area, near the old Delano place, at Fair Haven. They seemed very much out of place in what was still an old New England community. They segregated

themselves in the mill towns and had little to do with
their neighbours. I can still remember that the old generation shook their heads and used to say, "this is a new
element which will never be assimilated. We are assimilating the Irish but these Quebec people won't even speak
English. Their bodies are here, but their hearts and minds
are in Quebec."

Today, forty or fifty years later, the French Canadian
elements in Maine, New Hampshire, Massachusetts and
Rhode Island are at last becoming a part of the American
melting pot. They no longer vote as their churches and
their societies tell them to. They are inter-marrying
with the original Anglo Saxon stock; they are good,
peaceful citizens, and most of them are speaking English
in their homes.

All of this leads me to wonder whether, by some sort of
planning, Canada and the United States, working toward
the same end, cannot do some planning – perhaps unwritten planning which would not even be a public policy – by
which we can hasten the objective of assimilating the
New England French Canadians and Canada's French
Canadians into the whole of our respective bodies politic.
There are, of course, many methods of doing this, which
depend on local circumstances. Wider opportunities can
perhaps be given to them in other parts of Canada and the
U.S.; and at the same time, certain opportunities can probably be given to non French Canadian stock to mingle
more greatly with them in their own centers.

In other words, after nearly two hundred years with
you and after seventy-five years with us, there would
seem to be no good reason for great differentials
between the French population elements and the rest of
the racial stocks.

It is on the same basis that I am trying to work out

> post-war plans for the encouragement of the distribution
> of certain other nationalities in our large congested
> centers. There ought not to be such a concentration of
> Italians and of Jews, and even of Germans as we have
> today in New York City. I have started my National
> Resources Planning Commission to work on a survey of
> this kind.[63]

ESCAPEES FROM THE NAZI HELL: "UNDESIRABLES" IN CANADA

On May 20, 1943, Frederick Blair had this to say to a Dutch diplomat who wondered whether there was room in Canada for Dutch Jews scattered in other European countries: "Jews and other undesirable elements will never be admitted to Canada."[64]

Many English Canadians had generously offered to shelter Jews during the war, but only on condition they return to Europe afterward. A prominent Winnipeg Jew described the situation this way to a friend in Toronto:

> They fear the question of [Jewish] immigration as much as the
> Devil is said to fear holy water. They are all in favor of Canada
> offering "sanctuary for refugees" at the present time, but they do
> not wish this issue to be confused with the question of opening
> the doors of Canada to non Anglo-Saxon immigrants after the war.
> Many of them are in favor of refugees, but opposed to
> immigrants.[65]

James H. Gray, then publisher of the *Winnipeg Free Press*, saw the issue clearly and mocked the hypocrisy of Canadians: "It is unfortunately but decidedly untrue to say that the people of Canada are unanimous in desiring to see justice done to the Jews. . . . It is unfortunately but decidedly untrue to say that they desire to see all measures taken to relieve the plight of the Jews."[66]

The Hanna (Alberta) *Herald* warned its readers against those who would open even a crack in the solid wall of regulations which barred Jewish immigration. Why, it asked, were Jews the most hated people on earth? It hastened to add that Christians and humanists should steer clear of anti-Semitism.

In 1953, the Canadian Legion led a campaign against European "undesirables" sneaking into Canada. The Legion hoped for a new influx of ruddy-cheeked Caledonians and stout Englishmen.

Pressure also came from provincial leaders. T. D. Patullo, British Columbia's premier in 1939, advised Mackenzie King that the province wanted as few Jews as possible (as always, history has gently erased the indiscretion, and Patullo's name today graces a bridge in New Westminster).

But there is no question that Ottawa outdid the provinces in infamy. Here, in the capital city of the largest free country on the planet and one of the most thinly populated, it was decided to admit just under 4,400 Jews, the smallest quota of any country:

United States	200,000
Palestine	125,000
Great Britain	70,000
Argentina	50,000
Brazil	27,000
China	25,000
Bolivia and Chile	14,000

Throughout the war the Canadian government did everything possible to soft-peddle this appalling decision. It even convinced the influential *New Republic* magazine that its refugee policy demonstrated Canada's sterling virtue. This was accomplished by emphasizing the large overall number of refugees admitted (39,000 since 1933) while quietly setting aside the fact that almost none were Jewish. The *New Republic* used the overall figure to reproach America for its failure to adopt a similar policy.

This was another case of the United States taking an indulgent attitude toward Canada. But this time Ottawa was exploiting American credulity through a sophisticated campaign of lies and disinformation. Irving Abella and Harold Troper demonstrate that the supposed 39,000 Europeans welcomed by a sheltering Canada included 25,000 Axis prisoners of war, 4,500 German interns who had been booted out of England, and 8,000 temporary British evacuees. To paraphrase Mark Twain, there are lies, damn lies, and statistics . . . and Canadian government statistics.

Frederick Blair retired in 1943 with the highest government honours. His successor, A. L. Joliffe, maintained the anti-Semitic immigration policy until 1949. These were Joliffe's thoughts three months after the end of the war:

> The claim is sometimes made that Canada's immigration laws
> reflect class and race discrimination: they do, and necessarily so.
> Some form of discrimination cannot be avoided if immigration is
> to be effectively controlled in order to prevent the creation in
> Canada of expanding non-assimilable racial groups, the prohibit-
> ing of entry to immigrants of non assimilable races is necessary.[67]

Of the 65,000 immigrants admitted to Canada in the post-war period (1945–48), only 8,000 were Jewish. Along with them came a number of Nazi war criminals who had poured out their souls to the British secret service and been rewarded with a new home in Canada.

Mackenzie King had misjudged Hitler before the war, and indicated some anti-Semitic leanings. Did he show remorse after the war?

No such luck. Take this entry in his diary, written in 1946, when the facts about the Holocaust had become well-known. It's a reflection on his former teacher, the fervent Jew-hater Goldwin Smith: "I recall [. . .] Smith feeling so strongly about the Jews. He expressed it at one time as follows: that they were poison in the veins of a community . . . the evidence is very strong, not against all Jews . . . that in a large percentage of the race, there are tendencies and trends which are dangerous indeed."[68]

How is it possible that a man considered a great Canadian prime minister can have been so unmoved in his beliefs by the death of six million innocents? Can it be said that he possessed a conscience? Compassion?

The following year, in 1947, the full extent of King's racial intransigence became apparent. The post-war boom had created a serious manpower shortage, and the government contemplated liberalizing immigration laws so that the net could be cast wider than Northern Europe and the Commonwealth – or at least, the white part of it. This was King's reaction, as he expressed it in the House of Commons:

> The people of Canada do not wish, as a result of mass immigration, to make a fundamental alteration in the character of our population.
> Large-scale immigration would change the fundamental composition of the Canadian population. And be certain to give rise to social and economic problems of a character that might lead to serious difficulties in the field of international relations.[69]

That year there was a momentary flexing in the exclusionary laws. By special ministerial decree, 500 Jewish Holocaust orphans were admitted to Canada. But the official policy barring Jewish immigration remained in force for another year. Only those "who possessed the ability to adjust" (coded language meaning racial exclusion) were allowed to establish themselves here.

All of this is consistent with the view that Canada, throughout almost its entire history, has been a preserve of white-skinned people. The English-speaking majority inherited the idea from Great Britain, and took care to build an elitist society from which the persecuted and the inappropriately pigmented were excluded.

It is not wrong to say that Mackenzie King and Frederick Blair were responsible for the deaths of thousands of men, women, and children. These desperate souls had come to a fork in the road, with one path leading to Canada and the other to the extermination camps. King and Blair barricaded the first road. It is thanks to them that this country has the most shameful record of all the democracies where the saving of refugees is concerned.

Irving Abella was interviewed for the documentary film *Toward a Just Society* (referred to earlier). He emphasized that "Canada had perhaps the most miserly record of any Western country, of any immigration country in providing a haven to Jewish refugees from Nazi terror during World War II and before World War II."[70]

And then Mackenzie King dared to shift part of his shame onto Quebec! He claimed that he had to slam the door on Jews fleeing the Nazis because of particular opposition from Quebec. Considering the ample evidence of English-Canadian bigotry, this is especially intolerable.

Of course it is true that after 200 years of overt British and Canadian attempts to drown Canada's French population in a wave of non-French-speaking immigrants, Quebec was wary of any immigration policy emanating from Ottawa. But how vile of King to pretend that these ancient feelings had anything to do with Jews in particular. All the more so if one remembers that French Canadians and Jews in Canada had suffered the same kind of discrimination. As Morton Weinfeld puts it:

> The Jews are a small minority within Quebec; but the Québécois are an equally small minority within a predominantly English-speaking continent. To understand the situation of Jews in Quebec, it is thus important to recognize that we have here not a classic minority-majority relationship, but rather one between two groups, each of which is deeply marked by minority traits. . . . Both groups share parallel histories of minority struggle and perceived victimization, including a common exclusion by a dominant Anglo-Saxon group from key economic and social sectors in Quebec.[71]

To conclude this especially sombre chapter on contemporary Canada, it seems wise to give careful consideration to Gérard Bouchard's presentation to the colloquium "Jews and French Canadians in Quebec Society." He is talking about Quebec, but his observations apply even more urgently to the country as a whole:

Canada has hurt its own international image by an incessant and many-voiced harangue which stereotypes Quebec as the home of xenophobia, intolerance, racism, and anti-Semitism, pretending that these are typical French-Canadian qualities. Many francophones have unhappily internalized this stereotype, often without realizing it. They have come to believe that this indeed is who they are. And any number of spokespersons for the Jewish community have helped in this enterprise. They have violently, and rightly, denounced the anti-Semitism of French Canadians during the 1920s and 1930s. But they have also closed their eyes to the very same vexations and prejudices when these came from English-speaking Quebeckers. . . .

It is not surprising that it [the Jewish community] has wished to make use of this connection [to the English-speaking elite] to promote its interests. That certainly explains the discreet downplaying of the bullying and the rebuffs it suffered en route. And when all is said and done – or so, at least, we believe – the Jewish elites have ended up adopting the Anglo-Saxon elite's views about French Canadians. And the direct outcome of that is that we have come to feel (and still feel today) that francophones are subject to a greater vigilance where anti-Semitism is concerned than are their English-speaking compatriots.[72]

EPILOGUE

The government-sponsored *Heritage Minutes* regularly seen on television are designed to give the impression of a French and English mutual-admiration society in Canada. They do acknowledge the occasional bump in the road, the tiniest misunderstandings. But overall the *Minutes* connive with English Canada's ignorance of the crimes which have marked its history. For Quebeckers, they perpetuate the myth of a harmonious country-building project undertaken by the two founding peoples.

Quebec has a culture and an identity which are very well-defined. This is less true of the country's other cultures. And this shortcoming explains the federal government's ambitious project to create a Canadian identity, a national glue with greater emotional bonding power than one can reasonably expect from a national health-insurance program. Ottawa's current interest in history is part of this larger undertaking.

For some years it has laboured mightily to bring forth a national history which can be agreeably read by the French, the English, and every other colourful tile in the national mosaic. This purported history would have to be truthful yet universally satisfying, denuded of all difficulty and yet free of platitudes and political correctness. The circle squared.

Such a history is quite impossible in Canada. How can there be a consensual history when in fact there are two national histories, each antagonistic to the other?

It is much easier, one supposes, to concoct rosewater TV capsules about great Canadians and eye-boggling accomplishments. To deal with matters infamous and unjust is much less pleasant and certainly less amenable to a sixty-second format.

Within a few years after the Conquest, French Canadians had already figured out where they fit into the idea the English were hatching. They undermined it by quickly mastering the Parliamentary system. Then came the uprisings of 1837–38, which put an end to what we might call the era of politeness. The Act of Union was a straitjacket meant to immobilize the French as a permanent minority.

In many ways the 1840s were not unlike the period we've been living in since the 1960s: both ended with an upsurge of Quebec national affirmation. Today the sovereignist strain of Quebec politics, much like the historic entente between Baldwin and Lafontaine, menaces the deep and unequal structure of the Canadian political edifice.

Certainly the Quiet Revolution threatened English domination. Its object, after all, was to build upon the well-developed Quebec identity a state entirely different from that of English Canada. It's not surprising that English Canada challenged this, and that a competition began between what Maryse Potvin has called "two projects predicated on universal rights."[1]

English Canada is thoroughly (and arrogantly) convinced of the moral superiority of the state it has built. It insists that its state is built on universal rights, and that which is emerging in Quebec is not. The result, of course, is the current stalemate of Canadian politics.

This in turn explains the pushing and shoving, the temper

tantrums, the racist outbursts, the evident bad faith and general excess of the English-Canadian conversation about Quebec.

The bad example was set at the top. Did not Trudeau employ his full eloquence before the U.S. Congress to denounce Quebec's possible independence as a crime against humanity?

In truth, the two national projects are morally equivalent. If any difference exists between them, it is only that Quebec can build upon a better-defined national identity than English Canada may. In fact, English Canada, to the extent it exists at all, is dissolving into American-ness right before our eyes, like one of those movie special effects where a man turns into smoke. Off to one side is the heritage minister in her pointed cap, waving a wand and muttering magic spells to bring him back. But instead the smoke blows away to Schenectady.

As for Quebec, only the muse of history can tell if those who took up Papineau's torch will ever succeed in creating their own country.

This overview of the dark side of Canadian history stops at the end of the First World War, insofar as French Canadians are concerned. It only incidentally touches upon the plight of the native people. There is a chapter apiece concerning the Jewish and Japanese communities, but that is not to suggest that the injustices toward natives, like those toward blacks and other immigrant communities, do not merit similar attention. They also were subject to exclusionary and discriminatory policies endorsed by the majority of Canadians.

It is my intention to devote a second book to the story of these communities, and to pick up the tale of French Canada and carry it forward from 1920 to the present day. It will also examine the Canadian Ku Klux Klan and the racist extreme right, a phenomenon which today belongs almost exclusively to English Canada.

Normand Lester,
Outremont, October 2001

ENDNOTES

PROLOGUE

1. Allan Fotheringham, *Maclean's*, October 30, 1995, p. 88.
2. Ibid.
3. Barbara Amiel, *Maclean's*, June 1997; cited in Pierre Frisko and Jean Simon Gagné, "Le Québec vu par le Canada anglais: La Haine," *Voir*, vol. 12, no. 24, June 18, 1998, p. 12.
4. See Maryse Potvin's interesting analysis in "Les Dérapages racistes à l'égard du Québec au Canada anglais depuis 1995," *Politique et sociétés*, vol. 18, no. 2, 1999.
5. James McPherson, *Saturday Night*, March 1998.
6. William Johnson, *The Gazette*, September 1996; cited in P. Frisko and J. S. Gagné, op. cit.
7. Christopher Neal, *Cité libre*, February–March 1998; cited in P. Frisko and J. S. Gagné, op. cit.
8. Diane Francis, "Readers Support Tough Stance Against Quebec Separatists," *The Financial Post*, July 4, 1996; cited in Jean-Paul Marchand, *Conspiration? Les Anglophones veulent-ils éliminer le français du Canada?* Montreal, Stanké, 1997, p. 217.

9. *The Financial Post*, October 7, 1999, cited in J.-P. Marchand, op. cit., p. 217.

10. Diane Francis, *Fighting for Canada*, Toronto, Key Porter Press, 1996, p. 184–85.

11. *Le Soleil*, October 16, 1996; cited in J.-P. Marchand, op. cit., pp. 82–86.

12. Ray Conlogue, interviewed by Carole Beaulieu, "C'est la culture . . . stupid!" *L'Actualité*, March 15, 1997; accessible on <www.vigile.net/pol/culture/beaulieuconlogue.html>.

13. J.-P. Marchand, op. cit., pp. 112–13.

14. R. Conlogue, interviewed by Carole Beaulieu, op. cit.

15. Diane Francis, *The Financial Post*, November 14, 1995; cited in J.-P. Marchand, op. cit., p. 217.

16. Mark Bonokoski, *Ottawa Sun*, September 1997; cited in P. Frisko and J. S. Gagné, op. cit.

17. *Globe and Mail*, August 25, 1997, pp. A1, A4; cited in M. Potvin, "Les Dérapages racistes," *Politique et Sociétés* vol. 18 no. 2, 1999, p. 119.

18. *Globe and Mail*, August 30, 1997; cited in M. Potvin, op. cit., p. 122.

19. Jean Paré, "Opération Salissage," *L'Actualité*, March 1, 1997; cited in J.-P. Marchand, op. cit., p. 108.

20. Luc Chartrand, "Les 'Rhodésiens' masqués: Les Cercles de droite du Canada anglais sont en train d'inventer un racisme subtil, politiquement correct!" *L'Actualité*, April 15, 2000.

21. J.-P. Marchand, op. cit., p. 108.

22. Pierre Foglia, "Faut arreter de freaker," *La Presse*, December 16, 2000.

23. Ibid.

24. In a subsequent interview, Cotler noted that he did not receive the score. See also R. Conlogue, "Oh Canada, Oh Quebec, Oh Richler," *Globe and Mail*, June 26, 2002. Tr.

25. Mordecai Richler, *Oh Canada! Oh Quebec! Requiem for a Divided Country*, New York, Alfred A. Knopf, 1992, p. 88. Of the 103 works cited by Richler as references, only three are in French.

26. Gary Caldwell, "La Controverse Deslisle–Richler. Le Discours sur l'antisémitisme au Québec et l'orthodoxie néo-libérale au Canada," *L'Agora*, June 1994, vol. 1, no. 9; available on <www.agora.qc.ca/liens/gcaldwell.html>.

27. M. J. Milloy, "Rebel Without a Cause: A Response to the Politics of Pierre Falardeau's *15 Février 1839*," *Hour*, January 28, 2001.

28. Interview with Anna Terrana, federal Liberal Member from Vancouver, *Vancouver Sun*, July 1996; cited in P. Frisko and J. S. Gagné, op. cit.

29. J.-P. Marchand, op. cit., pp. 112–13.

30. Robert Lecker, *Saturday Night*, July/August 1996; cited in P. Frisko and J. S. Gagné, op. cit.

31. *The Suburban*, September 3, 1997, p. A1; cited in M. Potvin, op. cit., p. 117.

32. M. Potvin, op. cit. p. 117.

33. Michael Harris, *The Toronto Sun*, May 1998; cited in P. Frisko and J. S. Gagné, op. cit.

34. John Robson, "Why Levine Must Go," *Ottawa Citizen*, May 22, 1998; cited in M. Potvin, op. cit., p. 125.

35. *Ottawa Citizen*, May 21, 1998; cited in M. Potvin, op. cit., p. 127.

36. M. Potvin, op. cit., p. 108.

37. Robert Bothwell and J. L. Granatstein, *Our Century: The Canadian Journey in the Twentieth Century*, Toronto: McArthur & Co., 2001.

38. Anthony Appleblatt, *Saskatchewan and the Ku Klux Klan*; cited on <www.usask.ca/education/ideas/tplan/sslp/kkk.htm>.

Chapter 1: Payback Time

1. Acadie: Esquisse d'un parcours; Sketches of Journey; cited on <www.collections.ic.gc.ca/acadian/english/exile/exile.htm> and <www.publicbookshelf.org/public_html/Our_Country_Vol_1/ grandpre_bag.html>.

2. Cited in Jacques Lacoursière, *Histoire populaire du Québec*, vol. 1 (*Des origines à 1791*), Sillery, Septentrion, 1995, pp. 265–66.

3. Cited in Émery Leblanc, *Les Acadiens*, Montréal, Éditions de l'Homme, 1963, pp. 18–19.

4. Jean Daigle, "La déportation des Acadiens," *Horizon Canada*, vol. 1, no. 12, Saint-Laurent, Centre d'étude en enseignement du Canada, 1984, p. 267.

5. Letter from Charles Lawrence to the authorities in London; cited on <www.multimania.com/digagnon/raymonde.htm>. [This site has since been moved to <membres.lycos.fr/digagnon/raymonde.htm>. *Tr.*]

6. François Baby, "Fallait-il sauver le soldat Monckton de l'oubli?" *L'Action nationale*, August 1999; cited on <www.action-nationale.qc.ca/acadie/baby.html>. François Baby's article is worth citing at full length!

7. Ibid.

8. Cited in Naomi Griffiths, "The Acadian Deportation; Causes and Development," University of London (doctoral thesis), 1969, p. 176.

9. F. Baby, op. cit.

10. Cited in Dudley LeBlanc, *The Acadian Miracle*, Lafayette, Louisiana, Evangeline Pub. Co., 1966, p. 174.

11. F. Baby, op. cit. [The definition of genocide according to the UN Resolution 260 is in fact slightly different. *Tr.*]

12. The text of this letter can be read on the site <www.vigile.net/999/gervaismonckton.html>. [This page is no longer accessible. *Tr.*]

13. F. Baby, op. cit.

14. Ibid.

15. Mario Bettati, *Le Droit d'ingérence, mutation de l'ordre international* (The Right to interfere: Evolution of the international order), Paris, Éditions Odile Jacob, 1996, p. 275, cited in F. Baby, op. cit.

16. *Dictionary of Canadian Biography*, vol. 4, Toronto, University of Toronto Press, 1979, p. 540.

17. Cited in M. Bettati, op. cit., p. 298.

18. F. Baby, op. cit.

19. Cited in F. Baby, op. cit.

20. Stuart Reid, *Wolfe: The Career of General James Wolfe from Culloden to Quebec*, Cambridge, Mass., Da Capo Press, 2000, pp. 180–81.

21. Laurier Lapierre is a curious fellow who speaks English with a French accent and French with an English accent. He spent his career prettifying Canadian history, and there's little doubt he'll be rewarded with a Senate seat.

22. It won't be until 1952 that there will be another Canadian-born governor general, Vincent Massey.

23. Carl Waldman, *Atlas of the North American Indian*, New York, Facts on File, 1985, p. 106: cited in Peter d'Errico, <www.nativeweb. org/pages/legal/amherst/lord jeff.html>.

24. Patrick Couture, a teacher in Quebec, has a biographical sketch of Pontiac at <www.geocities.com/Athens/Ithaca/7318/PONTIAC.HTM> [This is now at<membres.lycos.fr/cousture.PONTIAC.HTM>. *Tr.*]

25. J. C. Long, *Lord Jeffrey Amherst: A Soldier of the King*, New York, Macmillan, 1933, pp. 186–87; cited in Peter d'Errico, op. cit.

26. This, along with the quotations from letters in the following paragraphs, are mentioned on Peter d'Errico's Web site: <www.nativeweb.org/pages/legal/amherst/lord jeff.html>.

27. Francis Parkman, *The Conspiracy of Pontiac and the Indian War After the Conquest of Canada*, Boston, Little, Brown, 1886, vol. 2, p. 39 (6th edition); cited in P. d'Errico, op. cit.

28. These letters are also reproduced on P. d'Errico's Web site.

29. This was a contemporary term for light cavalry.

30. Robert L. O'Connell, *Of Arms and Men: A History of War, Weapons, and Aggression*. New York and Oxford, Oxford University Press, 1989; cited in P. d'Errico, op. cit.

31. M. Wade, *The French Canadians: 1760–1967*, vol. 1, p. 49.

32. Ibid., pp. 52–53.

33. Denis Vaugeois and Jacques Lacoursière, *Canada–Québec. Synthèse historique*, Montreal, Éditions du renouveau pédagogique, 1973, p. 210.

34. Marcel Trudel, *La Révolution américaine, 1775–1783*, Sillery, Les Éditions du Boréal Express Inc., 1976, p. 55.

35. Ibid., p. 66.

CHAPTER 2: "BRITISH LIBERTIES," 1791–1811

1. Fernand Ouellet, *Le Bas-Canada, 1791–1840, changements structuraux et crises*, Ottawa, Éditions Université d'Ottawa, 1980, pp. 31–32. Also Denis Vaugeois, *Québec 1792: Les Acteurs, les institutions et les frontières*, Montréal, Éditions Fides, 1992, p. 66.

2. Louis-Joseph Papineau, *Histoire de la Résistance du Canada au gouvernement anglais*, Montreal, Comeau & Nadeau, 2001, p. 44.
3. Cited in Fernand Ouellet, op. cit., p. 21.
4. John Hare, *Aux origines du parlementarisme québécois, 1791–93*, Québec, Éditions Septentrion, 1993, p. 54.
5. Cited in Jean-Pierre Wallot, *Un Québec qui bougeait: trame socio-politique au tournant du XIXe siècle*, Sillery, Éditions Boréal Express Inc., 1973, p. 271.
6. Cited in ibid., p. 64.
7. J. Lacoursière and C. Bouchard, *Notre histoire, Québec–Canada*, Montréal, Éditions Format, 1972, p. 399.
8. *Le Canadien*, November 29, 1806, text attributed to Pierre Bédard, in J.-P. Wallot, op. cit.
9. *Quebec Mercury*, July 18, 1808.
10. F. Murray Greenwood, *Legacies of Fear: Law and Politics in Quebec in the Era of the French Revolution*, Toronto, University of Toronto Press, 1993, p. 222.
11. Letter of Monsignor Plessis, October 11, 1810.
12. Quoted in J.-P. Wallot, op. cit., p. 66.
13. This was erroneously given as Murray in the original. *Tr.*
14. Mason Wade, *The French Canadians, 1760–1945*, Toronto, Macmillan, 1955.
15. Ibid., p. 110.
16. Ibid., p. 111.
17. F. M. Greenwood, op. cit., p. 245.
18. M. Wade, op. cit., p. 113.

CHAPTER 3: THE BRITISH ASSASSINATE FREEDOM IN LOWER CANADA, 1820–1838

1. George Bell, *Rough Notes By an Old Soldier*, London, G. Bell & Sons, 1956, p. 162.
2. Jacques Lacoursière, *Histoire populaire du Québec*, vol. 2, Québec, Septentrion, 1997, pp. 208–9.

3. Allan Greer, *Habitants et Patriotes*, Montreal, Boréal, 1997, p. 121.

4. Quoted in Jacques Lacoursière, op. cit., p. 299.

5. Quoted in Jean-Paul de Lagrave, *Les Journalistes-démocrates au Bas-Canada (1791–1840)*, Montréal, Éditions de Lagrave, 1975, pp. 166–67.

6. *Gazette*, June 13, 1837; quoted in André Lefebvre, *La Montréal Gazette et le nationalisme canadien (1835–1842)*, Montréal, Guérin éditeur, 1970, p. 4.

7. Ibid., p. 1.

8. Ibid., p. 10.

9. Ibid., p. 35.

10. Ibid., p. 78.

11. *Gazette*, December 5, 1935; cited in ibid., p. 75.

12. *Gazette*, October 25, 1841; cited in ibid., p. 97.

13. Position adopted by the Montreal Constitutional Association, as expressed by Adam Thom in the *Gazette*, September 9, 1837.

14. *Gazette*, November 16, 1837, cited in Lefebvre, *La Montréal Gazette*.

15. *Gazette*, August 16, 1836; cited in ibid.

16. *Gazette*, August 1, 1835; cited in ibid.

17. *The Sherbrooke Farmer's Advocate*, ; cited in ibid., p. 157.

18. *Gazette*, March 24, 1836; cited in ibid., p. 157.

19. Gérard Filteau, *Histoire des Patriotes*, Quebec, Éditions l'Aurore/Univers, 1980, p. 260.

20. Quoted in J.-P. de Lagrave, op. cit., pp. 172–77.

21. Quoted in J. Lacoursière, op. cit., vol. 2, p. 299.

22. Quoted in Kyte Senior Elinor, *Les Habits rouges et les Patriotes*, Montréal, VLB Éditeur, 1997, p. 128.

23. G. Filteau, op. cit., p. 370.

24. M. Wade, op. cit., p. 185.

25. Ibid.

26. Quoted in G. Filteau, op. cit., p. 388.

27. M. Wade, op. cit., p. 190.

28. Ibid.

29. *The Montreal Herald*, November 14, 1838, cited in A, Lefebvre, op. cit.

30. Cited in L.-J. Papineau, op. cit., p. 38.

31. L.-J. Papineau, op. cit., pp. 55–56. (Footnotes in Hubert Aquin's edition, Leméac, 1968.)

32. Ibid., pp. 41–42.

33. M. Wade, op. cit., p. 183.

34. L.-J. Papineau, op. cit., p. 43.

35. M. Wade, op. cit., p. 206.

36. Ed. Gerald M. Craig, *Lord Durham's Report*, Toronto, McClelland & Stewart, 1963, p. 40.

37. Ibid., p. 23.

38. M. Wade, op. cit., p. 197.

Chapter 4: Montreal, 1849: The *Gazette* Calls for a "Racial Uprising"

1. Montreal *Gazette*, March 7, 1840, quoted in A. Lefebvre, op. cit., p. 171.

2. Quoted in A. Lefebvre, op. cit., p. 187.

3. *Missisquoi Standard*, reproduced in the Montreal *Gazette*, June 16, 1838; quoted in A. Lefebvre, op. cit., p. 187.

4. "A Staff Surgeon" (pseudonym of W. Henry), *Trifle from My Portfolio*; quoted in A. Lefebvre, op. cit., p. 187.

5. Montreal *Gazette*, October 27, 1838; quoted in A. Lefebvre, op. cit., p. 185.

6. Montreal *Gazette*, November 28, 1839; quoted in A. Lefebvre, op. cit., p. 185.

7. M. Wade, op. cit., p. 269.

8. Lionel Groulx, quoted in A. Lefebvre, op. cit., pp. 45–46.

9. *The Morning Courier*, February 15, 1849, cited in ibid.

10. Quoted in J. Lacoursière, op. cit., p. 45.

11. Extra of the *Gazette*, April 25, 1849, quoted in translation in Joseph Royal, *Histoire du Canada, 1841–1867*, Montréal, Beauchemin, 1909, pp. 308–310. Reproduced in *Une Capitale éphémère. Montréal et les événements tragiques de 1849*, texts assembled and presented by Gaston Deschênes, Sillery, Septentrion, 1999, pp. 100–104.

12. L. Groulx, quoted in G. Deschênes (ed.), op. cit., p. 51.

13. *Dictionary of Canadian Biography*, vol. 9, Toronto, University of Toronto Press, 1976, p. 258.

14. Clayton Gray, *Le Vieux Montréal*, Montreal, Éditions du Jour, 1964.

15. *La Minerve*, April 26, 1849, cited in A. Lefebvre, op. cit.

16. L. Groulx, quoted in ibid., p. 58.

17. C. Gray, op. cit., p. 67.

18. Gilles Gallichan in *Documentation et bibliothèques*, vol.36, no.1 (April–June 1990); quoted in G. Deschênes, op. cit., p. 97. This is the source of all my information about the parliamentary libraries.

19. *The London News*, June 11, 1849; quoted in G. Deschênes, op. cit., p. 96.

20. M. Wade, op. cit., p. 272.

21. L. Groulx, quoted in G. Deschênes, op. cit., pp. 73–74.

22. Hector Berthelot and Edouard-Zotique Massicotte, *Montréal, le bon vieux temps*, Beauchemin, 1916; quoted in G. Deschênes, op. cit., pp. 84–85.

23. Open letter by Guy Bouthillier, president of the SSJB, to John Ralston Saul, July 5, 2000.

24. G. Deschênes, op. cit.

25. Frederic D. Schwarz, *Awful Disclosures*, American Heritage, September 1999: <www.americanheritage.com/99/sep/timemachine/1849.htm>.

26. Ibid.

CHAPTER 5: THE HANGING OF LOUIS RIEL: A STATE CRIME

1. Donald Sprague, *Canada and the Métis, 1869–1885*, Waterloo, Wilfrid Laurier University Press, 1986, p. 82.

2. "Metis Nation History: Metis Culture 1869," <www.telusplanet.net/public/dgarneau/metis48.htm>.

3. J. Lacoursière and C. Bouchard, op. cit., p. 623.

4. Ibid.

5. Donald Sprague, op. cit., p. 89.

6. M. Wade, op. cit., p. 402.

7. Ibid., p. 403.

8. *Dictionary of Canadian Biography*, vol. 11, Toronto, University of Toronto Press, 1982, p. 743.

9. M. Wade, op cit., pp. 404–5.

10. *The Canadian Encyclopedia*, Toronto, McClelland & Stewart, 1999, p. 1655.

11. Quoted in Adolphe Ouimet and B. A. T. de Montigny, *Riel: La Vérité sur la question métisse*, Bibliotek multimédia: <www.microtec.net/~iandavid>. The original edition of this work was a manifesto published in 1889 under the title *La Vérité sur la question métisse au Nord-Ouest*.

12. "A Rebellion Diary," *Alberta Historical Review*, vol. 13, 1964.

13. Quoted in R. Rumilly, *Histoire de la province de Québec*, Montréal, Éditions Bernard Valiquette, vol. 5, p. 37.

14. Ibid., p. 36.

15. George R. D. Goulet, *The Trial of Louis Riel, Justice and Mercy Denied*, Calgary, Telwell Publishing, 2001, 1999, p. 45.

16. Quoted in R. Rumilly, op. cit., p. 46.

17. Ibid., p. 48.

18. Ibid., p. 63.

19. George Stanley, "Louis Riel," *Revue d'histoire de l'Amérique française*, vol. 18, no. 1, June 1964, Institut d'histoire de l'Amérique française. This excellent text is available on the Institute's Web site: <www.pages.infinit.net/histoire/riel.html>.

20. R. Rumilly, op. cit., p. 66.

21. Both cited ibid., p. 65.

22. Quoted in R. Rumilly, op. cit., p. 81.

23. G. Goulet, op. cit., p. 228.

24. Ibid., pp. 230–31.

25. Ibid.

26. Both quoted in R. Rumilly, op. cit., p. 102.

27. G. Stanley, op. cit.

28. R. Rumilly, op. cit., p. 111.

29. Ibid., p. 119.

30. M. Wade, op. cit., pp. 419–20.

31. R. Rumilly, op. cit., pp. 123–24.

32. Jean-Guy Rens, *L'Empire invisible*, Quebec, Presses de l'Université du Québec, 1993, vol. 1, ch. 2. Extract published on the Internet at <www.sciencetech.com/rech/th3.htm>.

33. Quoted in Daniel German, "The Political Game and the Bounds of Personal Honour: Sir Frederick Middleton and the Bremner Furs," *Saskatchewan History*, vol. 65, no. 1 (spring 1993), p. 14.

34. Ibid., p. 15.

35. *The Daily Witness* (Montreal), April 24, 1890; quoted in D. German, op. cit.

36. Chris Madsen, "Military Law, the Canadian Militia, and The North-West Rebellion of 1885," *Journal of Military and Strategic Studies*, University of Calgary, Spring 1998, <www.stratnet.ucalgary.ca/journal/1998/article5.html> (among the hundred works cited in the article's index, there is not one that was written in French).

37. G. Stanley, op. cit.

38. Ibid.

39. Alex Rough, *Canadian Orangeism: A Military Beginning*, 1991, <www.members.tripod.com/~Roughian/index-97.html>.

40. Dominic Di Stasi, *Orangeism: The Canadian Scene: A Brief Historical Sketch*, July 1995, <www.orangenet.org/stasi/htm>.

41. Ibid.

42. Information on links between fascist and Orange organizations can be found in a newsletter from Anti-Fascist Action – Stockholm, International News, February 25, 2001. The communiqué is available at <www.hafa-stockholm.antifa.net/nyheter/e01/eN0101225.htm#church>. [The Web site now appears to be inoperative. Tr.]

43. <www.grandorange.org.uk/choose.htm>.

CHAPTER 6: A HALF-CENTURY OF INFAMY, 1867–1918

1. Montreal *Gazette*, April 26, 1917; quoted in R. Rumilly, *Histoire de la province du Québec*, Montréal, Éditions Bernard, Valiquette, vol. 22, p. 57.

2. M. Wade, op. cit., p. 331.

3. *La Minerve*, July 1, 1867; quoted in J. Lacoursière, *Histoire populaire du Québec, 1841–1896*, pp. 191–92.

4. *The Globe*, July 1, 1867; quoted in J. Lacoursière, op. cit., p. 191.

5. George F. G. Stanley, *Acadiensis*, vol. 2, no. 1 (1972–73), pp. 21–38.

6. R. Rumilly, op. cit., vol. 6, p. 228.

7. M. Wade, op. cit., p. 423.

8. Ibid.

9. Quoted in J. Lacoursière and C. Bouchard, op. cit., p. 686.

10. Quoted in ibid., p. 688.

11. Quoted in ibid., p. 686.

12. R. Rumilly, op. cit., vol. 6, p. 74.

13. Speech given in Sohmer Park, April 4, 1893, in the BNQ electronic library.

14. R. Rumilly, op. cit., vol. 6, p. 264.

15. Quoted in Elizabeth Armstrong, *Le Québec et la crise de la conscription, 1917–1918*, Montréal, VLB Éditeur, 1998, p. 126.

16. Quoted in R. Rumilly, op. cit., vol. 7, p. 133.

17. Quoted in J. Lacoursière and C. Bouchard, op. cit., p. 720.

18. Quoted in R. Rumilly, op. cit., vol. 9, p. 178.

19. Ibid., p. 179.

20. Ibid., p. 123.

21. M. Wade, op. cit., p. 486.

22. Ibid.

23. Ibid., pp. 498, 505.

24. *The Toronto News*, November 8, 1900; quoted in R. Rumilly, op. cit., vol. 9, p. 261.

25. Quoted in J. Lacoursière and C. Bouchard, op. cit., p. 798.

26. Ibid., pp. 798–99.

27. Gérard Filteau, *Le Québec, le Canada et la guerre 1914–1918*, Montréal, Éditions de l'Aurore, 1977, p. 21.

28. *Dictionary of Candian Biography*, vol. 14, Toronto, University of Toronto Press, 1998, p. 1061.

29. M. Wade, op. cit., p. 638.

30. Ibid.

31. Ibid.

32. Quoted in G. Filteau, op. cit., p. 78.

33. M. Wade, op. cit., p. 653.

34. Ibid.

35. E. Armstrong, *The Crisis of Quebec, 1914–1918*, Toronto, McClelland & Stewart, 1974, pp. 121–22.

36. Quoted in J. Lacoursière and C. Bouchard, op. cit., p. 827.

37. Quoted in M. Wade, op. cit., vol. 2, p. 117.

38. J. Lacoursière and C. Bouchard, op. cit., p. 814 (French ed.)

39. Ibid., pp. 814–15 (French ed.).

40. G. Filteau, op. cit., p. 114.

41. R. Rumilly, op. cit., vol. 22, pp. 118–19.

42. Quoted in M. Wade, op. cit., vol. 2, p. 117 (French ed.).

43. Quoted in G. Filteau, op. cit., p. 118.

44. Ibid., pp. 118–19.

45. Quoted in J. Lacoursière, op. cit., p. 122.

46. M. Wade, op. cit., p. 751.

47. Ibid., p. 752.

48. E. Armstrong, op. cit., p. 208.

49. M. Wade, op. cit., p. 756.

50. G. Filteau, op. cit., p. 117.

51. Quoted in M. Wade, op. cit., pp. 754–55.

52. Ibid., pp. 756–57.

53. *Le Soleil*, December 22, 1917.

54. R. Rumilly, op. cit., vol. 23, p. 73.

55. G. Filteau, op. cit., p. 161.

56. *Les 30 journées qui ont fait le Québec. Le 24 juillet 1917. La Loi de la conscription.* Eurêka! Productions: <www.eureka-tv.com/francais/Realisations/television/30JourneesQuiOntFaitLeQuebec/Conscription1.htm>.

57. See *Québec: Printemps 1918* <www.telegraphe.com/printemps1918/index.html>. [The monument has since been completed. *Tr.*]

58. R. Rumilly, op. cit., vol. 23, pp. 76–77.

59. G. Filteau, op. cit., pp. 162–63.

CHAPTER 7: ANTI-JAPANESE CRIMES

1. The quotations in this chapter are drawn from the bibliography prepared by Linda Di Biase and Douglas Yancey, librarians of the University of Washington, and presented on the following Web site: <www.lib.washington.edu/subject/Canada/internment/intro.html>.

2. Cited in Ken Adachi, *The Enemy That Never Was: A History of the Japanese Canadians*, Toronto, McClelland & Stewart Ltd., 1977, p. 65.

3. Tom MacInnes, *Oriental Occupation of British Columbia*, Vancouver, Sun Publishing Co., 1927, p. 133.

4. Muriel Kitagawa, *This Is My Own: Letters to Wes & Other Writings on Japanese Canadians, 1941–1948*, Vancouver, Talonbooks, 1995, p. 9.

5. Ibid., pp. 9–10.

6. Genshichi Takahashi, quoted in Keibo Oiwa, *Stone Voices: Wartime Writings of Japanese Canadian Issei*, Montreal, Véhicule Press, 1991, p. 192.

7. Roy Miki and Cassandra Kobayashi, *Justice in our Time, The Japanese Canadian Redress Settlement*, Vancouver, Talonbooks, 1991, p. 81.

8. W. Peter Ward, *White Canada Forever: Popular Attitudes and Public Policy Toward Orientals in British Columbia*, Montreal, McGill/Queen's University Press, second edition, 1990.

9. Maryka Omatsu, *Bittersweet Passage: Redress and the Japanese Canadian Experience*, Toronto, Between The Lines, 1992.

CHAPTER 8: ENGLISH-STYLE ANTI-SEMITISM

1. H. W. Koch, *The Origins of the First World War*, New York, Taplinger Publishing Co., 1972, p. 349.

2. Lita-Rose Betcheman, *The Swastika and the Maple Leaf: Fascist Movements in Canada in the Thirties*, Don Mills, Fitzhenry & Whiteside, 1975, p. 45.

3. Ibid., pp. 51–52.

4. Gerald Tulchinsky, *Taking Root: The Origins of the Canadian Jewish Community*, Lester Publishing Limited, Toronto, 1992. pp. 231–38.

5. Richard Menkis, *From Immigration to Integration, The Canadian Jewish Experience: A Millennium*, published on the B'nai Brith Web site: <www.bnaibrith.ca/institute/millennium/millennium03.html>.

6. These campaigns targeted Jews. *Tr.*

7. Stephen Speisman, *The Jews of Toronto: A History to 1937*, Toronto, McClelland & Stewart, 1987, p. 322.

8. Ibid., p. 321.

9. Cyril H. Levitt and William Shaffir, *The Riot at Christie Pits*, Toronto, Lester & Orpen Dennys, 1987.

10. Karen R. Mock, *Countering Anti-Semitism and Hate in Canada Today*, The Nizkor Project, <www.nizkor.org/hweb/people/m/mock-Karen/countering-hate.html>.

11. L.-R. Betcheman, op. cit., pp. 51–52.

12. Ibid., p. 45.

13. Ibid., p. 100.

14. C. H. Levitt and W. Shaffir, op. cit.

15. S. Speisman, op. cit., p. 335.

16. Irving Abella and Harold Troper, *None Is Too Many*, Toronto, Lester and Orpen Dennys, 1983, p. xxx.

17. L.-R. Betcheman, op. cit., p. 102.

18. Ibid., p. 103.

19. I. Abella and H. Troper, op. cit. (Introduction to the 1986 edition), p. xi.

20. Richard Menkis, op. cit.

21. Benoît Lacroix and Stéphane Stapinsky, "Lionel Groulx: Actualité et relecture," *Les Cahiers histoires du Québec au vingtième siècle*, no. 8, <www.vigile.net/groulx/cahiers8pres1.html>.

22. Jacques Brassier, "Lionel Groulx," *L'Action nationale*, April 1993; cited in Gary Caldwell, "La Controverse Delisle–Richler: Le Discours sur l'antisémitisme au Québec et l'orthodoxie néo-libérale au Canada," *L'Agora*, vol. 1, no. 9, June 1994.

23. G. Caldwell, op. cit., p. 242.

24. Pierre Anctil, Ira Robinson, and Gérard Bouchard (eds.), *Juifs et Canadiens français dans la société québécoise* (conference proceedings), Sillery, Édition du Septentrion, 2000, p. 23.

25. James Gray, *The Winter Years: The Depression on the Prairies*, Toronto, Macmillan, 1966, p. 185.

26. Dave Renton, *Fascism and Anti-Fascism in Britain*, <www.dkrenton.co.uk/trent2.html>. Renton is a [former] senior lecturer in the history department of Edge Hill College. [*Tr.*]

27. Ibid.

28. For further information on this subject, see: John Costello, *Mask of Treachery: Spies, Lies, and Betrayal*, revised and updated, New York, Warner Books, 1990; Anthony Cave Brown, *Treason in the Blood*, New York, Houghton Mifflin, 1994; John Costello and O. Tsarev, *Deadly Illusions*, New York, Crown Publishers, 1993.

29. Paul Lashmer, "Revealed: Nazis' Friends Inside the British Elite," *The Independent*, Sunday, January 9, 2000.

30. Marc La Terreur, *Les Tribulations des conservateurs au Québec, de Bennett à Diefenbaker*, Québec, Presses de l'Université Laval, 1979, p. 11.

31. The current dollar figures were calculated with the aid of indexes from the Bank of Canada Web site: <www.bank-banque-canada.ca/en/inflation_calc.htm>.

32. The letter is located in the Bennett Collection of the National Archives of Canada in Ottawa. There is also a photocopy in the archives of the Canadian Jewish Congress in Montreal. Unless otherwise stipulated, all letters quoted may be founded in the CJC archives in Montreal, under the designation P0005 ARCAND, Adrien (collection).

33. Marc La Terreur, op. cit., p. 24.

34. Martin Robin, *Shades of Right: Nativist and Fascist Politics in Canada, 1920–1940*, Toronto, University of Toronto Press, 1992, p. 118.

35. L.-R. Betcheman, op. cit., p. 37.

36. Ibid., p. 45.

37. Correspondence between P. E. Blondin and R. B. Bennett, quoted in Martin Robin, op. cit.

38. *Globe and Mail*, January 5, 1938; quoted in L.-R. Betcheman, op. cit., p. 109.

39. Frederick Edwards, "Fascism in Canada," *Maclean's*, April 15, 1938, p. 66.

40. Ibid., p. 68.

41. Letter of Adrien Arcand to Daniel Johnson, Collection Adrien Arcand, Vanier Library, Concordia University, Montreal.

42. L.-R. Betcheman, op. cit., p. 127.

43. Quoted in the *National Post*, July 30, 2001, p. A12.

44. "*Goglu*," the name of one of Arcand's newspapers, is the French word for the bird which is called "bobolink" in English.

45. M. Robin, op. cit., p. 109.

46. Ibid.

47. Personal diary of Mackenzie King, p. 487a.

48. Luc Bertrand, *L'Énigmatique Mackenzie King*, Vanier, Les Éditions L'Interligne, 2000, p. 70.

49. Ibid., p. 75.

50. Quoted in L. Bertrand, op. cit., p. 83.

51. Unless otherwise indicated, all excerpts from Mackenzie King's diaries have been taken from I. Abella and H. Troper, *None Is Too Many*.

52. Quoted in Jean Gerber, "Too Close to Home," *Canadian Jewish News*, April 19, 2001, <www.cjnews.com/pastissues/01/apr19-01/features/feature1.htm>.

53. Quoted in I. Abella and H. Troper, op. cit., p. 37.

54. Luc Chartrand, "Dis-moi la verité! Le Mythe du Québec fasciste," *L'Actualité*, vol. 22, no. 3, March 1, 1997.

55. This description of Canadian immigration policy regarding Jews (1935–1945) is based on I. Abella and H. Troper's *None Is Too Many*.

56. L.-R. Betcheman, op. cit., p. 133.

57. I. Abella and H. Troper, op. cit., p. 230.

58. Ibid., p. 35.

59. *Toward a Just Society*, produced and directed by David A. Stein for the Canadian Council of Christians and Jews. The transcription of the video can be found at <www.interlog.com/~cccj/JustSociety/Default.html>.

60. Ibid.

61. Alan T. Davies, *How Silent Were the Churches? Canadian Protestantism and the Jewish Plight During the Nazi Era*, Wilfrid Laurier University Press, 1997; quoted in Sheldon Kirshner, "The Kirshner File," *The Canadian Jewish News*, April 23, 1998.

62. A misguided view: Hitler's policy was based on eugenics and directed against racial Jews, hence the killing of the Jewish-born nun, Saint Edith Stein, in Auschwitz [Tr.].

63. Quoted by Richard Cléroux in a column of May 12, 1998, on Canoe, <www.canoe.ca/CNEWSPoliticsColumns/may12_cleroux2.html>. [This link is now removed. Tr.]

64. I. Abella and H. Troper, op. cit., p. 147.

65. Ibid., p. 159.

66. Ibid.

67. Ibid., p. 199.

68. Quoted in G. Tulchinsky, op. cit., p. 238.

69. Quoted in the chronology of the Canadian Council for Refugees on <www.web.nct/~ccr/history.html>.

70. *Toward a Just Society*, op. cit.

71. Morton Weinfeld, *The Jews of Quebec*, quoted in Xavier Gélinas, *Notes on Anti-Semitism among Quebec Nationalists, 1920–1970: Methodological Failings, Distorted Conclusions*, <www.qsilver.queensu.ca/history/Papers/gelinas.htm>.

72. G. Bouchard, op. cit., pp. 24–25.

EPILOGUE

1. M. Potvin, op. cit.

BIBLIOGRAPHY

Abella, Irving and Harold Troper, *None Is Too Many*, Toronto, Lester & Orpen Dennys, 1983.

Adachi, Ken, *The Enemy That Never Was: A History of the Japanese Canadians*, Toronto, McClelland & Stewart, 1977.

Anctil, Pierre, Gérard Bouchard, and Ira Robinson, *Juifs et Canadiens français dans la société québécoise*, Sillery, Éditions du Septentrion, 2000.

Armstrong, Elizabeth, *Le Québec et la crise de la conscription, 1917–1918*, Montreal, VLB éditeur, 1998.

Bell, George, *Rough Notes by an Old Soldier*, London, Day & Son, 1867.

Berthelot, Hector and Édouard-Zotique Massicotte, *Le Bon vieux temps*, Montreal, Beauchemin, 1916.

Bertrand, Luc, *L'Énigmatique Mackenzie King*, Vanier, Les Éditions L'Interligne, 2000.

Betcheman, Lita-Rose, *The Swastika and the Maple Leaf: Fascist Movements in Canada in the Thirties*, Don Mills, Fitzhenry & Whiteside, 1975.

Bettati, Mario, *Le Droit d'ingérence, mutation de l'ordre international*, Paris, Éditions Odile Jacob, 1996.

Bothwell, Robert and J. L. Granatstein, *Our Century: The Canadian Journey in the Twentieth Century*, Toronto, McArthur & Co., 2001.

Brown, Anthony Cave, *Treason in the Blood*, New York, Houghton Mifflin, 1994.

Conlogue, Ray, *Impossible Nation: The Longing for Homeland in Canada and Quebec*, Toronto, The Mercury Press, 1999.

Costello, John, *Mask of Treachery: Spies, Lies, and Betrayal*, revised and updated, New York, Warner Books, 1990.

Costello, John and O. Tsarev, *Deadly Illusions*, New York, Crown Publishers, 1993.

Davis, Alan T., *How Silent Were the Churches? Canadian Protestantism and the Jewish Plight During the Nazi Era*, Waterloo, Wilfrid Laurier University Press, 1997.

De Lagrave, Jean-Paul, *Les Journalistes démocrates au Bas-Canada (1791–1840)*, Éditions de Lagrave, 1975.

Deschênes, Gaston (texts gathered and presented by), *Une Capital éphémère. Montrèal et les événements tragiques de 1849*, Sillery, Éditions du Septentrion, 1999.

Filteau, Gérard, *Histoire des Patriotes*, Montreal, Éditions l'Aurore/ Univers, 1980.

———, *Le Québec, le Canada et la guerre 1914–1918*, Montreal, Éditions de l'Aurore, 1977.

Francis, Diane, *Fighting for Canada*, Toronto, Key Porter Press, 1996.

Goulet, Georges R. D., *The Trial of Louis Riel: Justice and Mercy Denied*, Calgary, Telwell Publishing, 1999.

Gray, Clayton, *Le Vieux Montréal*, Montreal, Éditions du Jour, 1964.

Gray, J., *The Winter Years: The Depression on the Prairies*, Toronto, Macmillan of Canada, 1966.

Greenwood, F. Murray, *Legacies of Fear: Law and Politics in Quebec in the Era of the French Revolution*, Toronto, University of Toronto Press, 1993.

Greer, Allan, *Habitants et Patriotes*, Montreal, Éditions du Boréal, 1997.

Hare, John, *Aux origines du parlementarisme québécois, 1791–1793*, Sillery, Éditions du Septentrion, 1993.

Kitagawa, Muriel, *This Is My Own: Letters to Wes & Other Writings on Japanese Canadians, 1941–1948*, Vancouver, Talonbooks, 1995.

Koch, H. W., *The Origins of the First World War*, New York, Taplinger Publishing Co., 1972.

Kyte Senior, Elinor, *Les Habits rouges et les Patriotes*, Montreal, VLB Éditeur, 1997.

La Terreur, Marc, *Les Tribulations des Conservateurs au Québec, de Bennett à Diefenbaker*, Quebec, Presses de l'Université Laval, 1979.

Lacoursière, Jacques, *Histoire populaire du Québec*, Sillery, Éditions du Septentrion, 1995.

Lacoursière, Jacques and C. Bouchard, *Notre histoire: Québec-Canada*, Montreal, Éditions Format, 1972.

LeBlanc, Dudley, *The Acadian Miracle*, Lafayette (Louisiana), Evangeline Publishing Co., 1966.

Leblanc, Émery, *Les Acadiens*, Montreal, Éditions de l'Homme, 1963.

Lefebvre, André, *La Montreal Gazette et le nationalisme canadien (1835–1842)*, Montreal, Guérin Éditeur, 1970.

Levitt, Cyril H. and William Shaffir, *The Riot at Christie Pits*, Toronto, Lester & Orpen Dennys, 1987.

Long, J. C., *Lord Jeffrey Amherst: A Soldier of the King*, New York, Macmillan, 1933.

Mackenzie King, William Lyon, *Mackenzie King Diaries*, Toronto, University of Toronto Press, 1980.

Marchand, Jean-Paul, *Conspiration? Les Anglophones veulent-ils éliminer le français du Canada?*, Montreal, Stanké, 1997.

McInnes, Tom, *Oriental Occupation of British Columbia*, Vancouver, Sun Publishing Co., 1927.

Miki, Roy and Cassandra Kobayashi, *Justice in Our Time: The Japanese Canadian Redress Settlement*, Vancouver, Talonbooks, 1991.

O'Connell, Robert L., *Of Arms and Men: A History of War, Weapons, and Aggression*, Oxford, Oxford University Press, 1989.

Oiwa, Keibo, *Stone Voices: Wartime Writings of Japanese Issei*, Montreal, Véhicule Press, 1991.

Omatsu, Maryka, *Bittersweet Passage: Redress and the Japanese Canadian Experience*, Toronto, Between the Lines, 1992.

Ouellet, Fernand, *Le Bas-Canada, 1791–1840, changements structuraux et crises*, Ottawa, Éditions de l'Université d'Ottawa, 1980.

Papineau, Louis Joseph, *Histoire de la Résistance du Canada au gouvernement anglais*, Montreal, Comeau & Nadeau, 2001.

Parkman, Francis, *The Conspiracy of Pontiac and the Indian War after the Conquest of Canada*, Boston, Little, Brown, 1886.

Rens, Jean-Guy, *L'Empire invisible*, Quebec, Presses de l'Université du Québec, 1993.

Richler, Mordecai, *Oh Canada! Oh Quebec! Requiem for a Divided Country*, Toronto, Penguin Canada, 1992.

Robin, Martin, *Shades of Right: Nativist and Fascist Politics in Canada, 1920–1940*, Toronto, University of Toronto Press, 1992.

Royal, Joseph, *Histoire du Canada, 1841–1867*, Montreal, Beauchemin, 1909.

Rumilly, Robert, *Histoire de la province de Québec*, Montreal, Éditions de Bernard Valiquette, 1940.

Speisman, Stephen, *The Jews of Toronto: A History to 1937*, Toronto, McClelland & Stewart, 1987.

Sprague, Donald, *Canada and the Métis, 1869–1885*, Waterloo, Wilfrid Laurier University Press, 1986.

Thomas, Lewis H., *Dictionnaire biographique du Canada*, Quebec, Presses de l'Université Laval, 1982.

Trudel, Marcel, *La Révolution américaine, 1775–1783*, Sillery, Les Éditions du Boréal Express, 1976.

Tulchinsky, Gerald, *Taking Root: The Origins of the Canadian Jewish Community*, Toronto, Lester Publishing Ltd., 1992.

Vaugeois, Denis, *Québec 1792: Les Acteurs, les institutions et les frontières*, Montreal, Éditions Fides, 1992.

Vaugeois, Denis and Jacques Lacoursière, *Canada-Québec. Synthèse historique*, Montreal, Éditions du Renouveau pédagogique, 1973.

Wade, Mason, *Les Canadiens français, de 1760 à nos jours*, Montreal, Le Cercle du Livre de France, 1963.

Waldman, Carl, *Atlas of the North American Indian*, New York, Facts on File, 1985.

Wallot, Jean-Pierre, *Un Québec qui bougeait: Trame socio-politique au tournant du XIXe siècle*, Sillery, Les Éditions du Boréal Express, 1973.

Ward, W. Peter, *White Canada Forever: Popular Attitudes and Public Policy Toward Orientals in British Columbia*, 2nd edition, Montreal, McGill–Queen's University Press, 1990.

L'Encyclopédie du Canada, Montreal, Stanké, 1987.

ARCHIVAL MATERIAL

Arcand, Adrien, *Correspondence*, The Canadian Jewish Congress National Archives, Montreal, P0005 Arcand, Adrien (collection).

———, *Letter to Daniel Johnson*, Adrien Arcand Collection, Special Collections, Vanier Library, Concordia University, Montreal.

Bennett, R. B., *Fonds R. B. Bennett*, Public Archives of Canada, Ottawa.

MAGAZINES AND JOURNALS

Amiel, Barbara, Column, *Maclean's*, June 1997.

Baby, François, "Fallait-il sauver le soldat Monckton de l'oubli?" *L'Action nationale*, August 1999.

Bonokoski, Mark, *Ottawa Sun*, September 1997.

Brassier, "Lionel Groulx," *L'Action nationale*, April 1993.

Caldwell, Gary, "La Controverse Delisle–Richler. Le discours sur l'antisémitisme au Québec et l'orthodoxie néo-libérale au Canada," *L'Agora*, June 1994, vol. 1, no. 9.

Chartrand, Luc. "Dis-moi la vérité! Le mythe du Québec fasciste," *L'Actualité*, March 1, 1997, vol. 22, no. 3.

———, "Les 'Rhodésiens' masqués. Les cercles de droite du Canada anglais sont en train d'inventer un racisme subtil, politiquement correct!" *L'Actualité*, April 15, 2000.

Conlogue, Ray, interviewed by Carole Beaulieu, "C'est la culture . . . stupid!" *L'Actualité*, March 15, 1997.

Daigle, Jean, "La Déportation des Acadiens," *Horizon Canada*, vol. 1, no. 12, Saint-Laurent, Centre d'étude en enseignement du Canada, 1984.

Edwards, Frederick, "Fascism in Canada," *Maclean's*, April 15, 1938.

Foglia, Pierre, "Faut arrêter de freaker," *La Presse*, December 16, 2000.

Fotheringham, Allan, *Maclean's*, October 30, 1995.

Francis, Diane, "Readers Support Tough Stance Against Quebec Separatists," *The Financial Post*, July 4, 1996.

———, *The Financial Post*, November 14, 1995.

———, *The Financial Post*, October 7, 1996.

Frisko, Pierre and Jean Simon Gagné, "Le Québec vu par le Canada anglais. La haine," *Voir*, vol. 12, no. 24, June 18, 1998.

German, Daniel, "The Political Game and the Bounds of Personal Honour: Sir Frederick Middleton and the Bremner Furs," *Saskatchewan History*, vol. 45, no. 1, Spring 1993.

Harris, Michael, *Toronto Sun*, May 1998.

Johnson, William, *The Gazette*, September 1996.

Kirshner, Sheldon, "The Kirshner File," *The Canadian Jewish News*, April 23, 1998.

Lashmer, Paul, "Revealed: Nazis' Friends Inside the British Elite," *The Independent*, January 9, 2000.

Lecker, Robert, *Saturday Night*, July/August 1996.

Madsen, Chris. "Military Law, the Canadian Militia, and the North-West Rebellion of 1885," *Journal of Military and Strategic Studies*, University of Calgary, Spring 1998.

Martin, Lawrence, *Globe and Mail*, August 30, 1997.

McPherson, James, *Saturday Night*, March 1998.

Milloy, M. J. "Rebel Without a Cause. A Response to the Politics of Pierre Falardeau's *15 Février 1839*," *Hour*, January 28, 2001.

Neal, Christopher, *Cité libre*, February–March 1998.

Paré, Jean, "Opération Salissage," *L'Actualité*, March 1, 1997.

Potvin, Maryse, "Les Dérapages racistes à l'égard du Québec au Canada anglais depuis 1995," *Politique et Sociétés*, vol. 28, no. 2, 1999.

Rakoff, Vivian, *Globe and Mail*, August 25, 1997.

Robson, John, "Why Levine Must Go," editorial, *Ottawa Citizen*, May 22, 1998.

Stanley, George F. G., "Louis Riel," *Revue d'histoire de l'Amérique française*, vol. 28, no. 1, June 1964.

———, *Acadiensis*, vol. 2, no. 1, 1972–73.

Yaffe, Barbara, interview with Anna Terrana, *Vancouver Sun*, July 1996.

"A Rebellion Diary," *Alberta Historical Review*, vol. 12, 1964.

"MP Compares Bouchard to Hitler," The *Globe and Mail*, July 30, 1996.

VIDEO RECORDING

Toward a Just Society, produced and directed by David A. Stein for the Canadian Council of Christians and Jews. The video transcript is available at <www.interlog.com/~cccj/J>.

INTERNET PUBLICATIONS

Appleblatt, Anthony, *Saskatchewan and the Ku Klux Klan*, <www.usask.ca/education/ideas/tplan/sslp/kkk/htm>.

Di Stasi, Dominic, *Orangeism. The Canadian Scene. A Brief Historical Sketch*, July 1995, <www.orangenet.org/stasi/htm>.

Gerber, Jean, "Too Close to Home, *Canadian Jewish News*, April 19, 2001, <www.cjnews.com/pastissues/01/apr19-01/features/feature1.htm>.

Griffiths, Naomi, *The Acadian Deportation; Causes and Development* (doctoral thesis), <www.collections.ic.gc.ca/acadian/francais/fexile/fexile.htm>.

Lacroix, Benoît and Stéphane Stapinsky, "Lionel Groulx: actualité et relecture," *Les Cahiers d'histoire du Québec au XXe siecle*, no. 8, <www.vigile.net/groulx/cahiers8pres1.html>.

Lawrence, Charles, *Lettre aux autorités de Londres*, <www.multimania.com/digagnon/raymonde.htm>.

LeBlanc, Dudley, *The Acadian Miracle*, <www.collections.ic.gc.ca/acadian/francais/fexile/fexile.htm>.

McConnell, Brian, *The Canadian Twelfth. An Orange Celebration*, <www.firstlight_2.tripod.com/Twelfth.htm>.

Menkis, Richard, *From Immigration to Integration, The Canadian Jewish Experience: A Millennium*, <www.bnaibrith.ca/institue/millennium/millennium03.html>.

Ouimet, Adolphe and Benjamin-Antoine Testard de Montigny, *Louis Riel: La vérité sur la question métisse*, Bibliotek multimédia, <www.microtec.net/~iandavid>.

Renton, Dave. *Fascism and Anti-Fascism in Britain*, <www.dkrenton.co.uk/trent2.html>.

Rough, Alex, *Canadian Orangeism. A Military Beginning, 1991*, <www.members.tripod.com/~Roughian/index-97.html>.

Schwarz, Frederic D., *Awful Disclosures* book review, *American Heritage*, 1999, <www.americanheritage.com/99/sep/timemachine/1849.htm>.

Acadie, Esquisse d'un parcours, Sketches of a Journey, <www.collections.ic.gc.ca/acadian/francais/fcxile/fexile.htm>.

WEB SITES

Anti-Fascist Action – Stockholm. International News, <www.afa-stockholm.antifa.net/nyheter/e01/eN010225.htm#church>.

Baby, François, <www.action-nationale.qc.ca/acadie/baby/html>.

Bank of Canada, the, <www.bank-banque-canada.ca/fr/inflation_calc-f.htm>.

Beaulieu and Conlogue, <www.vigile.net/pol/culture/beaulieuconlogue.html>.

Canadian Council for Refugees, <www.web.net/~ccr/history.html>.

Canadian Institute of Historical Microreproductions, <www.canadiana.org/ECO/mtq?id=1046b9705&doc=38886>.

Cléroux, Richard, <www.canoe.ca/CNEWPoliticsColumns/may12_cleroux2.html>.

Couture, Patrick, <www.geocities.com/Athens/Ithaca/7318/PONTIAC.HTM>.

D'Errico, Peter, <www.nativeweb.org/pages/legal/amherst/lord_jeff.html>.

Gervais, Richard, <www.vigile.net/999/gervaismonckton.html>.

Grand Orange Lodge of Ireland, <www.grandorange.org.uk/choose.htm>.

Institut d'histoire de l'Amérique française, <www.pages.infinit.net/histoire/riel.html>.

L'Agora, <www.agora.qc.ca/liens/gcaldwell.html>.

Université du Québec, <www.sciencetech.com/rech/th3.htm>.

University of Calgary,
    <www.stratnet.ucalgary.ca/journal/1998/article5.html>.

University of Washington Library, <www.lib.washington.edu/subject/
    Canada/internment/intro.html>.

ACKNOWLEDGEMENTS

The author is grateful for permission to include the following extensive quotations in *The Black Book of English Canada*.

The excerpt on page 15 is from *Fighting for Canada* by Diane Francis (Toronto, Key Porter Books Ltd., 1996). Copyright © 1996 by Diane Francis. Reprinted by permission of the author.

The excerpt on pages 16–17 is from *Conspiration! Les Anglophones veulent-ils éliminer le français du Canada?* by Jean-Paul Marchand (Montréal: Stanké, 1997). Copyright © 1997 by Jean-Paul Marchand. Reprinted by permission of the author.

The excerpt on page 19 is from "Les 'Rhodésiens' masqués: Les Cercles de droite du Canada anglais sont en train d'inventer un racisme subtil, politiquement correct!" by Luc Chartrand (*L'Actualité*, April 15, 2000). Copyright © 2000 by Luc Chartrand. Reprinted by permission of the publisher.

The excerpt on page 33 is from "Fallait-il sauver le soldat de Monckton de l'oubli?" by François Baby (*L'Action nationale*, August 1999). Copyright © 1999 by François Baby. Reprinted by permission of the publisher.

The excerpt on pages 33–34 is from an article previously posted at <www.vigile.net/999/gervaismonckton.html> (Vigile-Québec, September 1999). Copyright © 1999 by Richard Gervais. Reprinted by permission of the publisher.

The excerpt on pages 44–45 is from *La Révolution américaine, 1775–1783* by Marcel Trudel (Les Éditions du Boréal, 1976). Copyright © 1976 by Marcel Trudel. Reprinted by permission of the publisher.

INDEX